What Happens Next?

Books by Vernon Coleman include:

The Medicine Men (1975)
Paper Doctors (1976)
Stress Control (1978)
The Home Pharmacy (1980)
Aspirin or Ambulance (1980)
Face Values (1981)
The Good Medicine Guide (1982)
Bodypower (1983)
Thomas Winsden's Cricketing Almanack (1983)
Diary of a Cricket Lover (1984)
Bodysense (1984)
Life Without Tranquillisers (1985)
The Story Of Medicine (1985, 1998)
Mindpower (1986)
Addicts and Addictions (1986)
Dr Vernon Coleman's Guide To Alternative Medicine (1988)
Stress Management Techniques (1988)
Know Yourself (1988)
The Health Scandal (1988)
The 20 Minute Health Check (1989)
Sex For Everyone (1989)
Mind Over Body (1989)
Eat Green Lose Weight (1990)
How To Overcome Toxic Stress (1990)
Why Animal Experiments Must Stop (1991)
The Drugs Myth (1992)
Complete Guide To Sex (1993)
How to Conquer Backache (1993)
How to Conquer Pain (1993)
Betrayal of Trust (1994)
Know Your Drugs (1994, 1997)
Food for Thought (1994, revised edition 2000)
The Traditional Home Doctor (1994)
People Watching (1995)
Relief from IBS (1995)
The Parent's Handbook (1995)
Men in Dresses (1996)
Power over Cancer (1996)
Crossdressing (1996)

How to Conquer Arthritis (1996)
High Blood Pressure (1996)
How To Stop Your Doctor Killing You (1996, revised edition 2003)
Fighting For Animals (1996)
Alice and Other Friends (1996)
Spiritpower (1997)
How To Publish Your Own Book (1999)
How To Relax and Overcome Stress (1999)
Animal Rights – Human Wrongs (1999)
Superbody (1999)
Complete Guide to Life (2000)
Strange But True (2000)
Daily Inspirations (2000)
Stomach Problems: Relief At Last (2001)
How To Overcome Guilt (2001)
How To Live Longer (2001)
Sex (2001)
We Love Cats (2002)
England Our England (2002)
Rogue Nation (2003)
People Push Bottles Up Peaceniks (2003)
The Cats' Own Annual (2003)
Confronting The Global Bully (2004)
Saving England (2004)
Why Everything Is Going To Get Worse Before It Gets Better (2004)
The Secret Lives of Cats (2004)
The Cat Basket (2005)
The Truth They Won't Tell You (And Don't Want You To Know) About The EU (2005)
Living in a Fascist Country (2006)
How To Protect and Preserve Your Freedom, Identity and Privacy (2006)
The Cataholic's Handbook (2006)
Animal Experiments: Simple Truths (2006)
Coleman's Laws (2006)
Secrets of Paris (2007)
Cat Fables (2007)a
Too Sexy To Print (2007)
Oil Apocalypse (2007)
Gordon is a Moron (2007)
The OFPIS File (2008)

Cat Tales (2008)
What Happens Next (2009)
Moneypower (2009)

novels
The Village Cricket Tour (1990)
The Bilbury Chronicles (1992)
Bilbury Grange (1993)
Mrs Caldicot's Cabbage War (1993)
Bilbury Revels (1994)
Deadline (1994)
The Man Who Inherited a Golf Course (1995)
Bilbury Pie (1995)
Bilbury Country (1996)
Second Innings (1999)
Around the Wicket (2000)
It's Never Too Late (2001)
Paris In My Springtime (2002)
Mrs Caldicot's Knickerbocker Glory (2003)
Too Many Clubs And Not Enough Balls (2005)
Tunnel (1980, 2005)
Mr Henry Mulligan (2007)
Bilbury Village (2008)
Bilbury Pudding (2009)

as Edward Vernon
Practice Makes Perfect (1977)
Practise What You Preach (1978)
Getting Into Practice (1979)
Aphrodisiacs – An Owner's Manual (1983)

with Alice
Alice's Diary (1989)
Alice's Adventures (1992)

with Donna Antoinette Coleman
How To Conquer Health Problems Between Ages 50 and 120 (2003)
Health Secrets Doctors Share With Their Families (2005)
Aninal Miscellany (2008)

Gordon Brown and the Labour Party have led us into a depression, turned us into a fascist country and made Britain the weakest nation in the developed world.

What Happens Next?

Vernon Coleman

Published by Blue Books, Publishing House, Trinity Place,
Barnstaple, Devon EX32 9HG, England.

Reprinted 2009

ISBN: 978-1-899726-14-1

A catalogue record for this book is available from
the British Library.

Printed by CPI Antony Rowe

Dedication

To Donna Antoinette. I'll always love you. (That's the one prediction I can guarantee.)

Contents List

What Happens Next?

It's difficult to believe that surveillance could become more intrusive than it already is: but it will. Millions believe the lies about 'protecting us from terrorism'. Calmly and without protest they are walking into the world that Orwell warned us about. The words 'Why should you object if you have nothing to hide?' will be their last.

The relationship between the police and the public has deteriorated rapidly in recent years. Arrogance, conceit, an over-close relationship with politicians (who have damaged the police with their emphasis on targets) and a failure at high levels to understand the very purpose of the police has led to a crisis that seems destined to deteriorate still further.

Faith in currencies depends upon belief and trust more than anything else. The world has lost trust in Britain and its currency. The Europeans have lost trust in the euro. And the world knows that America is up to the Canadian border in debt.

All valuable commodities are running out. The big developing countries (particularly China, India, Brazil and Russia) need vast amounts of everything. The world will recover from the coming slump but Britain won't. And so the rise in commodity prices will hit Britain hard (and will contribute to the inflation problem.)

The Chinese have discovered the joy of eating hamburgers. And everything else you might have heard about agriculture is irrelevant. Neither genetic engineering nor controlling the weather will prevent food prices from soaring.

What Happens Next?

What Happens Next?

Note

The conclusions and predictions in this book were devised by Vernon Coleman for his own use. They are offered here without any guarantees and without any recommendations that you follow any or all of them. If you make plans or investments on the basis of these predictions then you do so at your own risk.

PREFACE

The Beginning Of Troubled And Confusing Times

'Forecasts are dangerous, particularly those about the future.'
SAMUEL GOLDWYN

Readers who believe that we live in a fair and just society, in which politicians can be trusted to tell the truth and the BBC can be relied upon to provide a fair and full account of the news, should go away and read something else. I would recommend something by Beatrix Potter or Enid Blyton.

Anyone who voted for Tony Blair more than once, or who thinks that he, Brown, Prescott, Blunkett, Mandelson et al are decent, honourable human beings who have the interest of the country at heart, will probably be as disappointed with this book as was the reviewer of my book *Gordon Is A Moron* who concluded with the comment that the 'book is rather one-sided'.

We live in troubled and confusing times. These are the interesting times no one wants to live through. To live in Britain today is to live in the world of Lewis Carroll's Red Queen – the delightful monarch who always tried to believe six impossible things before breakfast. We all have to do that these days.

I doubt if any country has ever fallen so quickly and so far. When the Labour Government came to power in 1997 Britain still had good reason to remember its great days; reason to be proud. There was history in abundance and culture that had inspired the world. But in just over a decade Britain has become a laughing stock; a pathetic, tramp of a country, ashamed of its past, ashamed of its heroes, ashamed of its achievements, ashamed of its greatness. Britain has been destroyed by the politically correct and the multiculturalists but, most of all, it has been destroyed by those who have betrayed us and sold our birthright to the European Union.

Today, the biggest problems are invariably the unpredicted; things we either don't know about or haven't given much thought to. And there is virtually nothing that could not happen. I really don't think many things would surprise me. Sweden declares war on Ethiopia. Oh? Really? Wales has been bought by a Chinese trillionaire and will be floated round to Asia to enlarge Hong Kong. Gosh? When will it happen? Israel declares peace and love and invites all Palestinians in for tea and crumpets. OK. So, perhaps some things would surprise me.

But our greatest problem is that we are weakened, unprepared and poorly positioned to cope with future crises. We have no room for more disasters.

The world is going through the worst financial crisis in memory. It is, quite possibly, the worst financial crisis in history. Created by greedy bankers and weak politicians, the crisis affects the world. But no country has been damaged and weakened more than Britain. Thanks to one man, Gordon Brown, Britain is close to being destroyed. (In my book *Gordon is a Moron* I predicted that, as a result of Brown's mis-management of the economy, Britain would be in a worse position to face the economic crisis than any other country.)

What will happen next?

Things will continue to get worse because the idiots who caused our current problems are still in charge. And they are still making terrible mistakes. Indeed just about everything they do to try to deal with the problems created by their previous errors causes more problems. It's tempting to see conspiracies everywhere. I don't. I think the world is just run by idiots.

It's all gone wrong. It's all going to get worse. And I have, I am afraid, come to the conclusion that until more people care, there is nothing that you and I can do about it. Blair and Brown and the New Labour fascists (often working with and on behalf of the European Union fascists) have created a State that will not easily be dismantled. Why would several million excess civil servants willingly fire themselves?

There is no mercy, justice, honour or truth in the country any more. Respect (for people, property, the law or institutions) is so low that it cannot possibly go any lower.

The mass of people will never again be as rich as they thought they were. Public services (national and local) will never again be as good as they were. It is truly scary to realise that our hospitals, our schools, our roads and all other public services are on an unstoppable, downward slide.

All we can do now is look after ourselves and those dear to us.

The trouble is that people don't care enough, or perhaps don't have the courage to do anything even if they do care, or, worse still, still tend to believe what they are told. Whatever the cause, the result is that the Government and the EU seem to be getting away with everything.

You and I must, therefore, understand what is happening and what the consequences are likely to be and, more specifically, how those consequences may affect us and what we can and must do to protect ourselves.

The nation's debt is already horrendous. Taxes will rise for years to come. The truth (which no politician will tell you) is that things are probably never going to get better than they are now and will, almost certainly, get considerably worse. And then, when they've got worse, they will really start to deteriorate.

You think I'm exaggerating?

I wish I was.

We need a revolution. But this is unlikely to happen; partly because the politicians, the media and the police currently have all the power they need to suppress one, and partly because the vast majority of the people who would benefit from a revolution are too apathetic, too numb, to realise that they need one. And so things will continue to deteriorate. Political correctness, means-testing and multiculturalism, poor education, overbearing, zealous bureaucrats, fascist policemen, greedy, dishonest, selfish politicians will, together, all ensure that things continue to get much, much worse.

* * *

We want to know the future. It's human nature. And it's the

only way in which we can protect ourselves. To do this we always tend to rely on the 'experts' (those whom we think know best). Our ancestors relied on the sages, the witches and the interpreters of portents. Today we rely on economists, consultants, commentators, academics and, heaven help us, celebrities. We listen to what they have to say because they say it as though they know that they are right.

And we listen to those around us too. Human beings are social animals and we tend to believe what everyone else believes. Life is easier that way. Dissidents are unlikely to be popular with those among whom they live.

Never before in human history have things happened as fast as they are happening now. Never before have things been changing so fast. You need to know what's coming. And so do I. Only then can we make sound, wise decisions about issues which will make a huge difference to our lives (and, literally, our chances of survival).

If we rely on the media we will be misled. Sometimes we will be misled because the people whose advice we are taking are deliberately misleading us; sometimes we will be misled because the people supposedly advising us simply don't know the facts – or how to interpret them.

And so I decided to give myself the task of trying to predict what happens next.

Although, it may seem paradoxical it has never been more difficult to predict the future. It is true that we have greater access to information than ever before, and, of course, we have all the analytical powers of all those wretched computers. The world is full of experts offering conclusions and advice. They all seem confident enough (and, impressively the confidence doesn't even falter when they are proved wrong, wrong and wrong again).

The problem is that much of the information, many of the conclusions and most of the predictions we receive are distorted by commercial forces or self-righteous politically correct nonsense. The truth is hard to obtain. And the big picture is almost never available. The consequences of the credit crunch mean that today it is difficult to work out what is going to happen a day ahead – let alone a year or a decade ahead.

You can always get predictions from the Government, of course. The trouble is that Government predictions are usually wrong.

Politicians don't understand much of what is going on – and neither do civil servants. Things are made worse by the fact that the Labour Government has taken the inability to make accurate forecasts to a new low. This may, of course, be because they make the mistake of listening to their own spin, and looking at their own manipulated figures. Don't make any plans according to Government forecasts. You would be better taking advice from information provided by blind and arthritic monkeys throwing blunt darts at last year's copy of *Old Moore's Almanac.*

So I'm going to try to do the impossible: forecast the future in a book.

Of course, forecasting the future in a book is ridiculous. Things are changing so fast that television news programmes have to race to keep up. The Internet is awash with instant news and equally instant views. The Internet is instant and even it has a job keeping up.

A book takes months to write and months to print and then it hangs around for years. So, any author who tries to forecast the future in a book has to be barking.

And this, as you will, I'm sure, have noticed, is a book.

It is very daring to put down predictions in a book. Very few people do it for the excellent reason that it is easy to be wrong (either because events change or because past and present circumstances have been misinterpreted in some way) and when you are wrong it is easy for critics to sneer. Reputations can be lost very quickly. You can make eight accurate predictions and two that are proved wrong and still look very foolish. The Delphic Oracle was vague for good reason. And these days the world is far more complicated than it was then.

★ ★ ★

I've actually been studying the news, reading between the lines, and drawing conclusions for a long time.

My first non-fiction books were nearly all about medicine (*The Medicine Men*, *Paper Doctors*, *Betrayal of Trust*, *The Health Scandal*, *How To Stop Your Doctor Killing You*, etc). I learned to look behind the facade to find the real truth, and to make judgements based on the evidence I had uncovered. I learned to spot how researchers, drug companies and others were lying. I discovered how medical journals were used to distort the facts. I was astonished to discover how much doctors and researchers lie and mislead people. And I was even more astonished to discover that the vast majority of medical writers, both those writing for popular papers and those writing for medical journals, believed the lies and missed the truths behind them. They missed the truths because they were too ready to believe.

Knowing the truth in medicine is vital, of course. If you get the wrong information it can be fatal. It really doesn't matter whether your doctor is stupid or crooked: the end result is the same. Your chances of surviving or recovering will be substantially reduced and your chances of dying will be dramatically increased.

I found that most doctors got things wrong because they didn't go back to the original sources. They relied on what they had been told by drug company representatives, Government-employed bureaucrats and politicians – all of whom have a vested interest in putting forward a particular line and none of whom are likely to know the truth or where to find it (or even what it looks like). And medical journalists get things wrong because they rely on doctors for their information. And since doctors don't usually know the truth,, journalists inevitably get misled too. I found that I couldn't rely on medical journals and published research work either. I found that some of the most frequently quoted medical journals accepted research articles for money. The paper which looks as if it is independent may have been published because some corporation (usually a drug company) has paid for it to be published. Nearly all journals accept and rely on advertising (and it is difficult to remain open-minded when you will go bankrupt if you do). And finally most of the scientists who write journal articles have a vested interest in the product or treatment they are writing about. So, for example, many receive grants or payments for the work they do, or they own shares in the company making the product they are (allegedly) researching.

I've been digging out the truth for nearly forty years and I have made a lot of enemies in doing it. Over the years I learned all the tricks the drug companies and food companies use. I learned that researchers know that to please their masters they have to ask the questions which are most likely to give them the answers they want. And I learned that financially inconvenient results are ignored or shelved or overlooked. Evidence is suppressed or disguised.

Over the years my knowledge and techniques have enabled me to spot many problems ahead of other writers, and they have enabled me to warn my readers about many coming dangers. I've spotted numerous health truths, potential drug hazards and other hidden medical secrets. And I've repeatedly made myself unpopular with the establishment by sharing my discoveries with my readers.

Time and time again my predictions and forecasts have been ten, fifteen and even twenty years ahead of anyone else's. And, however unpopular they were to begin with, they've been proved right.

At the time most of my predictions were ignored, of course. But the predictions are there in black and white and they're not so easy to ignore now. (If you want to check out my older books, even the out of print ones should be available through public libraries.)

My books on medicine contain a huge number of warnings and predictions. But years ago I discovered that just about every medical issue I researched no longer took me into the heart of the medical establishment but into politics. The big decisions about health and medicine are made not by doctors but by politicians. And the politicians make decisions not according to the needs and wishes of the voters but according to the requirements of the lobbyists representing drug and food companies. Politicians and bureaucrats are bought by these people (sometimes for a campaign contribution, sometimes for a book contract with a nice advance, sometimes for a large lecture fee and sometimes for a few expensive lunches.)

Since I know how to find the truth about medical issues I also know how to find the truth about environmental, financial and geopolitical issues. The politicians, the journalists and the professionals in whatever area of life all use the same sneaky little tricks to enable them to hide the truth and to sell the most profitable lie.

Gradually, over the years, I started to apply the techniques I'd used to assess medical truths to enable me to look at other areas of life: politics and economics, for example. And I used the skills I'd acquired to enable me to make judgements about investments too. The predictions in this book are based not on reading tea leaves, or the positions of the planets, but on an analysis and interpretation of the evidence. I am using the same techniques I have used for years to assess medical risks and medical information.

★ ★ ★

What Happens Next? is my most ambitious attempt to look at the future. But as you read it you will, I suspect, find yourself drawing the same conclusions that I have drawn. In chapter after chapter I've lain down the evidence in a simple and straightforward way. It's not usually that difficult to interpret the evidence when it's all there in front of you. The main difficulty I had in writing this book was that events kept overtaking my predictions and I had to keep replacing and updating predictions and forecasts as they came true.

★ ★ ★

There are no references in this book. There is a good reason for this. A list of the books, articles, reports, videos, tapes and documents I've used would be ten times as long as the book itself and prohibitively expensive to print and post. (We rely on mail order sales because bookshops and libraries often refuse to carry my books. Those who have read my earlier books will know why.)

★ ★ ★

I made these forecasts to enable me to make my own plans. And, having done that, I wanted to share them with my readers. I have made a considerable number of accurate forecasts and predictions in the past and many readers have been kind enough to write and say that they found them useful. A number of readers actually wrote and asked for this book. After all, it isn't knowledge or information that gives power – it's how to use the knowledge that gives the power. By itself information is just that – information. Unless you know how to interpret it, the information is meaningless.

We have all been hit by a massive shock. We are, indeed, living in a state of national shock. We've hit a financial brick wall at full speed. And the consequences are, I believe, going to be long-lasting and dramatic. Moreover, the current financial crisis will segue directly into the peak oil crisis. Surviving what happens (and investing successfully) will require an ability to understand what is happening and to predict at least some of the possible consequences.

In the world of investing it is only necessary to make six out of ten good investment decisions in order to make a profit. I suspect the same is true of the forecasting business. If some of the predictions in this book turn out to be wrong then it should be clear fairly early on which they are. And the predictions which last the course should still be useful. If any or all of these predictions prove to be wrong then I hope that they might at the least be thought-provoking. It seems to me possible that even predictions which turn out to be wrong can be useful if they encourage readers to question reality and accepted perceptions.

This isn't a book which is designed to reach a wide audience or to change the world. This is a book which is designed to help my family of readers survive in an increasingly bizarre and threatening environment. Curiosity about what might (or might not) happen next is an inevitable part of life. If we have some idea of what is going to happen (or might happen) then we can prepare ourselves. Things will change, of course. And we must adapt whenever they do. ('When the facts change, I change my mind,' said John Maynard Keynes, the economist. 'What do you do, sir?')

Can we save our country? Can we stop Britain's great decline? I honestly don't know. I don't know whether enough people care enough for a bloodless revolution to be successful (though when I finish this book I intend to start work on a blueprint, a manifesto, for change). However, throughout the book I have tried to explain what you can do about these things, to protect yourself and your family.

Vernon Coleman, February 2009

Chapter 1

Britain: Sliding Towards Obscurity And Bankruptcy

Destroyed by an incompetent Government and greedy bankers, Britain is deeply indebted and doomed for generations to come.

It doesn't much matter whether you call it a recession, a depression, a slump or just a pretty miserable time for everyone: it's going to be bad.

And it's going to last a long time.

It doesn't matter who wins the next election. Britain is stuffed. This isn't just a blip; a hangover after a decade of greed and excess. What is happening is a period of significant structural change. And it is change that will affect Britain more adversely than any other country and that will last for years. It will last, indeed, until the world economy is devastated by the problems which will be created by the peak oil crisis.

With the possible exception of the Americans, Britons are now the fattest, least healthy, most illiterate people on the planet. We are top of the league tables for vandalism, binge drinking and fly tipping. We have the most congested roads in the Western world, the most dangerous, bug-ridden hospitals and the most complicated, and incomprehensible, tax laws. Our roads, cities, railway stations and airports are recognised worldwide as the dirtiest and most poorly run. We have more red tape than anyone else. We have the worst transport infrastructure in any country where people have access to television. When snow falls in London the buses stop running because the drivers are too wimpy to go out in the cold. We have more CCTV cameras than any other country. We come top of the tables for litter, drug abuse, pregnant teenagers and sexually transmitted diseases. We have the world's most complex railway timetable and the world's most incomprehensible fare structure. It is therefore appropriate that we also have the most unreliable railway system. (I was stunned in early 2009 to discover that Network Rail had just signed a contract to equip all trains with two way radios 'that work everywhere'. 'Once the system comes into network-wide use in three years,' reported the *Financial Times*, 'drivers will no longer have to climb out of cabs to talk to signallers by lineside telephones. That should smooth the process of dealing with disruption when the line is blocked or a train has broken down.' You think I'm joking don't you? I'm not. Today, every passenger on the train is ringing home on a mobile telephone and the driver can only communicate with the outside world by climbing out of his cab when he can find a lineside telephone.)

Our respect for the law is abused daily. We are monitored, regulated, fined and taxed more than any other nation on the planet. The people we employ to protect us are constantly coming up with new ways to punish us and oppress us. We're treated more like prisoners of war than owner-occupiers.

The Labour Government which took power in 1997 (and inherited an unusually strong economy) has weakened the economy, encouraged immigration, introduced taxes and benefits systems which have helped to destroy families, done their best to destroy the railways, done long-term damage to the farming industry, encouraged the nation's increased reliance on imports and alienated all the countries which do have oil supplies and who will, in the medium term, have the luxury of choosing the countries to whom they sell their oil. All of these things (and many more) will make things infinitely worse when the peak oil crisis arrives. Britain will be one of the hardest hit nations on earth when the oil starts to run out. The recession in Britain will segue neatly into the oil problem. Things will never be as good as they were – or as good as they are now.

★ ★ ★

The British Government boasts endlessly about the economic miracle which has enabled them to reduce unemployment figures but in reality, of course, their so-called economic miracle is nothing more than an absurd Ponzi scheme, destined to collapse. The reduced unemployment figures are a result not of prosperity but of massage, spin and the development of a variety of dishonest schemes designed to massage the figures down by putting the unemployed on 'schemes'. The figures have also been helped by allowing millions of cheats and fraudsters to take themselves off the unemployment register and describe themselves as long-term sick. And, of course, the only big employer who has been hiring recently has been the Government itself. (Since Labour acquired power in 1997 around a million manufacturing jobs have been lost. In that same period around a million new civil servants have been hired. The Labour Ministers might not be clever, honest or genuinely creative but they are crafty enough to realise that people who receive their monthly pay cheque from the Government, or whose survival depends upon Government benefits of one sort or another, are quite likely to vote for the Government every time there is an election. Civil servants don't want to vote for a Government which might cut back Government spending and the millions receiving benefits don't want to vote for a Government which might cut back the benefits budget.)

* * *

The Labour Government is like Tyrannosaurus Rex in that it has an extremely small brain and a very large body. The Government now employs so many people that huge quantities of them turn up for work and find there isn't anything for them to do apart from drink tea and make life as difficult as possible for the nation's real workers. In early 2009 one former Trade Minister claimed that the civil service could manage with half as many people.

It is often said that one of the problems with the City is that the place is run by twenty-year-olds who have little knowledge and virtually no experience. But the same problem applies in the civil service. It has been reported that half the Treasury staff have been there for less than three years. The vast majority have only ever known Brown and Darling as Chancellors. There isn't much grey hair in the Treasury. It is, perhaps, not so surprising that Brown is (and was) allowed to make so many egregious mistakes. Gordon isn't the only moron running the country. As a nation we have every right to feel browned off.

Since the Labour Party came to power they have filled all the important posts in the country with cronies and former flat mates. The country is run not by the best, most talented individuals but by people who happened to know Tony Blair, Gordon Brown and so on in their earlier lives. And the servants! You might think that the Labour Party would have cut back on servants. Not a bit of it. In early 2009, as the credit crunch crisis worsened, Downing Street was advertising for a butler to serve drinks to Cabinet Ministers and VIPs in the Prime Minister's residence. And Mandelson's office was advertising for someone to 'support' the new Business Secretary. Salary? £185,000 a year. (It's difficult to describe Mandelson as 'Lord Mandelson'. If the wretched and undeserving Mandelson has a peerage then everyone in the country should have one. They should be given away with cornflakes or petrol and their worthlessness should be made apparent to all.)

Public sector employees are invariably far less competent than their counterparts in private enterprise. For example, although a series of civil servants were recently conned by an art forger, the first professional art gallery expert who saw the forger's work laughed and immediately spotted the fake. Nevertheless, civil servants are rewarded far more generously than private sector workers. The average civil servant earned £22,160 in 2008 whereas the average private sector worker earned £20,716. The average civil servant also has a far superior pension, much shorter working hours, much less onerous working responsibilities, longer holidays, more job security, more flexibility and more time off.

Politicians and civil servants have gone berserk hiring management consultants and efficiency experts. Hundreds of millions of pounds of public money is wasted on idiots who have never run anything in their lives but who are hired as 'consultants' because that's how they describe themselves. Efficiency experts helped destroy much of industry. After management consultants told Railtrack to 'sweat their assets' there was a series of accidents. And the company collapsed. Management consultants advised Swissair to invest in other small, European airlines. Swissair duly went bust. The same so-called 'experts' (often young graduates who have never had a real job or earned any real money in their lives) are now destroying public life. In 2002 alone the number of mistakes in British hospitals rose by a quarter. In 2002, one London teaching hospital (allegedly staffed by the best doctors and nurses) made 135 mistakes every week when giving drugs to patients. A quarter of the mistakes were serious.

★ ★ ★

Thousands of highly paid civil servants do little or nothing all day. There are, for example, 500 civil servants at the Ministry of Defence who do not have an official role because they are waiting for someone to find them something specific to do. ID cards, the hugely unpopular scheme being forced on the country by the EU, will cost around £20 billion. (ID cards are not, and never were, anything to do with fighting terrorism, of course.). The NHS computer upgrade which was scheduled to start operating in 2005 is running rather late. The original cost was estimated to be £2.5 billion. The current estimate is almost ten times that. The scheme will offer no clinical benefits but will dramatically reduce patient confidentiality. Billions more could be cut from the Government's budget simply by not hiring outside consultants and by spending less taxpayers' money on advertising. And then there are, of course, the English Regional Assemblies which we pay for but which exist only to prepare England to be taken over and broken up by the EU. These, as I showed in my book *The OFPIS File*, already exist and, although they are entirely unelected, have tremendous power. (The EU throws money away in all sorts of strange directions. It's just given a grant for £850,000 to a Finnish dance project hoping to 'further the internationalisation of Finnish tango'. The whole EU becomes more like something out of the Goon Show every week.)

The British Government throws our money away at every opportunity. Did you know that the Government spent £12,000 of taxpayers' money on golf balls promoting British trade? Or that after being handed £20 billion of taxpayers' money the Royal Bank of Scotland spent £300,000 on a champagne junket for the very people who'd broken the bank? (Not difficult to see why or how they'd destroyed the bank.)

And then there's the wretched Olympics.

The London Olympics will be a sporting, commercial and economic disaster. They will be an expensive, disruptive, joyless and pointless excuse for thousands of people to fly thousands of miles and contribute enormously to the world's alleged climate change problem. There is no little irony in the fact that a Government which wants us all to worry about global warming, and which has led its country into penury, should plan to spend untold billions on an event which virtually no one wants and which the nation cannot possibly afford.

Thanks to Gordon Brown, and a bunch of greedy and largely anonymous bankers, Britain has headed into a perfect financial storm. The Britain of 2009 and beyond is going to be a very different place from the Britain we've got to know. Even the Chancellor of the Exchequer has admitted that we are facing the worst crisis in 60 years. We're heading away from a world of greed and acquisitions and loans and debts into a world where bankruptcies, repossessions and unemployment will rocket. Streets will be lined with boarded up houses and crime rates will soar.

★ ★ ★

If you have a safe job now then you should hold onto it. Unemployment is going to soar.

China and India and other Eastern nations are already 'home' for the world's manufacturing and service industries. Even though the Chinese and the Indians are getting richer they have a long way to go before they're as well off as the people of Britain. The average annual income in India, for example, is just £600.

And, by and large, they work much harder.

To that must be added the constant storm of red tape which makes life nigh on impossible for the entrepreneur trying to set up a business in Britain. By gold plating legislation from the European Union (see my book *The OFPIS File* for details) the British Government has made life exceptionally difficult for people trying to set up businesses in Britain. It's not going to get any better.

As an investor I'm not much interested in putting money into British manufacturing or service industries. If it can be done in China and India why would anyone try to do it in Britain?

For some years now most new jobs have been created by the Government itself. Of the total number of jobs created in Britain since 1998, two thirds have been in the public sector. Even when the nation was clearly in trouble, during 2008, the Government continued to hire more useless bureaucrats. In the final six months of 2008, around 300,000 private sector workers lost their jobs but 50,000 new public officials (complete with pension entitlements) were recruited. Even that hiring spree will have to come to an end as the Government runs out of money.

How high will unemployment go?

I have no idea.

But I am confident that it will be far, far higher than the Government expects. Four million? Five million? Most important of all, the unemployed will stay unemployed for a long, long time. Many people who are made redundant now will never work again.

I am also confident that Government Ministers will lie and fiddle the figures to try to disguise the truth. It is the only thing they do well.

And I am equally sure that as unemployment goes up the Government's income will fall still further.

* * *

It is difficult to think of anything the Labour Government could have done that would have made things worse. In the autumn of 2008 the financial markets were seriously considering the possibility that Britain might go bankrupt. That fear persists. It is now widely recognised that Britain, more than any other country, has been grossly mismanaged. The big problem is that Britain has for years been managed for the convenience and profit of politicians and bureaucrats. The needs of the citizens take a distant second place. We now have the greediest, most corrupt politicians and the most incompetent and craven civil servants we have ever had. Neither seem to understand the concept of regret or be able to bring themselves to apologise for the most egregious errors. All cling to honour when men (and women) of honour would have resigned. While they are in office our politicians are self-serving. And the minute they leave office they capitalise on their experience in a way that used to be frowned on as 'improper'.

It was Gordon the Moron whose policies resulted in ensuring that Britain dived headfirst into the credit crunch of 2008.

It was Gordon the Moron whose policies ensured that Britain was by then the weakest 'developed' country in the world. And the one guaranteed to suffer most from the crisis. The Bank of England, which taxpayers might have expected to have been having three kinds of hissy fit at what was happening, seems to have been too busy starching its collars to notice anything amiss.

Britain may never again be as prosperous as it was at the end of the 20th Century and the start of the 21st Century. Brown's imprudent economic policies have wrecked Britain's chances of surviving the economic tempest unscathed. The credit crunch bank problems (caused almost entirely by greed) and the housing problems (caused almost entirely by greed but partly by a fear among millions, whose faith in pensions had been destroyed, that buying a property was the only safe way to prepare for retirement) may last until the peak oil problems described in my book *Oil Apocalypse* hit us. In short, we must prepare for the hardest times anyone alive has ever known. When the Chancellor of the Exchequer forecast that Britain was heading for the worst financial crisis for 60 years he was being optimistic. Share and property prices in Japan have remained in the doldrums for two decades. It is perfectly possible that the same thing could happen in Britain (and, indeed, in much of the rest of the world). By then the global shortage of oil will be affecting our lives and the economy may never again rise.

My prediction (made in 2007) that Britain would suffer more than any other country from the coming crisis is now generally accepted by analysts and economic experts everywhere. For example, in December 2008, Commerzbank analysts pointed out that the economic evidence made a 'strong case for the UK ultimately suffering the worst recession in the developed world.' By early 2009, independent groups, bodies and organisations everywhere agreed that Britain was the least well-placed of all developed countries to cope with the global financial problems.

Whenever things seemed to be going well Gordon took the credit. When things went bad Gordon immediately blamed the global economy. Under the Labour Government an ever increasing share of public wealth has flowed into the military-industrial complex (just as it has for decades in America) and into a vast non-productive sector of financial manipulation which has changed debt into riches. The result is now a huge disparity between those at the bottom who are earning hardly enough to stay alive (less in many cases than those receiving benefit cheques from the Government) and those at the top, the irresponsible, ruthless, hubristic horde who have clawed their way to the top of financial and corporate structures (often by illegal methods) and made themselves super-rich. And there is another division too: between public sector workers and the rest of the population.

And it was Gordon the Moron, and his Scottish sidekick, whose incompetence ensured that Britain will end up in intensive care for at least one generation and probably more.

It was Gordon Brown whose policies, designed to punish the cautious and the prudent and to reward the incompetent and the feckless, will result in years of high taxes, soaring inflation and never ending debt. Britain is now borrowing around £150 billion a year. Public sector debt will exceed £1 trillion by 2012. And Brown's wasteful and pointless public spending will destroy, not boost, the economy. At what point will Britain need to beg for a loan from the International Monetary Fund? It can't be far away.

The Japanese spent the 1990s trying to overcome a recession with infrastructure spending. They ended up with more debts and a stuffed economy. And a stagnant stock market. Massive public spending in the USA in the 1930s failed to increase economic growth. Britain tried it in the 1970s and it failed. Brown is a tax, borrow and spend politician. His legacy, and ours, will be a ruined country. Don't expect things to get better in a hurry. In fact, don't expect things to get better. Brown should have cut taxes, cut Government spending, controlled wage inflation and allowed hopeless companies to go bust. He did exactly the opposite. Cutting Government spending in half would have helped. There is, I suspect, no chance of any Government doing that for a generation or two. And by then the Government won't have a choice.

Everything Brown has done since he became Chancellor of the Exchequer seems to have been designed to ensure that Britain ended up in a terrible mess. Did he did do it because he is a blithering idiot or because he's working for the Russians and wanted to destroy Britain? I don't have the foggiest idea. And to be honest I don't really care. All I know is that if anyone ever writes a lucid and dispassionate history of Gordon Brown's career they will doubtless conclude that the Scots git did more harm to Britain than anyone since the Austrian decorator with the daft moustache.

★ ★ ★

The problems of the so-called 'credit crunch' were caused by greed. The problems were caused by Americans, Britons and others spending more than they had, or could afford, and acquiring debts they could never hope to repay. It was greed which led people to take out mortgages (later defined as subprime) that they could never hope to service or repay. It was greed which led bankers to change the rules so that they could lend money to people who would never be able to pay it back. It was greed which allowed sellers and their agents to push house prices up higher and higher. And it was greed which encouraged politicians and those paid to supervise the banks to authorise all this spending and lending. The consumer boom of the early part of the 21st Century was built on a total contempt for the old-fashioned virtue of living within one's means and a total trust in the insane idea that house prices can only ever go up. That, of course, is the sort of economic nonsense upon which pyramid selling and Ponzi schemes are built. Labour had, said Gordon Brown, eradicated 'boom and bust'. Did he really mean that? Surely not even Brown was that stupid. Surely even the son of the manse must realise that although we have had the biggest boom in history it was built not on energy, initiative or hard work but on debt and so now the bust will be the worst bust imaginable. And as the son of the manse he must surely see just how the way he has led us means that we deserve the pain and the humiliation which awaits.

Governments had fun too, of course, merrily spending far more than they could afford on providing subsidies to their most enthusiastic supporters and pointless, overpaid jobs for their unemployable friends and starting wars they couldn't afford. No politicians in the world spent more wildly than the British Labour Government of the late 20th Century and early 21st Century. Under the reckless 'supervision' of Gordon Brown (the most reckless Chancellor to have ever lived) Britain spent, spent, spent with all the disregard for the future of Viv Nicholson (the famous pools winner).

'Had the Prime Minister been running a company instead of a country, he would be facing an inquiry into allegations of criminal negligence,' said a writer in the *Daily Telegraph*. It was nauseating to see the man who had created the mess preening himself and promising to save us all from the chaos he had created. The arsonist had put down his matches, picked up his helmet and axe and become the Chief Fire Officer. In early 2009 he was busy throwing more money at bad banks and furiously trying to persuade them to let him guarantee their loans. This, of course, was morally and economically absurd. What he should have been doing was guaranteeing savers' unlimited deposits in order to encourage the only people in the country with any money to have a little faith in the banks. But that would have meant pandering to the prudent and was, therefore, inconceivable. (One problem with not guaranteeing unlimited bank deposits is that potential housebuyers are reluctant to put the proceeds from one house sale into one bank account when they know that they will lose much of their money if the bank goes bust. House sellers and buyers can't rely on their solicitors' client accounts because these are just as vulnerable as anyone else's.)

So, what was Brown's primary solution to problems caused by the nation's binge spending?

He and his chancellor, fellow Scot Alistair Darling, decided to encourage people to spend more money. How do you spend your way out of a debt-induced crisis? More to the point, how could any sane person think up such a crazy idea? In a rational world men in white coats would have been waiting outside the House of Commons to take Brown and Darling off in straight-jackets.

But we do not live in a rational world.

Moreover, today the House of Commons is full of people who have never had proper jobs. In the bad old days most of the people in Parliament had practical experience of the real world. Many knew what it was like to create and build up a business. Others had worked in the professions.

Today, although there is a Minister in charge of the health service who used to be a postman, it is difficult to find an MP who knows what the word 'work' really means.

★ ★ ★

Brown and Darling decided that because Britain was in a mess through overspending they would spend more money – and encourage everyone else to spend more money too. It all began to sound as logical as the sort of distorted thinking used by the Venetians to elect a new Doge.

The Bank of England slashed interest rates in order to protect the greedy by reducing their mortgage payments. They seemed unaware of (or didn't care about) the fact that this would destroy the lives of those who relied on the interest on their savings to pay their bills.

It was time to spend, spend, spend again. A spendthrift was protecting spendthrifts at the expense of the prudent.

Now, it is true that under some circumstances, spending more money can help drag a country out of recession.

But this only ever works if the country has some money put aside 'for a rainy day'.

You can't ever spend your way out of a depression by spending money you don't have.

It's as daft as expecting a bankrupt to spend his way out of penury by borrowing more money and buying more things he doesn't need. Brown's efforts have made things worse. Brown has encouraged debtors to enjoy their debt; he has encouraged those who don't care about being in debt and he will increase the length of time people remain in debt. His actions will create more long lasting stress, poverty and bankruptcy than if he had done nothing at all. It is, indeed, difficult to think of ways in which Brown could have designed policies destined to do more harm, and to prolong the crisis which started in 2007 and 2008, than the ones he has introduced.

* * *

Failure, disintegration and decay are integral parts of our lives. Without them we end up with a planet full of rubbish and with companies that need supporting by taxpayers because they aren't good enough to look after themselves.

Politicians know this, of course.

Nevertheless, Britain, Europe and America seem committed to saving their car industries from the consequences of their own errors. (Actually, in Britain's case that means saving the bits of the foreign car industry that are in the UK.)

The argument in favour of saving the car industries is simple and, by now, traditional: they are too big to be allowed to fail. If car companies go, other industries suffer. For example, if there are less cars then there is less need for car dealers. Haulage companies don't have as much work moving parts and cars around the country. And with television stations and newspapers hugely reliant on the car industry for advertising revenue it is clear that anything which adversely affects the car industry will have an adverse effect on the economy in general. (In America, local TV stations get at least 25% of their advertising from the car industry.)

But the big car companies have been losing money either because they have been making and selling cars that people don't want to buy or because they have been making them inefficiently. They have been doing something wrong. And giving them money wasn't intended to cure their problems but to cover up the mess they had made of their businesses. It will also enable them to cut prices in an attempt to gain sales – and that will drag healthier rivals into insolvency too. The crisis that developed in 2008 could and should have been used as an exercise in catharsis; a chance to rid the world of failed industries and methods and to develop and nurture new replacements that would work efficiently, effectively and profitably. We needed politicians to be brave and to make brave decisions. Instead they turned out to be and do just the opposite. Sadly, it was no great surprise.

The truth is, and has been for years, that the Japanese and the Chinese can produce better cars far more cheaply than Britain can. Not surprisingly, these are the cars that people want to buy. Renault is planning to produce a £3,000 car built in Romania and in 2009 an Indian car company will sell a new car for under £1,500. How? Because instead of paying £30 an hour or more for manual labour (as American car companies do in Detroit) the Indians are paying workers 50 pence an hour.

Of course, it is also possible to argue that the car industry has been making too many cars and should now turn to making other things. There is now one car on the road for every adult in America. The most telling headline I've seen for some time appeared in the *Financial Times* in February 2009 and said simply: 'Out-of-work ships used as storage for unsold cars.' Nothing summed up the global recession more effectively.

The grossly inefficient American car industry resisted the wishes of consumers and persisted in making huge, oil guzzling monsters that no one wanted to buy because they are expensive to run and bad for the environment. The big three American car makers continued to make obsolete, petrol hungry vehicles long after the public demand for them had fallen. They made poor quality cars, they ignored the fact that the price of oil would inevitably rise, they ignored the need for cars which were more environmentally friendly, and they ignored the fact that they were competing with car manufacturers in Asia. The whole industrial mess was made worse by poor designs, huge pension fund debts, massive health insurance liabilities and absurdly inflexible and costly union working agreements. The average car worker in America earns 1.7 times as much as the average working American.

It is true that car industries are important (one in ten American jobs is supported by the car industry) but giving car companies government money won't help them survive or cure their long-term problems. The British Government should have learnt its lesson from its repeated, doomed (and expensive) attempts to save the British car industry. Bailing out companies which are failing doesn't work; it is invariably driven not by a genuine need to save the economy but by short-term political motives.

But politicians, who always feel a sense of affinity with people who are greedy and lazy, don't want a lot of overpaid, lazy car workers to lose their jobs and so they will use taxpayers' money to bail them out.

Great. That will help a lot.

Bailing out companies that are failing is unfair to everyone – especially the companies which don't need bailing out but who will be weakened both by the taxes they have to pay to support the failures and by the fact that they are being forced to compete on an uneven playing field. By the end of 2008 just about every trade group in Britain was demanding financial support (in the form of grants or loans) for its members.

It was, as expected, the car industry, with all those unhappy employees living in marginal constituencies, which got Government money.

Or did it? When, in January 2009, Lord Mandelson, a perfect accomplice for Brown and his gang of incompetents, announced that he was giving the car industry a £2.5 billion lifeline, the industry and unions seemed ungrateful in their response. If they'd known just how ungenerous the lifeline really was they might have been even more churlish. Most of the £2.5 billion came in the form of guarantees to back loans. More than half of that came from European Investment

Bank loans, which had been announced in the autumn of 2008. And the rest was dependent on approval coming from Brussels, which the Government said it hoped would not take months. Naturally, the British Government cannot give or lend money to British industries without approval from the European Union.

The same stupid policies were, it seems, being adopted everywhere.

In Italy it was announced that taxpayers would buy 50 million euros worth of cheese, in order to prop up northern Italy's cheese-making industry. Why did the cheese-makers need propping up? There are too many of them. There are 400 makers of Parmigiano Reggano around the city of Parma. There is so much of the damned cheese that it sells for less than it costs to make. Unless the Italian Government chooses to subsidise cheese-makers for ever there will still be too much of this cheese and too many people making it.

The wise move would, of course, be to allow a few cheese-makers to go bust. If the Government wanted to intervene it could help them find new work. They could, perhaps, make a different kind of cheese. Or make wheelbarrows, clocks or yoghurt. Forcing taxpayers to keep failing businesses alive is mad. It gives subsidised firms an unfair advantage and means that the weak survive while the strong (which would otherwise survive and thrive) will fail.

Britain is full of businesses which are surplus to requirements. Do we need more houses? Do we need more banks? More bankers? More shops? More cars? More hedge funds? Of course we don't.

Japan prevented bad businesses from failing in the 1990s. Two decades later they are still getting over that error. And yet Britain, the rest of Europe and America are now making exactly the same mistake.

You have to let failures fail.

Joseph Schumpeter prescribed corporate Darwinism, where the well-run businesses thrive and the poorly run ones fail. The badly-run business, or the business with an inadequate raison d'être, will fail, giving the entrepreneur with a genuinely good idea the chance to expand.

By supporting the weak at the expense of the strong Brown has weakened the economy enormously. It seems likely that both the American and British Governments will continue with this doomed policy. They should have been supporting new businesses and the low paid workers in manufacturing industries. Instead, by increasing Government spending and increasing the size and extent of the Government payroll, they increased their respective national debts and made things considerably worse for the medium and long-term. They sold the future for short-term political advantage. Our world is changing. We need political leaders with imagination, courage and wisdom. We have Gordon Brown.

★ ★ ★

Much of the West is now bankrupt. America has accumulated huge trade deficits. Europe has strangled business with bureaucracy. The UK, which has gold-plated EU legislation and now has the world's most incomprehensible tax system and most extensive maze of red tape faces the worst future of any nation.

In contrast, much of Asia has low debt, huge foreign exchange reserves and a massive trade surplus. The centre of financial power is moving east, away from New York and London. As the financial crisis of 2008, born of years of greed and financial mismanagement, opens up and develops further so the West will get weaker and weaker.

When central banks in Asia stop buying US government bonds, the USA will be near the end. When China abandons the dollar the temporary upwards blip, which has interrupted a secular decline, will come to a sudden and probably spectacular end. When oil is traded in a currency other than US dollars the end will finally arrive for America. And the 'special relationship' British politicians like to boast about won't be worth a dime.

The growth of Asian countries (and other BRIC countries, Russia and Brazil) can be judged by the fact that even with the global recession, car sales around the world hit an all-time record of around 59 million in 2008.

Of those 59 million, 14 million cars were sold in BRIC countries. And the significance is that in 2008 the Americans didn't buy that many cars. For the first time in history the BRIC countries were buying and selling more cars than America. The importance of this can be judged by the fact that as recently as 2005 America sold ten million more cars than the BRIC countries. The world is changing at a phenomenal rate. Car sales in Brazil are rising at a rate of 30% a year. Russia will be Europe's biggest car market within two years. The Indian car company Tata, sells a car for well under £2,000 and is sponsoring Ferrari in Formula One.

But the real significance of all this is in a simple three letter word: oil.

All these cars which are being sold need petrol.

And the oil is running out.

★ ★ ★

Investors George Soros, Jim Rogers and Marc Faber have all suggested that the West is in its worst financial crisis for decades because the economic baton is being passed from West to East. We are, perhaps, at a crossroads where Western destruction is being replaced, or, rather, offset, by Eastern creation. As one part of the world waxes, so the other wanes.

The West – America, Britain and Europe – is in a secular decline. The East – China and India etc – is on the rise. Russia, Brazil and Africa are rising too. The future belongs to Asia in general and China in particular.

We need a Foreign Secretary who can build a decent (and possibly special) relationship with these countries.

We have David Miliband, surely the best known graduate of the Peter Mandelson School of Veracity And Integrity.

Incidentally, is Miliband really as big an idiot as he seems to be? Is anyone as big an idiot as Miliband seems to be? The banana brandishing boy has all the charisma and gravitas of a train-spotter. Who in their right mind would make this grinning buffoon Foreign Secretary?

The Labour Party has, since 1997, given us Britain's worst ever Chancellor of the Exchequer (Gordon Brown), the worst ever Home Secretary (David Blunkett), the worst ever Prime Minister (Tony Blair) and the worst ever Foreign Secretary, (David Miliband).

I suppose the Labour Party can be proud of that. They haven't got anything else to be proud of.

Actually, there is one more achievement that will last long after the Labour Government has disappeared into history.

Distrust of politicians.

Today, no one expects politicians to tell the truth about anything. Blair and Brown and Mandelson et al did that. We had some pretty ropey politicians before 1997 but it was the post 1997 bunch which finally removed any lasting hope that politicians might be trusted.

Today, no one expects politicians to do anything other than lie and cover their own backs. Peter Mandelson is the poster boy for politicians these days. Lie, spin and cover your back. Lie, spin and cover your back. Lie, spin and cover your back. And take the money.

It's a legacy of a sort, I suppose.

★ ★ ★

The Labour Party will not be forgiven by the middle classes who now realise (belatedly) just how much damage has been done to their wealth, lifestyle and country by politically-correct, multicultural, means-testing, target-mad lunatics. Savings have been destroyed, pensions turned into shadows and economic misery spread generously around. It is hardly surprising, perhaps, that the Labour Party is throwing money at the scroungers and the parasites, the long-term malingers and the public sector workers.

The Labour Party no longer pretends to do anything but please a very small group of people – the public sector workers, the unemployed and the people claiming sickness benefits. A modern political party does not need to win one vote from a person with a real job in order to win an election. Private sector workers, the people who actually create the nation's wealth, are effectively disenfranchised. The country is run by people who are 'takers', who contribute nothing but who take a great deal. I have long believed that Brown has been deliberately enlarging this group in order to protect his own party's electoral success.

The Government now spends £680 billion a year of our money. And much of it (most of it, indeed) is wasted on projects and people who provide nothing of value to our society. Most of it is spent doing nothing else other than ensure that Gordon Brown and his cohort can retain power. The Labour Party doesn't give a damn about upsetting the middle classes they were originally so keen to court because they know they have lost their vote. And they know they no longer need it; they have created their own support base.

★ ★ ★

The real aim of politicians should be justice. Our modern

politicians do not understand the concept, let alone believe in it. Politicians have discovered that the medium really is more important than the message. Indeed, the message doesn't matter very much at all. It is easier to sell a good-looking politician with a smile and bad policies than it is to sell an ugly politician with a frown and good policies. Politicians have discovered that depth and effectiveness are irrelevant. All that matters are superficial emotions. Tie strings to a puppet with a beaming grin and you can sell false ideas to enough people to gain, and retain, power. The unholy trinity of the modern politician consists of lies, denial and spin.

Our politicians promise us a better future but they are only concerned about a better future for them, not us. The only thing our politicians stand for is themselves. Politicians have always been the most contemptible of men. The most pathetic and easily bought, but today's politicians can be bought for a two week holiday in a nice villa, a pension, the chance to mix with celebrities and the promise of a well-paid directorship of an American company.

People accept the newspeak and the lies and the deceits and allow themselves to be manipulated because they don't believe that anyone can possibly lie to them as much as politicians do, and because they are frightened of what is happening and they want to put their head under the blanket and let someone take charge and create a better world. And so they accept tanks at Heathrow airport and believe, sort of, that they are needed to stop terrorists hijacking aeroplanes. And they aren't demonstrating in the streets because they are frightened. And when Gordon Brown and his idiotic friends tell them that they can save them from a darkening world, they want to believe. They don't go out into the streets to demonstrate because they know they will be arrested as terrorists but they also don't go out because they feel it won't do any good and they believe that maybe Gordon really can make things better – because he says he can.

Our politicians are self-serving chancers with no skills and, on the whole, very little training or job experience. The real-life job experience of the last ten years of Labour Government has included one minister who had a few years as a bar steward and another who worked as a postman. Hardly any have had genuine long-term experience of employment in the private sector.

As for their advisers – well, George Osborne, the current Shadow Chancellor, was at the age of 24 a Government Advisor on BSE. His training for this vital post? He is the son of a rich wallpaper manufacturer. He read history at university. His first choice was a job on a national newspaper as a journalist. But he failed to get such a job. So he got a job advising the Government on BSE.

★ ★ ★

It is the trend these days for former Labour ministers to take highly paid jobs with companies which have some relationship to their former political posts. In some cases the Ministers concerned were involved in creating a financial and regulatory climate which has helped the companies they join. In previous books I have often successfully predicted the jobs Ministers would take. (It isn't difficult.) This is called 'putting your snout in the trough'. Here are some examples, taken at random:

1. David Blunkett, former Home Secretary, took a job as adviser to a company offering identity card technology.
2. Hilary Armstrong, former local government minister, took a job with a French owned company which has won contracts to collect rubbish from British households.
3. Patricia Hewitt, former Health Secretary and Trade secretary, took jobs with Alliance Boots, Cinven and BT.
4. Alan Milburn, former Health Secretary, took jobs with Lloyds Pharmacy and PepsiCo UK.
5. Ivor Caplin, former defence minister, took a job as a consultant to a company called MBDA which sells weapons to the Ministry of Defence.
6. Charles Clarke, former education secretary, took a job with LJ Group which sells technology for science and engineering education.
7. Melanie Johnson, former public health minister, took a job as adviser to the Association of British Pharmaceutical Industry.
8. Stephen Ladyman, former Minister of State for Transport, became an adviser to ITIS Holding, which sells traffic data to the Department of Transport.
9. Nick Raynsford, former housing minister, took a job with Hometrack.

10. Tony Blair, former Prime Minister and a 'pretty OK sort of war criminal', took numerous jobs with people offering him vast amounts of money. (Seven years ago, when I predicted that Blair would choose to support Bush's illegal invasion of Iraq, I asked if his enthusiasm for the USA was perhaps 'personal' and inspired by an ambition to find well-paid jobs on leaving office.) Within his first two years after leaving Downing Street he reportedly made £15,000,000. He was charging more for a speech (£250,000) than anyone else on the planet. And then there was his salary as Middle East Special Envoy (you might have noticed his important silence during Israel's bombing of women and children in Gaza). For some reason which escapes me British taxpayers paid £700,000 for Blair to hire an entire floor of the American Colony hotel in East Jerusalem.

Were these people hired for their enormous skills or for their special knowledge and contacts? As far as I'm aware big companies weren't queuing up to offer these people highly paid positions before they became Ministers.

* * *

As for the House of Lords. Well, Blair replaced a bunch of perfectly decent lunatics who were gentlemen, if barking, with a chain gang of crooked nonentities and sycophants.

* * *

It may be difficult and painful to accept but economic failure is an essential and cathartic part of a healthy economy. Badly-run companies must die so that they can be replaced by well-run ones. (As an incompetent himself, Brown presumably has great sympathy with people who have risen far beyond their capabilities.) By bailing out failures and allowing the incompetent men and women responsible for the failures to stay in power, Brown has simply extended the length and depth of the recession. Japan made the same mistake and has, as a result, endured twenty years of stagnation. By trying to limit the damage done you ensure that damage lasts longer. And the psychological damage to employees, investors and entrepreneurs is long lasting. If Brown had allowed house prices to fall at a natural rate to their natural level (probably falling to around half of their peak level in two or three years) then everyone could have got on with their lives. And the market would have recovered reasonably quickly. New buyers would have queued up to buy houses. The cycle would have restarted. But by interfering with nature, Brown has ensured that the housing collapse will last twice or three times as long as it might have done. He has created an exceptionally bad cycle, ensured that prices will fall far further than they need have done and ensured that no one with more than half a brain will want to buy domestic residential property for decades. What Brown (and indeed the American leadership) failed to understand was that in a financial crisis it is healthy, and indeed essential, to let some bombed out businesses fail.

* * *

Brown has always been an idiot. He proved his incompetence very early on. Soon after becoming Chancellor he decided to sell English gold so that he could delight the EU by buying some euros. A foolish, short-sighted notion. And a badly timed one since gold was near its all time low. But making a simple mistake wasn't enough for Brown. He had to make things worse for the nation by announcing beforehand that he intended to sell vast amounts of gold.

The inevitable happened.

If you owned a large stock of umbrellas and you told the world that you were going to sell them all then the price of umbrellas would fall. If you owned a number of flats in a building, and you announced that you were going to dump the lot, the price of flats in that building would collapse. You don't need to be an economic genius to work that out.

But that's just what Brown did. Having decided to sell the nation's gold he told the world his plans. And subsequently sold the gold at the lowest possible price. It was a kindergarten bloomer that cost the country billions. But it was typically Brown and best summed up in a single word: moronic.

Sometimes it's difficult to avoid wondering if Gordon might not be doing it all on purpose. We know he loathes the English. Maybe he really wants to destroy England. He's certainly making a very good job of doing just that.

Or maybe he's just gone mad and needs locking up. It was, remember, Gordon who claimed to have brought down the price of oil and who promised to bring down the price of food. (Or, was it the other way round? I'm beginning to get confused by his fantasies.) And it was a presumably sober Gordon Brown who genuinely seemed to mean it when he told the House of Commons that he was saving the world.

★ ★ ★

One of Brown's big problems is that he has too little experience of the real world. You could tell Brown knew nothing of the real world when, just before he left the job as Chancellor, he restricted commercial property tax relief in a stupid attempt to discourage property owners from holding onto empty buildings. Brown (and whatever idiot advised him) thought that by not giving tax relief on empty buildings he would force them to renovate the buildings and to relet them. In the real world the owners of empty properties suddenly found that they had to pay vast amounts of tax for the privilege of holding onto their buildings. And so they demolished them. All over the country the bulldozers were called in. And buildings were knocked down because it was cheaper to do that than it was to pay extortionate amounts of tax on them. It was Brown's version of the window tax of the 1700's – a tax brought in to charge householders more for having buildings with lots of windows. (Householders got round the tax by bricking up some of their windows. Stonemasons and bricklayers did well out of it, and the nation was left with a lot of old buildings which still have bricked up windows.)

In November 2008, after claiming that the country was soundly based to face the future, Brown and Darling introduced all sorts of schemes which they seemed to think would help the economy. And they showed just how out of touch they are.

First, they made the tax system even more complicated by introducing another tax band designed to charge high earners more tax. Thanks to Brown's decade of mismanagement, Britain already had the most complex tax system in the world. Brown and Darling made it worse. And, in the view of most independent experts, the changes will result in lower tax revenues because the people affected will either dump some of their money into their pension fund or they just won't bother earning more money once they reach the new band.

Second, they cut 2.13% off shop prices by cutting 2.5% off VAT for 13 months. Whatever tiny advantage this might have offered to shoppers was far, far outweighed by the damage it did to businesses.

Put aside the fact that this decision was clearly designed to encourage more consumer spending (the cause of the problem in the first place, of course) rather than help businesses, I couldn't help feeling that this was a perfect example of the way politicians simply don't understand the real world.

(Indeed, very few journalists seemed to understand that this was an appalling idea.)

Dealing with VAT is one of the big nightmares for all businesses – large and small. The whole VAT system has made businessmen and women unpaid tax collectors. Keeping VAT records, and filling in VAT forms, is a terrible burden. It takes up much time and effort. Darling's decision to cut VAT from 17.5% to 15% on December 1st 2008 sent shivers down my spine and made me give thanks that my business no longer sells any items which have VAT on them.

Most businesses set their tax year to coincide with the Inland Revenue's tax year which runs April 5th to April 4th. So the Government's VAT cut meant that VAT would change in one tax year and then change again in the following tax year.

If Darling had thought up a way to make life difficult for businesses, and to tip thousands more into bankruptcy, he couldn't have made a better job of it.

The fact that both Parliaments and the civil service are all packed with people who have no experience of real life, and who have never lived or worked in the real world, means that businesses in Britain will continue to struggle and will, during the long recession ahead, fail in ever increasing numbers. Most countries make things and export them. They make cars, television sets, plastic toys, bras, and computers. What does Britain make and export? Guns, landmines and whisky. And that is about it.

The Labour Government's response was a typically statist solution. What they should have done, of course, was to encourage existing industry and coming entrepreneurs. Reducing red tape would have been a good start.

★ ★ ★

Matthew Parris of *The Times* described the Pre-Budget Report as a case of 'pissing expensively into the wind'.

I was sitting in a cafe in Paris when I heard of the VAT cut and my immediate response was to ask the waiter to send over a pint of vin chaud. The VAT rate change was such an obviously stupid, stupid thing to do.

It was stupid for three reasons.

First, it was never going to make consumers start spending again. At the time when the 2.5% cut in VAT was announced, the British high street was decorated with signs announcing cuts ranging between 20% and 95%. I doubt if there was a shopper in Britain who would have given a second glance to a poster announcing a cut of 2.5%.

Second, the cut seemed specifically designed to make life difficult for small businesses at a time when most of them were fighting for their lives. Shops and businesses were given four days to change the prices on all their stock. Four whole days. The total bill of changing all the prices was estimated at £300 million but that was probably a conservative guess. Shopkeepers had to reprint price labels. Mail order companies had to reprint catalogues. Companies with websites had to pay a small fortune to have their site reconfigured. Tills had to be reprogrammed. Restaurants and cafes and pubs had to reprint menus. The cut of 2.5% was designed to last from 1st December 2008 to 1st December 2009. Businesses were given the task of organising their accounts with two separate VAT rates in two consecutive years.

When the media finally realised just what chaos the Chancellor had introduced I wasn't surprised to hear that many people running small businesses had simply decided to ignore the cut and to leave their prices as they were.

'This is the worst possible time for us to divert man-hours to a non-essential exercise, it being the busiest time of the year and the most challenging financial period we've faced,' said one angry entrepreneur, quoted in the *Financial Times*, who pointed out that he would have to do everything in reverse when the temporary VAT reduction was eventually withdrawn.

'It is costing people and causing headaches, but it is not going to make a jot of difference to the economy,' said another.

Third, it cut tax revenues by a significant amount at a time when the country's debts were already building up to a terrifying level. Cutting this minuscule amount from VAT cost the country £12.5 billion.

If Brown had understood or cared for the economic future of the country he might perhaps have followed the example of the Prime Minister of Singapore, Lee Hsien Loong, who cut his pay and that of all civil servants by a fourth saying that the Government should tighten its belt.

Brown's whole policy was based on a rather outdated and discredited theory by Keynes. Keynesians say that when people stop wasting their money, the government has to step in and waste it for them. His plan (if we can call it that) was that we should sacrifice the long-term for the short-term by spending every penny we couldn't afford in order to get the economy moving again. And so the Government carried on planning for the Olympics, hiring new employees and generally chucking money around.

They were, of course, making more mistakes.

First, the Keynsian theory really requires that you spend money on stuff that improves society – like building new bridges, roads and hospitals. Giving money to banks so that bankers can continue to enjoy their huge bonuses isn't the same thing at all. Second, when your problem is caused by spending too much money (i.e. more than you have) you can't cure the problem by spending even more money that you don't have. You can only spend your way out of a recession if you have savings you can call on. Britain didn't have any money saved because Brown had spent it all hiring consultants to wander around telling the dumber citizens how to eat five vegetables a day and how to give up smoking.

Of course, if Brown and his chums had enough experience of the real world they might have realised this. But Brown and his chums had spent most of their entire working lives cocooned in a bizarre world where everything is paid for by public money which just rains down from heaven in a never ending stream. When the stream looks as if it's drying up you just put taxes up. Easy.

By the end of 2008, Britain's problem was that no one in Government seemed to realise that the mess the country was in was their fault. Just like the bankers who seemed to think that their banks had lost billions of pounds because it had been stolen away by some evil tooth fairy, so Brown seemed to want to blame other people. It was all the fault of the Chinese, or the Americans or the Venezuelans or little green men from Mars.

For a decade Brown had claimed that Britain was prosperous because his policies had made it so. No mention of the fact that the prosperity was based on debt. No mention of the fact that Britain had been dragged along by the rest of the world. It was all down to Brown's genius. But now that things had gone badly wrong it was all someone else's fault. None of it was Brown's fault.

Indeed, in one telling moment in the House of Commons Gordon Brown actually announced to the nation that he was saving the world.

That's what he said.

Just why men in white coats didn't rush in and take him away is just one of the many mysteries which will puzzle me until I am no longer here to worry about such things.

The problem with living in cloud cuckoo land is, of course, that unless you put a foot back down on the earth you can't take a real step forward towards solvency and prosperity. Unless you acknowledge that you've made mistakes you will never face reality.

And so Gordon, who far from single-handedly saving the world has single-handedly destroyed Britain, will, until he relinquishes the post he was never elected to hold, continue to create policies which will make things worse.

And by the time he goes off to start a new career advising banks or presenting television programmes, the country will be in such dire straits that it will take generations to put things right.

There is something grotesque, even obscene, about the way Brown portrays himself as the world's saviour. Brown made Britain the weakest and most vulnerable nation in the world. He should be tried for treason. He has done more damage to Britain in general, and England in particular, than any other individual I can think of – including Adolf Hitler. (Unlike Brown, Hitler was at least elected leader of his country.) If I thought he had the intelligence I would suspect him of deliberately destroying the country in order to satisfy the secret requirements of those who want a World Government.

'Egotism is an infirmity that perpetually grows upon a man,' wrote Hazlitt, the English essayist, 'till at last he cannot bear to think of anything but himself, or ever to suppose that others do.'

He could have been writing about almost any member of the Labour Government at any time since 1997.

The superboom of the end of the 20th Century and the first few years of the 21st Century has left the door wide open for a fearful and distressed society to welcome a world in which governments and companies become as one.

That, just in case you've forgotten, is the official definition of fascism.

★ ★ ★

The failure of politicians or civil servants to understand how vulnerable many businesses were, and just how dangerous the financial crisis was likely to be for the survival of thousands of small businesses, was exemplified by the fact that within hours of announcing the VAT change the Government announced proposed legislation allowing councils to levy a supplement on business rates to pay for local economic development projects.

And, on the same day, they announced another raft of proposed employment legislation (as instructed by the EU) designed to make life considerably harder for entrepreneurs. The new measures introduced flexible working rights for 4.5 million employees and new rights giving millions more employees the right to 'request' that they be allowed to undergo training while being paid. While entrepreneurs were digesting that lot it was announced that the Government owned Post Office had decided to raise the cost of postage by 10% – far more than the official inflation rate.

Within days things got even worse when the European Court of Justice announced that employees on long-term sick leave would, in future, be entitled to take all the holiday they may have accrued when they returned to work. Workers who left after being on sick leave would have to be given their holiday pay for the period when they were off sick. This all came on top of existing legislation insisting that employers who terminated an employee's contract should pay wages for the full notice period – whatever the employee's offence.

And then, just as entrepreneurs were digesting that (if they were luck enough to spot it amongst the reams on new legislation) there came another blow. In January 2009, the Health and Safety Offences Act 2008 came into force. It increased the maximum fine that can be imposed in lower courts to £20,000 and made it possible for certain offences, which could previously only be tried in the lower courts, to be tried in both the lower and the higher courts. The Act also increased the number of offences that can result in imprisonment for employers. I wonder how many small business owners know which Health and Safety offences merit imprisonment. And I wonder how many know what the laws are and how easily their business can be destroyed?

Who are the people who make up these rules? They're highly paid, they're in secure employment and they have never met a pay roll out of their own pockets.

If the Government had deliberately decided to destroy as many businesses as possible it could not have made a better job of it. Indeed, it does sometimes seem to me that the Government and the EU want to get rid of small businesses completely. From their point of view this makes sense. Entrepreneurs are difficult to control. Governments (and the EU) can negotiate and deal with big businesses far easier than they cope with small businesses. Fascism is, after all, a marriage between the statism and capitalism. Corporate bureaucrats understand and work well with state bureaucrats.

Peter Mandelson, for the Government, told the BBC that 'flexible working can give employers and employees valuable flexibility, helping to keep businesses profitable and to keep people at work.'

The director-general of the Institute of Directors said: 'The argument the Government is making that this proposal will help the country get through recession quickly is frankly absurd.'

The bottom line is that before this mess is over, more than 1,000 small businesses will be going bust every week. Partly as a result of that, the overall unemployment figure will far exceed three million. And the cost to the taxpayer will be horrendous. Most worrying of all it is small businesses which grow into big ones. If you destroy small businesses, which has for a long time seemed to be the avowed aim of the Labour Government, there won't be any big ones. Thanks to the Government, the next few years aren't going to be about growth but survival. And businesses are going to cut corners as often, and as sharply, as they can in order to try to survive. As individual companies try to raise cash by cutting jobs, capital spending and inventories this will inevitably have a damaging effect on the country. One company's expenses are another company's income. One company's cutbacks mean that another company will stop making any profits – and will have to cut back further.

★ ★ ★

We have a newly devised class system with politicians and civil servants on top and everyone else down below. Our society has been destroyed by social engineering: a toxic mixture of political correctness, multiculturalism, institutional targets and means-testing.

Here's an example of the new 'them and us' class system that the Labour Government has created.

The Government is allowing politicians, officials and competitors attending the Olympic Games to have traffic priority in and around London. Some traffic lanes will be reserved for the Olympic VIPs. Just as we now have 'bus lanes' so we will soon have 'limousine' lanes. The M4, A40 and other major arterial routes through London will have lanes closed to everyone who isn't a registered Olympic VIP. Special Zil lanes (named after the roads reserved for Soviet-era Politburo members and KGB officers) will be made by the Olympic Delivery Authority. London Mayor Boris Johnson has given the lanes his full blessing. I bet he has. Will the traffic lanes revert to normal use after the Olympics? I very much doubt it. Ministers (who will use the reserved traffic lanes) will so much enjoy their ability to move about without having to wait in traffic queues that they will retain the special lanes after the 2012 games have finished.

The Government and civil service now seem to regard the electorate as nothing more than a source of revenue. For example, the Government made a £499 million profit out of the floods which destroyed much of England in 2007. Although the Government handed out £36 million in building grants it made £535 million in VAT on housing repairs resulting from the flood damage. The damage was a result of two Government policies: allowing builders to put houses on flood plains and allowing changes to rivers and waterways.

★ ★ ★

The long-term outlook for Britain is appalling. High inflation, huge tax rises and more fascism. Gordon Brown promises another 100,000 jobs. That's the good news. The bad news is that the 100,000 new jobs are all in the public sector. More nappy folding advisors on £50,000 a year. Since Labour took over the country, one in seven private-sector jobs has disappeared. The nation's currency is falling in value. House prices are collapsing. Nothing is going to improve because the mass of people are too tired, too bullied, too browbeaten and too frightened to do or say anything. As Thoreau wrote: 'the mass of people lead lives of quiet desperation'. That has never been truer than it is now.

Britain has been ruined by bureaucratic jobsworths who enjoy the power given to them by a gang of politically correct, statist, fascist-quasi-liberal-self-proclaimed-do-gooders dedicated to such disastrous theories as multiculturalism, social targets and means-testing.

Thanks to a dozen years of Labour Governments we are now living in a cesspool of fraud, deceit and institutionalised dishonesty; a septic tank of despair; a quagmire of poverty, disease, hypocrisy and corruption. Britain has, beyond any shadow of doubt, become a fascist country, run by a fascist Government and controlled by a fascist police force.

And it's going to get worse. Much, much worse.

* * *

There are now around 1,200 quangos in Britain. These unelected public bodies employ more than 700,000 people and cost taxpayers £101 billion a year. There are so many of these damned busy body organisations that no one can keep track of who they are, what they do or why they are even in existence. Most are simply stuffed to the gills with friends of the Labour Party. It's the modern way politicians reward their faithful friends, supporters, canvassers, hangers-on, neighbours, relatives and flat-mates.

When the Labour Party came to power in 1997, Gordon Brown promised a 'bonfire of the Quangos' to reduce public sector costs. It was a typical Gordon Brown promise. In 2003 the Parliamentary Public Administration Committee called for the Government to create a comprehensive list of quangos; detailing their spending and staff numbers. The Government did nothing. The only list we have was created by the TaxPayers Alliance.

Quangos are now breeding like rabbits. There is, for example, the British Potato Council. Why do we need that one? If potato farmers want a lobby group let them set one up and pay for it. There is the Equality and Human Rights Commission (now part of the problem and not a solution). We would all be better off without that.

Government Departments have had to hire huge numbers of

staff simply to open the envelopes containing the reports sent in by all these quangos. The Department of Business, Enterprise and Regulatory Reform (previously known as the DTI and before that known as something else) has oversight of 68 quangos and, in order to deal with these wretched organisations, employs 244,000 staff. A quango called Transport for London employs an army of expensive staff; 232 of whom are paid over £100,000 a year. The chief executive takes home almost £500,000 a year. In one recent year, the chairman of the South East England Development Agency spent £51,489 on 'executive cars' and taxis. And the agency spent £600,000 running ten overseas offices and participating in a property trade fair on the French Riviera.

'Nobody,' said Milton Friedman, 'spends other people's money as carefully as he spends his own.'

There are eight regional development agencies, given to us by the Labour Government (with some encouragement from Brussels) and they cost us £2.3 billion a year to run.

Why?

Well, maybe you should ask the European Commission.

But I rather doubt if you'll get any more of a reply than I did.

Worst of all the wretched quangos keep growing. The ones that exist demand ever more money. New quangos spring up like weeds in a summer garden. And there is no accountability. No one measures their usefulness or effectiveness. But the taxpayer keeps paying the bills.

Name one quango you wouldn't like to be without.

I can't.

They should go. All of them. And the people who sit on them, bleeding the taxpayer dry, should be fired and put to useful work. Britain's public lavatories are a disgrace and desperately need attention.

* * *

The Chancellor and the Prime Minister and the Governor of the Bank of England keep telling us that 'we will come through this'.

Of course we will.

What, pray, is the alternative?

But what matters is what sort of state we are in (both as a nation and as individuals) when we do come through it. And everything the politicians and the public sector workers are doing is ensuring that we come through this crisis in a very weakened state.

The fundamental problem is, of course, that the economy is (like everything else) run by people whose actions are inspired by their own personal (or party) requirements, rather than by the needs of the nation, and who usually only react to immediate problems and who do not plan or act strategically.

⋆ ⋆ ⋆

In January 2009 a YouGov poll showed that 40% of the population thought that Gordon Brown and Alistair Darling were the best people to lead the country through the recession. I would have been less horrified, and less surprised, if I had read that 40% of the population thought that Noddy and Big Ears were the best people to lead the country through the recession. Or that the Isle of Wight is actually a meringue nest. It is worrying to know that you are living in a nation where 40% of the population is stark raving bonkers. These people walk around and look like normal, living people. They watch Big Brother, read books by Jordan and think speed cameras cut accidents and vaccines prevent disease. The existence of these people, and the fact that they have votes and opinions, frightens the life out of me.

⋆ ⋆ ⋆

Will Britain go bankrupt?

It has for some time been acknowledged that Britain could go bankrupt. If this happens the Government might not be able to honour its financial obligations regarding gilts and national savings.

Countries don't often go bankrupt. But it does happen. (Argentina was a recent example.) There are several countries currently on the brink of bankruptcy. Both Britain and America are high on the list.

In December 2008, the cost of protecting against default by the British Government rose dramatically in the UK. In February 2008, it cost £8,000 to insure £10,000,000 worth of UK Government debt against default over a five year period. By December 2008, it cost £110,000 for the same insurance cover. In other words investors had decided that by the end of 2008 the likelihood of the

British Government being unable to honour its obligations had risen around 14 times.

By December 2008, it cost more to insure the UK against default than it cost to insure some of the UK's banks (such as HSBC and Lloyds).

This matters because Brown and Darling are planning a good deal of 'unfunded spending' (spending money they have to borrow). And in order to pay for all that spending they intend to raise £135 billion a year until 2013. (That's three times as much as the Government had previously been borrowing). And they intended to raise all that money by selling gilts.

Overseas investors are beginning to worry that if they buy gilts they might not get their money back because the UK Government might go bust.

★ ★ ★

The world's economic crisis started because people and governments everywhere were spending too much money. Billions of consumers had got into the habit of spending money they didn't have on stuff they didn't need. A grotesque explosion of buying things turned into a grotesque explosion of debt. Consumers were spending money they earned (and saving none if any); they were spending money they acquired by re-mortgaging their houses; and they were spending money made available through their credit cards. Governments were simply spending money they had created by turning on the printing presses. And they were using the money to hire thousands and thousands of utterly pointless advisers and consultants and spin-doctors – all of whom went onto the public payroll.

In the autumn of 2008 all this went sour. The greed and stupidity which led to the subprime crisis resulted in an international crisis. The problem was originally caused in the USA but bankers, politicians and consumers everywhere were also responsible.

As the crisis deepened people became aware that they might lose their jobs. House values crashed (and so banks were no longer prepared to lend money against them). And banks pulled back credit card lending.

Crunch.

The engine driving the economy forward hit the buffers.

People stopped buying stuff. So people making stuff found they were no longer earning any money. And people digging stuff out of the ground so that people making stuff could use it to make more stuff found that they were suddenly receiving less for the stuff they dug out of the ground than it was costing them to get it out.

A global mega crisis caused by too much spending.

People and governments spending money they didn't have on stuff they didn't need. (And didn't even really want.)

Governments around the world decided to combat the problem by spending more money. And by encouraging consumers to spend more money.

For once in their lives politicians actually wanted to create inflation. (Printing money is what causes inflation.)

It all seems like madness. And it is.

Money is, fundamentally, fairly simple stuff. It's a way of swapping labour for goods. It's a way of keeping score. It rewards the most productive use of capital. It helps us measure how we value our time and our labour.

But by protecting bad investments and bad industries (such as the banks and the car manufacturers) governments have damaged the whole purpose of money: they have devalued the principle of money. By handing money over to banks which were run by stupid, greedy people (and by leaving the stupid, greedy people in place) governments have rewarded failure and removed the element of risk which is an essential part of capitalism. Money that should have been used on sensible, productive projects has been wasted on speculative, unproductive, pointless projects. And greedy, stupid people have been rewarded for their greed and stupidity.

By following a policy of spend, spend, spend (the policy that Gordon Brown was so proud to call his own) governments have made things much, much, much worse.

★ ★ ★

There is a real risk that if the global recession continues and becomes a depression then countries will start to look more and more for ways to protect themselves from the mess. The jobless will demand that politicians introduce protectionism to ensure that they get work again. Import tariffs will be introduced. Barriers will be erected everywhere. America is particularly likely to do this. It is a solution that American politicians move towards very easily. And it is what happened in the 1930s when protectionism and devaluations were rife as countries determined to play 'beggar thy neighbour' to the death. Nationalism will return. And so will racism.

There is one country in the world which is, thanks to the policies of its Government, certain to suffer more than any other.

That country is Britain.

The debt Britain has acquired under Brown's disastrous leadership will lead to persistently high unemployment, reduced public expenditure (with a consequent massive reduction in the quality and quantity of public services), higher taxes, higher prices, a reduced standard of living, lower house prices, high inflation, high interest rates, widespread poverty and lower growth.

The Government has no idea what is going on. Ministers and civil servants have lied and spun so much that they don't have the foggiest idea what sort of state the country is in. The accurate information required to make good, sound decisions simply wasn't there when it was needed.

The Government has lied so much that the truth is buried, way out of reach.

★ ★ ★

'The buck stops here.'

SIGN ON THE DESK OF USA PRESIDENT HARRY S.TRUMAN

★ ★ ★

In 2008, the oil price soared and plummeted, sterling nearly collapsed, volatility reached levels rarely if ever seen before, cash deposits were threatened, companies were going bankrupt as though it was in fashion, banks had to be nationalised and equities fell around 40%. For investors, 2008 was the second worst year in 312 years. Highly paid investment managers were happily boasting that they had beaten their competitors by losing only 35% of their customers' money. The stock market crash of 2008 was the third worst bear market in European history and the second worst in America. Companies were facing their worst earnings recession in at least 40 years.

Now, Britain faces insolvency; the collapse of the currency; the sort of inflation seen in South America and Zimbabwe; falling living standards; a collapse in public services and a decline in our status in the world. Our economy will stumble and shrink for some years to come. House prices will fall, fall again and then, just when it seems impossible for them to fall again, they will fall again. Shares will meander, fall, rise, fall, rise and go pretty much nowhere for years to come. There is a worrying risk that Britain is now entering the sort of era that has bedevilled Japan for the last two decades. In October 2008, the Japanese Nikkei index reached its lowest point for 26 years. Shareholders who had held onto their shares for over a quarter of a century without seeing any gain whatsoever must, by then, have surely been feeling rather disillusioned with the idea that, in the long run, equities are the best investment. The Japanese market hit 30,000 in January 1990. In October 2008 it was between 7,000 and 8,000 – the lowest it had been since 1982. Anyone who bought Japanese shares in 1990 would have been sitting on a huge loss a generation later.

And in Britain the next generation will be faced with higher and higher taxes and fewer and fewer public services. 'Screw the unborn,' could be Labour's watchword. The future is gloomier than even Labour politicians think it might be.

All thanks to Gordon the Moron.

Spanish philosopher George Santayana wrote that character is an omen of destiny and that the more integrity we have, the nobler our destinies are likely to be.

Our destiny has been ordained by Gordon's character and is unlikely to show many signs of nobility. What can go wrong will go wrong and what will get worse will get worse. Anyone relying on our current batch of politicians to get us out of this mess (a mess they got us into to) is doomed to disappointment. They are going to make everything worse. Much, much worse.

Sadly, one of the big problems in Britain today is that we, as citizens, have allowed the politicians to take away our power. We have allowed ourselves to be lied to and deceived and we have allowed our politicians to take power (and to sell it on to the European Union). The result is that, today, politicians can do what they like with us. If they (or their minions) tell us that we cannot take a book with us onto an aeroplane we meekly accept that. If they tell us that a mother cannot take milk for her baby onto a plane then we accept that too. If the police shoot an innocent man seven times in the head we accept that when we are told it was done for our own good. If our Government tortures people we accept that. If our Government starts wars so that America can steal oil we accept that.

★ ★ ★

'Doing nothing is not an option,' seems to be the Labour Government's latest mantra.

Why not?

Doing nothing would do less harm.

★ ★ ★

We need to remember Japan went bust nearly twenty years ago. Property has collapsed to around a tenth of its value in the late 1980s. Interest rates in Japan have been zero for years. And the Japanese Government has spent around a trillion dollars trying to encourage investment. It has all failed. And now, facing pretty much the same problem, the British Government is following the Japanese plan. It's an old, old plan. (Not, as Gordon Brown would apparently have us believe, something he thought up in the bath.) And it comes from an old Christmas cracker motto: 'Spend your way out of a recession'.

But such a daft scheme can only work if you have loads of cash to start with. And unfortunately for Gordon and Britain we didn't have loads of cash.

The only effective way to get out of the mess Gordon got us into is to fix the balance sheet. And that means saving more and spending less. It means putting up taxes and cutting services.

But Gordon didn't want to do that. It's not the best way to win an election. And Gordon wants to win an election more than he wants to save the country. In fact, he is prepared to destroy the country to give him a vague chance of winning an election.

If, as I suspect, the global recession ends elsewhere before it ends in the UK then commodity prices (including the prices of fuel and food) will soar as people elsewhere resume their consuming habits. The result, when taken in conjunction with the collapse of the pound, will be massive inflation in the UK.

★ ★ ★

So, how bad can it get?

How bad can you imagine it could get?

It will be worse than that.

Chapter 2

America: The Long Decline Obama Won't Halt

America's period of world supremacy has been relatively short. Self-serving and violent, it has made enemies everywhere and its decline is now inevitable.

America has become two nations: the very rich and the poor. An estimated 36.5 million Americans live below the official poverty line and that figure will probably exceed 50 million within a year or two. Many Americans only avoid starving by relying on food handouts. Rich Americans drink bottled water. Poor Americans drink the stuff that comes out of rusted pipes. Each year more than 3.5 million people who drink water from the tap fall ill from Escherichia coli poisoning and from over 40,000 sewage spills. No wonder the posh people drink water bottled in France. Of the 756 steel deck bridges which cross American waterways at least 80 urgently need repairing. How urgently? Well, one of them fell into the Minnesota river recently, killing 13 school children. No money for bridges. Plenty of money for bombs.

'What a wonderful country this is,' said George W. Bush, when told by one American that she had three jobs.

America is in serious trouble. The borrowing binge and the greed which created the world's greatest ever financial crisis has left most of its banks close to bankrupt.

'The President has said the dollar is strengthening because it's a safe haven,' said legendary investor Jim Rogers. 'That is just balderdash. The US is bankrupt.'

★ ★ ★

In America, industrial output and wages have both been falling for years.

But although the currency has fallen it has not yet collapsed.

Why?

It hasn't collapsed because people keep spending.

When an American consumer buys a Chinese television set he pays for it with dollars.

The Chinese company then stockpiles the dollars it receives. And it uses the excess dollars to buy American Government bonds as an investment. The Chinese company wants to keep its money in dollars because if it sells the dollars then the value of the dollar will fall. And if the value of the dollar falls then American consumers won't be able to afford to buy any more television sets.

And so the world economy is built on debt.

The American Government keeps printing money. The American consumer keeps borrowing money and spending it in China. America's debt grows. China's store of dollars grows. The result is that China now owns America's future and occasionally American politicians do a little chest beating and moan about this in various ways. There have even been lunatics in America talking of a war with China. (That would be a very big mistake, and quite certainly the last one America would ever make. The Chinese have a big and superbly equipped army. The Americans have lost a lot of wars in recent years, but if they start a war with China it will last less than a week and it will be the last one they ever start.)

★ ★ ★

In 2006, Americans spent more money than they earned. Generally speaking this is not, as Mr Micawber would confirm, a wise thing to do. Before 2006, the last year when Americans spent more than they earned was 1933. That was not a good year for America. Things today are worse, however, since Americans now owe more than they did back in 1933. Most Americans currently have few or no savings to tide them through a difficult time. The rich Americans just spend their money and assume that more will come their way. The poor Americans (by far the largest group of course) struggle to survive and don't get a chance to save anything.

Where has all the money come from?

Rising property prices.

America's residential housing stock was worth around $10 trillion in 1999. By 2006 it had doubled to $20 trillion. America's perceived growth has been nothing more than an expansion of its debt. Just like Britain.

The American national debt is now $8.8 trillion (at the time of writing it was $8,883,212,488,519). It was $5.7 trillion when George W. Bush first arrived in the White House.

In the first quarter of 2007, American Gross Domestic Product (GDP) growth fell well below the rate of population growth. This means that Americans are getting poorer. (There is less money to be shared among more people.) In the USA as in the UK, while the poor and the middle classes got poorer the super-bubble for the rich kept expanding into the early years of the 21st Century.

Personally, Americans now owe a staggering $16 trillion dollars – much of it borrowed against their homes since 2001. No more is America the land of the free. Today it's the land of the debt slaves. Personal savings in America are running at minus $140 billion annually. In other words, instead of saving for the future, Americans have been digging into their savings and spending them. They have been borrowing money from banks and credit card companies so that they can continue pretending to be rich.

★ ★ ★

'There is no question about it. Wall Street got drunk and now it's got a hangover. The question is: how long will it take to sober up?'

George W. Bush (speaking without realising that he was wearing a 'live' microphone).

★ ★ ★

Globalisation magnifies economic problems. When American banks sold huge mortgages to people who couldn't possibly ever afford to pay them back the consequences were felt by banks, depositors, shareholders, pensioners and workers throughout the world. As a direct result of the greed of American bankers and brokers people all over the world will face higher taxes, greater unemployment and more regulation and statism. There will also be a dramatic and long-term rise in inflation.

★ ★ ★

It isn't just the banks that are in trouble. The American nation itself is pretty well bankrupt – both financially and morally. The American Government used nearly nine trillion dollars in the autumn of 2008 in its attempts to halt the financial crisis.

By the end of 2008 the credit crunch crisis had, if you put the money into today's dollars, already cost the country nearly three times as much as the whole of World War II. In fact, the credit crisis of 2008 has, as I write, cost America more than the Korean War, the Marshall plan, the invasion of Iraq, the Vietnam War, the race to put a man on the moon and World War II. The public debt had grown to nearly 200% of GDP (gross domestic product) resulting in many foreign governments actually worrying that America itself might go bankrupt. (As a comparison it is worth noting that the Masstricht Treaty requires member states of the European Union to reduce their public debt to no more than 60% of GDP).

More than 100% of America's public debt is held by foreign investors and they're getting very worried. The International Monetary Fund published a study showing that countries which have more than 60% of their public debt held by non-resident foreigners run a high risk of currency crisis and insolvency, or debt default. And that's all the official, Government debt. American private debt (money owed by individual Americans) is also more than 100% of GDP. The country most worried by all this? China. Much of China's accumulated currency reserves are in US dollars.

★ ★ ★

One of the problems in America is that corruption is now endemic. You think I'm exaggerating? Here are two examples:

1. Half of the past eight governors of the state of Illinois have been indicted and several of them have been sent to prison.
2. There are 535 members of the USA congress. The last time I looked 75% were lawyers. According to the Harry Schultz Letter: seven of the 535 have been arrested for fraud, 19 have been accused of writing bad cheques, 117 have directly or indirectly bankrupted at least two businesses, three have been in prison for assault, 36 have been arrested for spousal abuse, 14 have been arrested on drug-related charges, 84 have been arrested for drunk driving, 21 are currently defendants in

> lawsuits, eight have been arrested for shoplifting and 71 cannot get a credit card because of bad credit. Remember I am referring here not to the inmates of one of the tougher American prisons but to the United States of America Congress. The congressmen recently voted themselves a $15,000 a month pension for life, even for those congressmen and women who have served just one term.

No one much notices these things. No one cares. It's the way things are. It is hardly surprising that banking and investment institutions are awash with crooks.

★ ★ ★

Things are made worse for America by the fact that the nation's bullying and imperialist attitude (as it robs its way around the world) has created much anger.

Anti-Americanism is rising and is probably the fastest growing phenomenon on the planet. Since the Second World War, America has ruled the world by force, exerted in its own interests rather than in attempting to promote international peace. America's uncritical support of Israel has further damaged its reputation. I doubt if any nation has ever been loathed quite as much as America is loathed. When the world's richest nation uses the money it steals from poor nations to help it flout international law, distort the truth and disregard world opinion then the world as a whole is in great peril. (I dealt with these issues in my books *Rogue Nation* and *Confronting The Global Bully*.) American protectionism has impoverished countries around the world. American companies have bullied whole populations into poverty. No big nation gives as little of its wealth in foreign aid.

And as America becomes weaker and weaker so anti-Americanism will become increasingly overt. America is on an irreversible downside slide. The dollar was strong during the credit crunch crisis of late 2008. But it won't be long before America will implode. As America declines the Americans (who are the most parochial people on the planet) will keep their investments within the USA. But as America declines so world power will shift to China, India and Russia.

It will not, of course, be the first time that power has shifted from one nation to another.

During the two World Wars of the 20th Century, Britain spent every penny it could lay its hands on. America took advantage of Britain and grew in wealth and power as Britain declined in both. Britain saved the world twice and was enfeebled and bankrupted by the effort. In 1940, USA still had not recovered from the Great Depression which followed the 1929 Wall Street crash. But America grew in economic strength as it ruthlessly took financial advantage of Britain during World War II. The Second World War ruined the UK and made America rich. America profiteered and did very well.

The special relationship between the USA and the UK has always worked in one direction only. Israel is the only country to which America (through its powerful Jewish lobby) feels any genuine affinity and loyalty. Britain's relationship with the USA has for years been built on the individual interests of our leaders. Time and time again Britain has been betrayed by the USA.

America has been declining since the 1970s. The disastrous economic events of 2008 finished America off. The American Government is so much in debt (as a result of its military adventures and the greed of its bankers) that its power has gone.

The USA was successful and strong throughout the 20th Century because of its huge natural resources – especially oil. Access to its own supplies of natural resources allowed America to take advantage of European inventions such as the train, the aeroplane and the motor car. (Despite American claims none of these were invented in America or by Americans.)

Now those valuable home-grown resources are running out. The oil has pretty much gone. And America is on the slide. The American transport system is 97% dependent on oil and more than 90% of the oil supply is controlled by foreign governments. The result is that America is going to suffer more than any other country in the world – and certainly far more than any of the major nations in Europe.

The UK, France, Germany, Spain and most countries in Europe have extensive railway services. And, despite the activities of the ludicrous Dr Beeching, most decent sized towns in Britain still have a railway station of their own. It is possible to travel around Europe by train without too much inconvenience. America doesn't have that sort of railway network. In America, people either fly or drive.

And flying and driving are going to be increasingly expensive and eventually impossible for ordinary people.

Even without the oil running out America is heading for serious economic problems. It is heading for an economic depression that will make the 1930s look like a long holiday. There will, within a few years, be a meltdown of the American dollar that will be reminiscent of the collapse of the German mark during the Weimar Republic in the 1920s.

The coming Great American Depression will lead to the end of Medicare and Social Security in the USA. America will simply not be able to afford these programmes. The disintegration of American society will lead to civil unrest, to rioting and to enormous levels of violence. Thanks to the powerful pro-gun lobby in the USA, a lot of the unhappy citizens will be armed. Everyone will be looking for someone to blame. The liberals will want to blame the Bush family and the Zionist neocons. The republicans will look abroad and will want to blame bin Laden. Extreme left wing groups and environmentalists will blame big business. Everyone will blame someone. The rioting will lead to lynching. America will break up into separate states.

The collapse of the German economy led to the rise of Hitler and the Third Reich. It is impossible to predict just what will arise out of the ashes of America. But it probably won't be very pleasant.

★ ★ ★

When Barack Obama was elected President of the USA it was difficult to avoid the feeling that something biblical had happened. Crowds in Chicago and elsewhere seemed to be lifted up into a state of mass hysteria at the prospect of Obama running the country.

But what is really going to happen?

I am afraid I am considerably more sceptical about Obama's prospects. I have for some time regarded him as another Blair (and we all know how that worked out in the end). My fears and suspicions weren't helped when one of the first things Obama said when elected was that it would not be possible to do everything he wanted to do in 'the first four years'. I couldn't help being reminded of Blair, whose first action, as he walked into Downing Street, was to start planning his next election victory. Indeed, Obama reminds me very much of Blair (and, indeed, of Bill Clinton upon whom Blair based his political persona). All hype and superficiality. The adoration of

Obama reminds me of nothing so much as the adoration of Blair. I fear it will be as badly misplaced.

Obama has considerable experience of electioneering and very little experience of actually running anything. He is a man of many words and gestures. But what do they really mean? He is a graceful man and as a speech maker his timing is immaculate. Many speakers raise their voices at the end of a phrase or a sentence. This makes the speaker sound as though they are slightly uncertain; as though they are half asking a question. But I noticed that Obama does the opposite. He lowers his voice at the end of important phrases and sentences and this makes them sound like proclamations from on high, rather than political promises. It is, I believe, the single most important secret of his astonishing success. He is a man who has grasped the way that an empty promise, wrapped in purple prose, and accompanied by a lowering voice and a look of sincerity, can appear to be filled with substance. His understanding of the media, and how to use it, is second to none. But he seems to have spent most of his adult life preparing himself for high office. He has never run any public body of note. He was elected because he is a good speaker and had considerably more charisma than his main opponent, but running a declining superpower in a time of great economic crisis requires different skills to those needed to criss-cross the country in a private jet adorned with a campaign logo. I fear that his inexperience as a leader and manager will make him vulnerable to the wiles of the lobbyists and manipulators who abound in Washington. A clever speaking style won't save America or the world. (Incidentally, Margaret Thatcher had a secret vocal trick that worked well for her. She always breathed in mid-sentence when debating or being interviewed. This enabled her to keep talking and breathing and prevented anyone else from speaking unless they were prepared to interrupt her and appear rude.)

There's a lot of sizzle with Obama, but is there any steak? Will he be stronger than George W. Bush or just as pliable? Will he be able to withstand pressure from the Zionist lobby which will pressure him to support Israel, however reprehensible its behaviour? Israel's slaughter of Palestinian children in early 2009 horrified and alienated thinking, caring people throughout the world. The spin and self-righteous posturing which accompanied the murder made things worse. But America and Obama refused to condemn Israel. Indeed, days before the inauguration, the House of Representatives, dominated by Obama's party, voted 390-5 to back Israel's massacres in Gaza. As a senator, President-elect Obama raised no objection to $22 billion worth of weapons – including a missile which sucks the air out of the lungs, ruptures livers and amputates arms and legs, being hurried to Israel. And Obama is surrounded by people from 'Zionists-R-Us'. His Vice-President and Chief of Staff are both Zionists and so there is unlikely to be much change in America's policy of support-whatever-they-do for Israel. Indeed, Obama has already promised that Jerusalem will be Israel's capital, which was very nice of him.

Within days of the expensive inauguration in early 2009, Obama was already proving a disappointment to many of his most eager devotees. They were sad that he seemed disinclined to prosecute Bush or Cheney as war criminals. And he was breaking many promises that people thought he'd made. If they'd looked at the small print a little more carefully they would have noticed that he'd left himself what *The Economist* politely called 'wiggle room'. *The Economist* also reported that during his campaign Obama described himself as 'a blank screen on which people of vastly different political stripes projected their own views'. His major skill was that he managed to convince a lot of people (some with very different hopes and expectations) that their most urgent aspirations were also his.

And within weeks the scandals were already appearing. First, several former lobbyists were selected for senior position within the Obama administration despite the President's insistence during his campaign that 'lobbyists will not run my White House'. He appointed a former lobbyist for Raytheon, the arms contractor, as deputy defence secretary. And a former lobbyist for Goldman Sachs was appointed Chief of Staff for the Treasury secretary.

Second, there were the resignations as some appointees were discovered to have somehow missed paying fairly huge amounts of tax. This is the sort of thing that ordinary people go to prison for, but it is the sort of thing politicians like to shrug off with a 'silly old me' look. George W. Bush lost two nominees for high office in his administration after it emerged that they had not paid taxes. Bill Clinton lost two nominees for tax scandals. But within days of starting to build his administration Obama, Mr Clean, had three nominees embroiled in tax problems. One, Tim Geithner, whose job included responsibility for the Internal Revenue Service, admitted more than $34,000 of late tax payments. Another, Nancy Killefer, withdrew after announcing that she too had been late in paying taxes. Ms Killefer had previously been heavily involved in the management of the IRS and had sat on a board which pushed the agency to crack down on high-income tax cheats. Tom Daschle, a Washington power broker who withdrew from his proposed position as health secretary after revelations of $140,000 of skipped taxes, had been a supporter of high taxes and unforgiving attitudes towards tax evaders when he was a senator. 'Tax cheaters cheat us all,' he had said, 'and the IRS should enforce our laws to the letter.'

My suspicion that Obama might turn out to be a massive disappointment, and that he would continue producing wishy-washy campaign promises when the markets, the nation and the world needed specific, targeted action to deal with very real problems was supported in February 2009. Sadly, it seemed that the financial community was similarly unimpressed by Obama's attempts to deal with the very real problems overwhelming the United States of America.

★ ★ ★

Things aren't helped by the fact that America is in a terrible mess. I refer not just to the housing market, the stock market, the banks and the car industry but to the nation's ever-growing debt and its massively inflated currency. The national debt has gone up so much that in October 2008 the National Debt Clock in Times Square ran out of digits. Obama can't cut American interest rates (there isn't far to go down from 1%). He can't raise taxes (without turning a depression into a real disaster). And he can't cut spending without disappointing the people who voted for him and who believed he could work miracles. On the first day of Obama's Presidency, a day when the world is supposed to be filled with hope and heavy with expectation, the American stock market, that cruellest and sharpest of commentators, that most ruthless of judges, sank like a stone.

One of Obama's first appointments was that of Larry Summers as part of his economic team. I suspect that Summers, former Treasury Secretary under Bill Clinton, is famous for two things.

First, having advocated (in 1991, when he was World Bank chief economist) 'polluting' African countries for economic benefit. Second, suggesting (while president of Harvard University) that women are inherently worse at science than men.

So, now you know.

I think Obama will turn his back on free trade and protectionism will come back in a big way. The American Government has for years protected huge swathes of American industry (particularly its farmers). This has done enormous damage to the rest of the world. In the dying days of his Government, Bush effectively nationalised great chunks of the financial industry and took steps towards nationalising the failing American car industry. A wise president might try to unravel those. I doubt if Obama will. On the contrary I think he will follow the politically easy route of introducing more protectionism (forcing American manufacturers to use American steel for example). This may please the voters but it will, of course, result in other countries retaliating. The idea of a global market place will crumble. Speaking at the World Economic Forum in Davos, early in 2009, the leaders of both China and Russia lectured the leaders of the West and blamed them for leading the world into a global financial crisis. Most notably, one of the Russian President's advisers likened America's planned economic policy to the 'beggar thy neighbour' protectionist policies of the 1930s. 'Of course,' he said, 'Mr Obama expects the Chinese or Russians to buy US Treasury Bills. That is pretty selfish and philosophically it is protectionism.'

If the Russians and the Chinese don't buy US Treasury Bills (and why should they?) the USA is going to have to have even bigger problems with massive unemployment, high interest rates and painfully high inflation. In the end, things will become so bad in America that Americans will be smuggling themselves across the border into Mexico to find work. The Americans will at some point have to stop being nasty to the Chinese. They will have to recognise that the Chinese own America and that it is not polite to be disrespectful to your landlord.

Naturally any country which has aligned itself with America (and American greed and imperialism) is likely to suffer too.

Now, which country could that be, do you think?

Chapter 3

How Greedy And Incompetent Bankers Wrecked The World

The world's bankers have almost destroyed capitalism. Their greed and stupidity have devastated the lives of millions. And yet they remain unrepentant – and as greedy as ever.

In June 2007, the Bank for International Settlements reported that the total value of global derivatives in existence was $415.2 trillion. This was money and credit. And it was just under 800% of global GDP. Which means that bankers, pension companies and investment companies (the guys buying the £10 million London houses) were playing with eight times the value of everything made and every service provided, on the entire planet. It reminded me of the games of Monopoly I used to play when I was a boy. The money, the properties, the debts – none of it was real. It was a make believe world.

Nothing about this absurd state of affairs started alarm bells ringing in the Government or at the Bank of England. It should have. That's what we pay them for.

How did highly paid specialists not realise that if banks were allowed to drop their lending standards, securitise bad loans (without any transparency) and then sell the new securities to hugely leveraged institutions and hedge funds which then sold on the stuff they'd bought to individual investors who didn't have the foggiest idea what they are buying, you might end up in trouble?

The banking fiasco was always going to go wrong – though it

was astonishing that so many bankers screwed up at the same time. It was amazing that such a high proportion of highly paid bankers got their risk quantification so completely wrong.

And now that it has gone wrong it is going to take a decade or more to unwind; it is going to take ten or fifteen years to repair the damage done to confidence, to trust and to the bank balances of financial institutions. This problem has been developing for more than a decade. You can't put right in weeks or months a problem that has taken that long to develop. The problem will affect Britain more than any other country. This isn't because the bankers in Britain were much greedier or more stupid than the bankers elsewhere, but because we had just had ten years with Gordon Brown running the country's finances.

During late 2008, it became clear that highly paid bankers didn't always seem to know quite as much about their corporate finances as one might like to feel they knew. Never before had stupidity paid quite so well. Running a bank was more profitable than robbing one (with much the same result for the customers).

Reading about the antics of some of the bankers who created the so-called 'credit-crunch', I found it increasingly difficult to understand why these people weren't going to jail. Most of them seemed to be keeping their jobs and the untold millions they had given themselves in the years before their hubris destroyed the system. They showed no sense of shame and seemed unwilling to apologise for their greed.

In September of 2008 the chief executive of the American Insurance Group (AIG) learned that Moody's, a rating agency, intended to lower the company's credit rating unless it raised at least $30 billion in capital. This produced a panic inside the AIG headquarters where bankers on salaries which would make professional footballers envious apparently found this something of a shock. (Investment bankers and footballers will surely be bracketed together as the two most obscenely overpaid groups of people in our modern world – demanding massive fees and yet contributing nothing to society. One British footballer who was offered £24 million to kick a ball around for three years was so disgusted by the offer that he threatened to leave the country and take a job abroad.) AIG begged insurance regulators to borrow $20 billion from subsidiaries but, after spending all night poring over the books, bankers found that AIG actually needed $40 billion to survive. Gosh. This seemed to shock everybody involved even more. Days later bankers lifted their heads from the accounts and announced that the shortfall was closer to $65 billion than $40 billion. (Imagine your bank manager's tone if he found that your understanding of your finances was this wishy washy.) Lawyers drew up papers for a bankruptcy petition from the world's largest insurance company. But the American Government felt that they couldn't let AIG go bust because the consequences would be just too dramatic. Drivers wouldn't be insured. Homes around the world wouldn't be insured. Pension funds would go zonk. Pensioners would be thrown into the streets. Other banks would go bust. The whole financial caboodle would collapse. And so the Fed asked some big investment banks (which were themselves not in the best of health) to help arrange $75 billion in loans. The banks sucked in air, shook their heads and said sorry, they couldn't help. Good job really, within another 72 hours the experts (and I use the word loosely) had decided that the amount of money AIG needed wasn't $75 billion but $85 billion. Or possibly more. The American Government speeded up the printing presses and offered to find $85 billion before things got out of hand.

Were the executives responsible for this shambles overwhelmed with shame?

Not a bit of it.

Just one week after the US Treasury saved AIG from certain failure with a multi-billion dollar bailout, executives from the company went for a week long luxury retreat at the St Regis Resort in Monarch Beach, California and spent $200,000 on rooms, $150,000 on meals and $23,000 on the hotel spa. Since AIG had been bailed out with money from American taxpayers it was American taxpayers who paid for this bailout party. And although AIG announced that senior executives would get no bonuses for the year, the company quietly disclosed that it would, instead, make what it called 'retention payments' of up to $4 million to 168 executives. AIG claimed that the payments were necessary in order to keep key members of staff. Just why they wanted to keep people who had, presumably, also been key in the company's decline wasn't made clear. And since the financial services industry in America was downsizing as fast as it could go it did not seem very likely that many of these people would be choosing to leave.

Elsewhere, bosses of banks which were clinging on by their corporate fingernails, or which had gone bust, were still running their ruined companies. And they were still making truckloads of money.

In 2008 the American Government allowed Lehman Brothers to go bust because they needed to show bankers that they wouldn't always be bailed out. But the politicians and civil servants may not have been aware of the consequences. Lehman had so many fingers in so many pies that, for example, money market funds (theoretically the safest investments anyone can make) actually lost money. A dollar invested in some money market funds became worth less than a dollar. When that happens, stuffing your money under the mattress looks extremely sensible. And that, of course, is what people did: withdrawing their money from the banks in vast quantities.

The chief of Lehman Brothers took home nearly half a billion dollars in 'total compensation' between 1993 and 2007. In 2007 alone he 'earned', or was paid, about $45 million. That's around $17,000 an hour. Would he have done it for less? My bet is yes. For that money Richard Fuld drove the 158-year-old company into the ground, creating financial chaos around the world and sending thousands of bankers home clutching the detritus from their desks in cardboard boxes and black plastic sacks. If Fuld had been a success it might, just might, be possible to argue that he was worth the money. But the company failed. The bank went bust owing a far from modest $639 billion. The biggest bankruptcy in history by miles. A lot of ordinary people lost their savings. Why the hell wasn't Fuld offered employment sewing mailbags? Why didn't someone go round to his house with a fleet of trucks and take back the money he'd been given?

It wasn't just Fuld who was shovelling money into his wallet with gay abandon. The *Financial Times* in London reported that five days before it went bankrupt Lehman Brothers rushed out third-quarter figures showing that whereas revenues had gone from $4.3 billion the year before to minus $2.9 billion, total 'compensation' of employees had fallen hardly at all, dropping from $2.1 billion to $2.0 billion. According to The *Daily Telegraph* Lehman Brothers made a profit of $4.2 billion in 2007 but paid out nearly $6 billion in bonuses. You would think, wouldn't you, that highly paid people who handled money for a living would have heard of our dear friend Mr Micawber?

Just days before Lehman went bust, executives who left the bank were given millions of dollars in leaving presents. Just why a bank should feel the need to give huge gifts to ex-employees is beyond me, though I'm sure the recipients were grateful.

Some bankers from Lehman Brothers were seen weeping on television, bemoaning the loss of their overpaid jobs. I'm not surprised. After Lehman went bust it was revealed that new graduates, with no banking experience, had been hired at a first year salary of £58,000, with a bonus and a 'golden hello' of approximately £20,000. Three days before Lehman went bust the bank paid a cash advance of $25 million to a new employee hired to be 'global co-head of fixed income'. The $25 million was an advance on the new employee's pay for 2008 and 2009. The bank said that the advance payment was 'intended to facilitate retention and engagement in his new role'. In other words Lehman paid their new employee a great chunk of his massive salary, in advance, in order to encourage him to 'engage' in his new role. Difficult to believe. I wonder how many modestly paid coal miners and bus drivers get their considerably more modest salaries paid a year in advance? (And I wonder which is the hardest, most taxing work: digging out coal, driving a bus or being co-head of fixed income investments.)

Maddest of all, however, was the fact that after Lehman went bust, Barclays Bank handed out $2.5 billion in bonus to ex-Lehman employees it wanted to hire. Nomura doled out $1 billion to ex-Lehman employees in London. It was no wonder that members of the public and politicians were repulsed. Investors and pensioners around the world had lost their savings because of the mismanagement of the company. Ordinary employees (typists, cleaners, etc) had lost their jobs. But the bankers who had created the mess, and who were responsible for unimaginable hardship and financial pain, emerged from the Lehman wreckage richer than ever.

Incidentally, those who believe that America is Britain's closest ally should know that Lehman transferred $8 billion from its European operations to the USA where up to 10,000 staff at the bankrupt bank's New York office were set to receive $2.5 billion in bonuses. Transferring the money meant that it was hard to pay UK workers their final salaries.

The greed was still evident as 2008 disappeared into the sunset. Financial institution Merrill Lynch, which was taken over by the Bank of America, made a $15.3 billion pound loss during the fourth quarter of the year. You might imagine that the boss of Merrill Lynch might be grateful to Bank of America and anxious to do everything he could to make his gratitude clear. Not a bit of it. Just days before the closing of the sale of Merrill Lynch to the unfortunate Bank of America, Merrill Lynch decided to accelerate the payment of nearly $4 billion in employee bonuses. The bonuses were paid out as Bank of America sought additional funds from American taxpayers so that they could close the deal. The words 'greed' and 'arrogant' simply aren't expressive enough. 'Greedy bastards' gets closer, though. Merrill Lynch didn't do much better over the whole year of 2008: they lost $42.2 billion and managed to negate all the profits the company had made over the previous 25 years. John Thain, the quarter-witted boss who authorised the bonuses said he did so to ensure that the bank kept its good people. What good people? The bank had just gone bust! And even if the bank had any people worth keeping, where were they going to go? Banks weren't hiring. Perhaps the boss was frightened that his bankers would give up their million dollar a minute pay cheques to take jobs driving taxis. The truth is that banking is not difficult to learn or to do and the vast majority of bankers have for years been absurdly overpaid for what is, in essence, as undemanding mentally as it is undemanding physically. Sportsmen, singers and film stars are highly paid because of their talents, skills, experience, charm and established fan base. They provide entertainment pleasure for millions and produce millions in profit for their sponsors. Bankers, on the other hand, receive huge salaries and bonuses simply because they are working where the money is. It's like workers in a chocolate factory having access to an endless supply of free chocolates. The events of 2007 and 2008 have proved beyond doubt that bankers are of modest intelligence and modest skills.

Despite the massive, bank-shattering losses, Merrill Lynch's 60,000 workforce were paid an average of $250,000 for their incompetence and general ability to lose money. Most of the loss was charged to the British-based end of the business with the result that it will be years before whatever is left of Merrill Lynch ever pays any tax in the UK.

And then there was Citigroup – another huge American bank which was reliant on public support. The bosses at Citigroup were about to purchase a $50 million executive jet with bail-out money provided by American taxpayers until the Treasury secretary 'expressed strong opposition to the move'. (I'd love to have been in the room during that conversation.)

Bankers everywhere were moaning that their lifestyles required massive annual bonuses. They did not make clear just what god they felt decreed that spotty, ignorant, arrogant bank clerks should be paid millions for shuffling other people's money about. It did not seem to occur to any of them that decent, hard working people had seen their investments and savings destroyed because of the venal activities of incompetent bankers.

George W. Bush had to nationalise the two biggest mortgage firms in America, with the result that more than half of American homes were by autumn of 2008, owned by the American Government. 'Who would have imagined that when the most right-wing of neo-cons leaves office, 50% of the Land of the Free will effectively be a council estate?' asked one newspaper columnist.

Shareholders in these two huge firms, Fannie Mae and Freddie Mac, lost their shirts, blouses and underwear but the departing Chief Executive Officers, the guys who had created the mess, did well. Fannie Mae's boss received $9.3 million in severance pay, retirement benefits and deferred compensation. The former boss of Freddie Mac left with around $14 million, thanks to a clause added to his contract just before Freddie Mac went under for the last time.

It was, perhaps, hardly surprising that growing numbers of politicians finally decided that banks needed more controls and that there should be a cap on employees' bonuses. Those who liked to describe themselves (in novelist Tom Wolfe's phrase) as 'masters of the universe' had shown that they would have been far better described as 'idiots of the universe'.

As an aside it is worth pointing out that it hasn't only been bankers who have exhibited Olympic medal-winning levels of greed.

In January 2009, Google announced that it was offering to exchange its employees' stock options for new ones at a lower strike price. They had done this because existing options were 'underwater' (they were of no value). Management always claim that they do this to discourage staff from leaving, though just why Google felt this necessary at a time of deep recession was not made clear. The point was that Google was making a mockery of incentive schemes by severing the link between employee performance and the share price. The idea behind options is that employees are given an opportunity to buy shares at a particular price and then, if the share price rises, they can buy at the lower price, sell and make a profit. It's a way of rewarding employees if the company is successful. Google, in my view one of the least responsible and most ethically-challenged companies on the planet, was changing the rules so that its employees would benefit even though the share price had not gone up.

In the UK, the directors of Bellway, the UK's fourth largest housebuilder, paid more than £630,000 to top executives in bonuses in spite of a sharp fall in its share price. The directors were given bonuses worth 55% of their salaries in a year when sales fell by 50% and shares in the company lost 28% of their value. According to Peter Montagnon, director of investment affairs at the Association of British Insurers: 'Management had targets and abandoned them when it became clear that they were not going to meet them. They decided to pay bonuses anyway.' Shareholders voted against the bonuses but were told their vote didn't mean that the directors had to give the money back.

(When bankers, company directors and Government employees try to excuse their huge salaries they always claim that the salaries are necessary in order to prevent people moving to other jobs. Just what other jobs are these people going to do? Would hospital bosses, town hall executives or company directors really prefer to be flipping burgers?)

★ ★ ★

When British banks started imploding in 2008 the general feeling in the media seemed to be that we should feel sorry for the thousands of bankers being made redundant. Really? And just who did the journalists think caused the whole darned mess?

In the middle of the banking crisis an awards bash for 100

HBOS employees was celebrated with a fireworks display costing £10,000. (According to the *News of the World* it then turned into a cocaine-fuelled orgy.) The day before announcing a £45 billion loss Royal Bank of Scotland bosses spent £50,000 on a champagne banquet to celebrate Scottish Burns Night. In 2009, the part-time chairman of RBS was being paid £750,000 a year plus a £1.5 bonus if he hit an undisclosed target (in other words did his job properly). RBS, a complete failure as a bank, was by that point 70% owned by taxpayers and the chairman, Sir Philip Hampton, was yet another overpaid civil servant.

In January 2009, it was announced that the staff of Northern Rock, the failed building society/bank which had to be rescued by taxpayers, would receive 10% of their salaries as a bonus for doing their jobs – despite the fact that the bank was still making a loss. On the same day that this was announced, the Government revealed that there were almost two million people unemployed in the UK. Only in a country run by Gordon Brown, a man steeped in debt and failure, could such a thing happen. Northern Rock's finance chief left the company almost £1,000,000 richer after barely a year's work. And the boss of the taxpayer-owned bank was being paid £3,000 a day.

(We should not forget that under Gordon Brown's patronage it has become normal for civil servants to receive huge bonuses for hitting their targets, or nearly hitting them, or, indeed, getting nowhere near them. In 2008, Whitehall bonuses totalled £128 million. In 2009, the staff at the Financial Services Authority, surely the most incompetent and entirely useless Government body ever created, celebrated their failure to regulate the banks effectively, or to protect the interests of taxpayers, with magnificent pay rises and, almost unbelievably, huge bonuses. So it's a bit tricky for Gordon to say 'no' to the vast army of civil servant bankers who want huge bonuses for taking the trouble to get out of bed, totter into work and do their jobs.)

A few days later another failed bank, Halifax Bank of Scotland, which had been rescued by Lloyds Bank, handed £2,000 holiday vouchers to 1,000 of the staff who had helped it fail. Sir Fred Goodwin, who left the Royal Bank of Scotland in disgrace after apparently pretty much destroying it single-handedly receives an annual pension of £703,000. That's £703,000 every year until he snuffs it. The fact that the man whose talent was hubris and whose name is bracketed with subprime mortgage lending as a significant cause of Britain's recession is not acquiring a liking for porridge and learning to pick up the soap with his toes proves just how much is wrong with British justice these days. Goodwin was described by *The Times* as 'possibly the world's worst banker' and by *The Sun* as 'criminally incompetent'.

In late February 2009 there was a furore when details of Goodwin's pension finally emerged and politicians demanded that he abandon some of his claims against the nation. (I half expected to hear someone suggest that, in order to avoid paying the pension, Goodwin be hung. It would have certainly been a cheap and doubtless popular option.) I had included details of Goodwin's absurd pension arrangements in an early draft of this book, which I'd written before Christmas 2008, so I have a suspicion that the row over the pension arrangements (triggered by an alleged BBC scoop) was used as a well-designed distraction to take public attention away from the fact that the Royal Bank of Scotland's huge, toxic debts had become the responsibility of the British taxpayers and were, indeed, so massive that they might eventually bankrupt the country.

In America, in January 2009, much of the $140 million donated to fund the biggest Presidential inauguration in history, came from banks that had received taxpayer-funded bail-outs. Astonishingly, 79% of Wall Street workers said they received a bonus for 2008, despite the mess they had made. Even more astonishingly, almost half said they were dissatisfied with the amount they had received. Is it any wonder that nearly four out of five Americans have no faith in their country's financial system?

★ ★ ★

In the autumn of 2008, some British and American bank bosses announced (with much trumpeting) that they had frozen their salaries. Some even announced that they were foregoing all or part of their annual bonuses for a year. They made these announcements as though taxpayers should be grateful for their sacrifices.

These bastards were the venal idiots who had, through their unbridled greed and rank stupidity, pushed millions of ordinary, hard working folk into everlasting penury. These bastards were the people who closed down branches and left communities without banking facilities, the people who forced customers to hang on the phone for ages before getting a chance to speak to a rude, unhelpful, ignorant call centre operative several thousand miles away. These bastards were the people who sold overpriced insurance products, who sold customers unsuitable investment products, who hit unsuspecting customers with hidden and unfair charges. These bastards were the greedy idiots whose efforts had cost taxpayers billions in whatever currency you like to talk. These bastards were the greedy idiots whose failure to follow regulatory standards had resulted in countless workers having to spend another ten, fifteen or twenty years working at low paid jobs before they could afford to live on their pension. These were the bastards who had bullied their customers and snarled at them whenever they erred. These were the bastards who took reckless risks with the customers' money – so that they could boost their own personal multi-million pound bonuses. These were the bastards who worked out a system which ensured that if the bank made money (or even seemed to make money) then they would be paid huge bonuses but that if the bank lost money then they would still find a way to give themselves huge bonuses. These were the bastards whose incompetence and greed destroyed the banking system, damaged the economy and caused economic distress worldwide.

Directors (and Government regulators) allowed employees to take huge gambles with depositors' money; giving them massive bonuses as a huge percentage of any short-term success, even when the risks were long-term. The employees took no risks at all with their own money. The incentive to take big risks with other people's money was huge. The rewards and risks of ownership and the management of capital had been divorced. Directors, regulators and Government Ministers all knew this and did nothing.

And just how big a sacrifice were the bank bosses making?

Well, of the first $125 billion of taxpayers' money given to American banks, $105 billion went as bonuses to rich American bankers – the very people who had caused the problem in the first place. It is as though the Government handed out bundles of cash to robbers and muggers. And the same thing happened in Britain. The rich and well-connected, the Government's chums, walked away with their pockets stuffed with taxpayers' money. Billions of pounds worth of money that Brown had gouged out of taxpayers was funnelled straight into the vaults of the banking elite. It is hardly surprising that the bankers leapt on Brown's proposals, and were delighted by his generous offer to bail them out.

Krzysztof Rybinski, former Deputy Governor of the National Bank of Poland summed it up best: 'Imagine that there is a wild party, a long one,' he wrote. 'Every time the alcohol supply dries up, the central bank shows up and keeps the party going and going, and people get more and more addicted to partying and drinking. At some stage, the drunken crowd demolishes the premises and the party is over. Hank (USA Treasury Secretary Hank Paulson) and Ben (USA Chairman of the Federal Reserve System, Ben Bernanke) show up and ask who did the most damage. John, people say, broke four windows and smashed the table. Great, says Hank, John will get $300 – who is next on the did-most-damage list? Tim, the crowd cries, he sprayed paint all over the place and burnt the sofa. Excellent, says Hank, Tim will get $250. Who is next? In a few days, the next party will begin. People are planning to show up in large numbers. Not only can they have a lot of fun (while others – obviously jerks and dorks – will go to work every morning) and drink for free – they will also get free cash handouts when the party is over. How do you like the Paulson plan?'

It became clear, as the crisis went on in late 2008, that modern politicians don't make decisions according to careful thought-out plans based on an analysis of the facts. They make on-the-hoof decisions that are driven by expediency and selfishness. The bail out of the failing HBOS, through a takeover by Lloyds Bank was designed to satisfy Scottish voters and to help protect the political interests of Brown, Darling and the Labour Party in Scotland, rather than to show concern for the needs and rights of investors, English staff or customers. The deal was apparently made during a chat at a cocktail party. Lloyds was apparently persuaded to make a promise not to axe Scottish jobs in order to satisfy the political needs of the Labour party.

In reality, of course, the bankers who created the mess should have been fired. They should have then been arrested, put in the stocks for a year and sentenced to 80 years hard labour. Arranging for Lloyds Bank (a solid, financially secure English institution) to take over HBOS (a bankrupt, financial mess) was lunacy. The result was always going to be an even larger mess and the ruination of a magnificent, English, banking institution. Everyone but the people involved could see that. But the bankers were greedy for power and the Prime Minister was desperate to retain political popularity in Scotland. Astonishingly, it subsequently appeared that the Scots running the Government were so desperate to save the incompetently run Scottish banks that they poured billions of pounds of taxpayers' money into the banks without anyone from the Treasury checking the health of the banks they were rescuing. Scottish banks and Scottish politicians have ruined England and the rest of Britain.

★ ★ ★

Will the world's banks continue to do stupid things?

Of course they will. They will continue to do stupid things because they are still being run by the same greedy, self-serving stupid people. No one in banking has paid the price for the greed they have shown. The evidence is horrifying. For years, bankers have been making fortunes by cheating manufacturing companies, investors, pensions and everyone else around them. In 2008, as the subprime crisis unfolded, a relatively small number of obscenely highly paid American bankers took home $18 billion in pay and bonuses. For every dollar American companies raised via initial public offerings (money that was needed to expand their businesses) bankers took 57 cents in fees and about half of that was paid to bankers in bonuses. In other words, for every dollar that businesses raised, bankers personally helped themselves to a quarter merely for setting up the deal. That's not taking a 'fee'; that's stealing. And, worse still, they raised their 'fees' through the roof by valuing new stocks at ludicrous prices. For example, bankers valued the company eToys at $11 billion even though it lost $2.46 on every dollar's worth of toys it sold.

The greed wasn't just common in America and Britain, of course. It was global greed. Josef Ackermann, the chief executive of Deutsche Bank, is, according to the *Financial Times*, well known in Germany for 'setting his bank the goal of earning a pre-tax return on equity of 25%.'

I cannot imagine how a large, mature corporation can possibly earn a return of 25% a year without ripping off everyone with whom it comes into contact. I'm not alone. Germany's senior Protestant Bishop attacked Ackermann by claiming that such a goal drove up profit expectations to unsustainable levels. 'In the current circumstances,' said the Bishop, 'money has become a god.'

'The issue which has swept down the centuries, and which will have to be fought sooner or later, is the people versus the banks,' said Lord Acton, who served in the House of Commons from 1859 to 1865 and was subsequently an advisor to William Gladstone.

How right he was. And how sad it is that our politicians did not seize the moment when it came.

Instead, the government bailouts in America and Britain ensured that the banks are still being run by the same greedy idiots who created the mess of 2008.

And bankers, regulators and politicians will continue to avoid facing the real long-term solution: keeping commercial banks and investment banks quite separate. Bankers should be told: 'You can run a commercial bank or an investment bank.' None of the people with the power to order this change grasp that this is what people want, and that it would give investors, depositors and entrepreneurs confidence. Nor, of course, do they understand that it would be the right thing to do.

★ ★ ★

I had very little sympathy, I'm afraid, with inept and greedy bankers who set up complicated schemes designed to gouge million dollar bonuses out of ordinary people's savings. It was their fault that their banks went bust and it showed extraordinary chutzpah that they should imagine for a moment that taxpayers' money should be used to bail them out.

Is the Government going to bail me out if I print too many copies of a book and fail to sell them? Is the Government going to throw money in my direction if the response from an advertisement proves disappointing? I suspect not.

I feel sorry for the cleaners, receptionists and secretaries working for the bankers whose businesses went bust. But I refuse to feel sorry for the bankers at the top. Most of them have feathered their nests with vast quantities of folding stuff. And it was their greed which led to the problem. In 2008, around 4,000 British bankers received bonuses of more than £1,000,000 a year. Such unwarranted distributions lead to resentment and anger.

I feel sorry (a little bit) for unintelligent house buyers who were, at the peak of the housing market madness, tricked into borrowing far more money than they could ever hope to pay back. (I only feel sorry for them a little bit because only the most deeply stupid could not have known that their purchases were absurd and the payments way beyond their means. I don't feel sorry at all for the intelligent but greedy borrowers.)

I feel genuinely sorry for the trusting private investors and pensioners whose savings have been decimated by the selfish greed of a few incompetent and utterly self-serving bankers. Making money (or even holding onto it) can be particularly difficult when the men given the responsibility for holding the stakes go bust. If I lose money because I buy a high risk investment, or because I make a mistake and choose to put money into a company which is selling umbrellas just before a seven year drought, then that is my fault and I can live with it. But if I lose money because the bank holding my investments (or my spare cash) goes bust then I think I have a right to feel aggrieved.

And I feel genuinely sorry for the men and women running small businesses whose chances of surviving through the difficult years have been dramatically reduced by what has happened.

After studying what happened in 2007 and 2008 I got the distinct feeling that a conversation between a recruiter and a prospective senior bank employee might have gone something like this:

Recruiter: 'Do you have any banking qualifications?'

Applicant: 'Well not actually any qualifications, per se.'

Recruiter: 'Do you have any banking experience?'

Applicant: 'Oh yes! I've had a bank account for many years.'

Recruiter: 'Splendid. That's marvellous. And do you have any other qualities which might be relevant?'

Applicant: 'I love money. Absolutely love it.'

Recruiter: 'Marvellous. You sound perfect. When can you start? Would a million a year be acceptable?'

Applicant: 'That would be lovely.'

Recruiter: 'And a huge pension and a stonking great bonus every year?'

Applicant: 'Even better. Perfect. I'd like that.'
Recruiter: 'Right. Good. When can you start?'

* * *

In the UK the British Government, unpopular, panicking and utterly out of its depth, struggled to deal with the crisis which reached a head in September 2008 with the impending collapse of HBOS – just a year after the collapse of another British bank, Northern Rock.

Because HBOS has many Scottish employees, and because the Prime Minister and Chancellor of the Exchequer are both Scottish and have parliamentary seats locally, instructions were given that the company's headquarters – and many of its employees – must be retained if the takeover of HBOS by Lloyds Bank was to be allowed. The sad result of this political chicanery is that many employees of Lloyds Bank (which had itself done nothing wrong) will find themselves in the dole queues while employees of HBOS (which would have almost certainly gone bust) will be retained.

Doctors always teach relatives that they should not provide too much support for alcoholics who refuse to seek help for their fundamental problem – their addiction to alcohol. Giving them money and protecting them from embarrassment or more serious problems is known as 'enabling' and is considered unhelpful because it prolongs the agony.

The problem for the British Government was that before the crunch of 2008 there were more finance sector workers in Britain than there were construction workers, farmers and factory workers combined. Thanks to Brown's destructive policies Britain had become a nation of overpaid bank clerks.

The massive over-staffed and hugely expensive regulators Brown had put in place did nothing to prevent the carnage. Even though they could, and should, have prevented it. The Financial Services Authority (FSA) in the UK (set up by Brown) has 2,665 highly paid members of staff and a budget measured in hundreds of millions. The Desperate Dan Pie Eaters Club did as much to protect investors and depositors. The idea that the idiots at the FSA will now sort out the problem and rescue us from the mess we are in is, frankly, laughable.

In their greed the bankers dreamt up all sorts of crafty investments which no one really understood. They merrily sold these to pension funds, colleges, municipal government and to widows and orphans everywhere. They leveraged and flipped and churned. They stripped and securitised. It was all flimflam. A thousand Ponzi schemes.

As one commentator put it, the average investor would have been better off at the racetrack. Bookies take about 20% of the gross. In the City, the worst of the wide boys were skimming 50% to 80% of every pound of profit. And when investments went wrong it was the widows and orphans who carried the loss. Ordinary investors, who still trusted banks and investment companies, never stood a chance.

Of course, profits aren't a bad thing. Industries use them to expand, to build new factories and to create new products. But the finance industry just distributed the profits among the chosen few. A billion here. A billion there. And the bankers and investment advisors bought third and fourth homes, fleets of cars, private aeroplanes and yachts with three helipads.

In the 1980s, the businesses of banking, broking and insuring produced around 10% of corporate profits in the UK. The money was paid for arranging financing and wearing pinstripe suits very nicely. This was much the same sort of figure as was common in other developed countries. By the time of the great Financial Crash of 2008 around 35% of all the corporate profits in Britain and America came from these nebulous, parasitic service industries. In America in 2007 corporate profits reached $6 trillion. Wall Street took $2 trillion of that. Bankers and brokers don't make anything useful. They don't even make electric nose hair clippers. Bankers and brokers merely exist to enable the real producers in a country to do what they do. Bankers are facilitators. Their task (a remarkably simple and straightforward one) is to bring together savers and borrowers.

The dramatic expansion of the financial sector has puzzled many people. George Soros, the hedge fund manager observed: 'The size of the financial sector is out of proportion to the rest of the economy.'

When the crash came, and the banking and investment company profits tumbled, the Governments of the UK and the USA decided that they had to give the bankers some taxpayers' money in order to keep them going. Governments in both countries had become addicted to the taxes they received on the profits made by banks and investment companies. Britain's financial industries contributed about a third of the nation's corporation tax in the year 2000. And then there was the money paid by individual bankers and brokers in tax. And the money they spent on buying houses, yachts and champagne. And so politicians threw vast amounts of public money at the bankers in the hope that they would be able to keep the taxes coming.

Ironically, the explosion in the number of bankers and investment professionals (and in the fees they charged and the bonuses they gave themselves) also led to an increase in the number of financial crises. The emerging market debt crisis. The unexplained stock market crash of 1987. The USA savings and loan debacle. The Asian crisis. Various oil crises. The implosion of the American hedge fund Long-Term Capital Management. The dot.com bubble. The more bankers there were, the more chaotic the system became. Bankers created their own cycle of booms and busts. Speculators didn't just observe: they also participated. And their actions influenced what happened next.

And there was the problem that the professionals knew more than the ordinary investors and used that extra knowledge to give them an edge. Regulators tried to stop 'insider trading' (where an investor takes advantage of special knowledge) but they failed miserably. Bankers, brokers, fund managers and analysts just got richer and richer. And the ordinary investor (and his pension fund) stagnated.

At the end of the 1990s and the early part of the 21st Century the investments made by ordinary men-in-the-street investors went nowhere while bankers made (literally) billions in fees, commissions and trading profits. Bankers and financial intermediaries were allowed to capture too big a share of the profits from each country's growth. And the British Government, excited by the taxes it was raising (and, possibly, by the donations and parties being given by the mega rich) encouraged this policy of taking from the poor and the middle classes and giving to the very rich. As financiers have become increasingly crooked and crafty so their share of the overall cake has increased. And the investment world has become unstable.

★ ★ ★

The money taken by bankers and brokers has been called 'the croupier's take' by Charlie Munger (Warren Buffett's partner). And various groups of people share this money.

Bankers charge a percentage of the total value of a deal whenever there is a merger or an acquisition. They charge commissions when shares are bought or sold. They make money from the spread (the difference between the price paid by a buyer and the price received by a seller). They charge up front fees. And they increase their take by doing lots of churning (buying and selling for no good reason other than to increase the manager's profits). In 1965 the annual turnover of British equities was worth 10% of nominal Gross Domestic Product. In 2007 turnover had grown to almost 300%. Fund managers constantly swap their holdings with other fund managers. The managers are getting very, very rich by buying and selling, buying and selling, buying and selling and taking fees and commissions every time they do so. In 2007 the value of equities traded on UK markets amounted to well over £4,000 billion. That is about three times as much as the nation's Gross Domestic Product.

And then many fund managers started helping themselves to a share of any profits that might be made.

It is hardly surprising that most investors have made no money at all on their savings in the last ten years. The average investor who puts £10,000 into an investment programme or a pension plan in 1997, and who was expecting his money to grow, will be lucky to have that much left today – a dozen years later.

Things got worse when bankers realised that they could make even more money by repackaging quite ordinary banking arrangements. And so they turned ordinary residential mortgages into collateralised debt obligations (CDOs). These were the basic cause of the financial crisis we are now in. By turning ordinary household mortgages into structured loans the banks could sell them to other banks, to pension funds, to insurance companies and to investment funds all over the world. The buyers were simply told they were buying property-backed investments that would pay them a regular return on their money. Greedy and lazy fund managers snapped up the CDOs without ever really finding out what they were buying.

The banks found this profitable. But they needed more mortgages to sell on. And so they started lending money to people who couldn't afford to buy a car let alone a house. And thus we had the subprime crisis.

Unbelievably, everything was then made even worse by the American Government which removed the element of risk for investors. Fed chairman Alan Greenspan rescued the stock market (and bankers) when the hedge-fund Long-Term Capital Management faced bankruptcy. He repeatedly rescued the markets whenever it looked as though bankers might make a loss. Greenspan acquired a reputation for bailing out the investment industry. The problem of 'moral hazard' was born. Investors thought that they just couldn't lose money.

And the American and British Governments allowed hedge funds, private equity funds and investment banks to charge huge fees. Politicians and regulators were so besotted by the new financial industry that they even allowed individual fund managers to pretty well avoid paying tax. Many of these new billionaires paid less tax than the people they hired to clean their offices.

And so a hugely unstable financial system was created.

As the bankers and fund managers became ever greedier so they thought up more and more ways to make money out of ordinary investors. They created swaps, options and a whole alphabet soup of new financial devices that were designed for one purpose only: to make more money for rich bankers. There seemed to be no end to the number of derivatives that could be created and sold. In September 2008, the value of shares around the world was around $40 trillion. But bankers were holding $1,000 trillion worth of derivatives based on these shares.

It was utter madness. A whole system has been organised not to help borrowers and lenders get together but solely to make huge, obscenely huge, amounts of money for a few very greedy, ruthless people.

The public, the pensioners, the ordinary investors did not benefit at all from any of this. Indeed, on the contrary, they just lost more and more money.

Then, when things went wrong and the bankers found themselves in the mire they turned to their governments. 'We've screwed up. Give us money,' they cried.

And the American and British Governments handed over great wodges of taxpayers' money so that the bankers could continue to enjoy their expensive lifestyles.

Our banks and building societies were run like casinos. Regulators did nothing. Politicians did nothing. The Bank of England did nothing. The cautious, the careful and the prudent will pay for this for years to come. But the executives who caused this chaos are still rich. The ones who have retired went off with fat pensions and barrowloads of cash. The regulators all have their jobs. No one at the Bank of England resigned. And the politicians just claim the credit for trying to sort out the mess they should have prevented.

★ ★ ★

High street banks, the other sort of bank, used to be the ones which issued cheque books and sent out rude letters about overdrafts.

But under Brown's 'supervision' the bosses of the boring high street, commercial banks (the sort sometimes also known as business banks, retail banks and clearing banks) and the former stodgy building societies thought they'd make bigger bonuses if they got involved in some of the more exciting stuff. The money little old ladies saved and handed to their bank for safe keeping was given to Ferrari-owning pimply youths in expensive suits so that they could gamble on buying complicated financial derivatives which they obviously didn't understand.

The banking crisis which hit Britain in 2008 developed because commercial banks (the high street banks which run current accounts and deposit accounts, issue cheques and do other boring but essential financial stuff) got greedy. Or, rather, the people who run them got greedy. And they began operating as investment banks – taking huge risks and investing wholesale in what they hoped would be hugely profitable financial jiggery pokery but which they clearly didn't understand. The problem was compounded by the fact that the people running the banks obviously didn't have a very good ability to see the big picture. None of them seemed to be aware that lending had got out of hand (even though this was quite apparent to many lay observers – myself included). They were so focused on their bonuses that they simply didn't realise the extent of the risks they were taking. It is difficult to see why this wasn't criminal negligence on the part of senior executives and directors and I suspect that I am not alone in feeling that a considerable number of bankers should be spending less of their time on the golf course and more of it sharing small rooms with large men with tattoos.

Ordinary, 'vanilla-flavoured' banks should borrow money from people who have spare cash and lend it to people who need money to start small businesses or buy houses. That's how ordinary high street banking works. But the profits from that sort of banking weren't enough. And the bankers who ran the high street banks wanted to wear silk suits and mix with flash bastards in the hospitality suites at Lord's and Royal Ascot. So, they got into investment banking.

If they had been told: 'you can be one or the other but you can't be both' then the country wouldn't be in the mess it is in now.

Investment bankers and hedge fund operators would have lost a ton of money but, quite frankly, no one except the distributors of exotic Italian cars and expensive French champagne would have noticed or cared very much.

★ ★ ★

The mess of 2008 was created as a result of the bursting of a gigantic bubble in property which developed in the USA and in parts of Europe (particularly the UK but also Ireland and Spain). Things were made infinitely worse by new and very sophisticated financial derivatives which virtually no one (including the people trading them) understood. Greed, incompetence and irresponsibility and an interest only in short-term profits, exhibited en masse by people who thought they were cleverer than they turned out to be, led to financial chaos and proved that banking is far too important to be left to unregulated, unrestricted bankers.

In their search for greater and greater profits Wall Street bankers discovered the joys of securitisation. They repackaged ordinary loans into bonds and then sold the bonds on to banks in Europe. As the number of good mortgages ran out (there is, after all, a limit to the number of solvent would-be home owners) banks started lending more and more money to people who never stood a chance of paying it back (the subprime market). This pushed up house prices still further and convinced everyone that making money out of property was as easy as falling off your wallet. European bankers (particularly ones in Britain) became the fall guys; merrily gobbling up all the rubbish the American banks could produce. By autumn 2008 it was clear that European banks had more writedowns than American banks (even though the primary problem started in America). Wall Street successfully exported more than half of its financial toxic waste. Make no mistake about it, the credit crunch which led to so much damage in Europe was made in America.

Banks, run by men and women earning millions a year, borrowed money and lent it in bits to people who couldn't afford to borrow it because they didn't have jobs or had very poorly paid jobs but who wanted to buy smart houses they really couldn't afford. These were clearly risky loans but the rich bankers liked making the loans because the interest the poor people were supposed to be paying added up and enabled the bankers to pay themselves huge bonuses worth millions more.

The banks which had lent the money to the poor people then bundled the loans together and sold them to other highly paid bankers who had borrowed money to buy them. These bankers paid a lot for the right to own these loans because even though the first lot of bankers were taking a cut there was still a lot of interest to be shared out, and when you borrow billions and lend billions there is enough interest to give yourself hundreds of millions in bonuses. The bankers thought there wasn't any risk in any of this because if you lend out enough money most of the people borrowing it are surely going to be able to pay it back. And besides, they thought, the people were using the money to buy houses (which always goes up in value) so, if the people borrowing the money failed to pay back their loans, the banks could take over the houses, sell them and make even more money.

The banks which had bought packages of loans then split up the loans again, and mixed them up and stirred them and shook them until no one had the faintest idea what they entailed and sliced the loan mixture into new packages which they sold to yet more banks and investment companies and hedge funds, all of which had borrowed loads of money so that they could buy the loans and make money out of the interest that the poor people were supposedly paying and even if they didn't it didn't matter much because the money had been lent to people buying property and property always goes up in value.

You might have thought that the Government would have realised that this was dangerous. Battalions of vastly overpaid regulators exist to protect us from financial idiocy and dishonesty and from bankers who aren't bright enough to be left alone to sort the used clothing in a charity shop.

If you had thought this you would have been wrong.

Because no one did anything.

Until it was too late.

And then a Treasury Committee at the House of Commons grilled four disgraced former bank bosses and had the unusual pleasure of being able to take easy possession of the high moral ground.

★ ★ ★

Bankers weren't the only people who became greedy. Consumers got greedy too. Some wanted to buy houses they couldn't possibly afford. Others wanted to get rich by leveraging up and wheeling and dealing in buy-to-let properties. Most of the people doing this probably didn't understand what leveraging meant. They certainly didn't understand the consequences.

You might think that in a sensible world the people who borrowed money they could never afford to pay back might have learned a lesson.

But I doubt that.

Consumers will continue to borrow more than they can pay back and will continue to spend more than they earn. Both the British and American governments have bent over backwards to comfort, protect and reassure the greedy millions who bought houses they could not afford. In 2007 and 2008, for the first time in history, personal debt in the UK was more than the entire value of the economy. Even if people changed their attitudes this sort of problem would take a long time to unwind. In 2007, at the height of the credit boom, British people borrowed £130 billion to help them meet their spending habits. Many borrowed it against the value of their absurdly overvalued houses. They blew the loot on ipods and television sets, cars and scented candles. As a result of all this leveraged spending the British economy grew by 3% and Gordon Brown took the credit for it. It wasn't until the credit crunch really hit in the summer of 2008 that borrowing plummeted by more than 80% – virtually overnight. Even then the spending habit was hard to give up. The British couldn't borrow so they sold shares, bonds and cashed in their pensions. They spent £80 billion between the summer and Christmas 2008. And now there isn't anything much left. In order to maintain spending in the coming years (as Gordon Brown wants people to do) Britain's Micawber families will have to borrow £130 billion a year. They can't. Gordon Brown will keep spending money the Government hasn't got but among ordinary citizens consumption will fall. The economy will shrink.

Politicians will continue to behave as stupidly as they have in the past. In autumn 2008, the British Government announced that in order to overcome the financial crisis it was going to force British banks to continue to lend at 2007 levels. Politicians seemed unaware that the crisis had been caused by the banks lending too many people too much money in 2007. The politicians did everything they could to create the crisis and then did everything they possibly could to make things worse. (Which resurrects the question: are our politicians incredibly stupid or are they deliberately trying to destroy the country? It's one or the other.) Bullying the half-nationalised banks to continue to lend at the same reckless rate as before can only be compared to giving a convicted pyromaniac a can of petrol and a box of matches for Christmas. The only people who have truly suffered as a result of the banking crisis and the resultant depression are the thrifty, the hard working, the people who put aside a little money for a rainy day and the people who have invested their money in pension funds. They have seen their investments, their pensions and their savings halved (or worse) in just a few months. Even allegedly safe investments have disappeared. And, now that interest rates are approaching zero, the income from their bank accounts has dived.

No one has been punished for their greed and stupidity. The greedy haven't learned any lessons. Even those who borrowed more than they could possibly afford seem to prefer to blame the banks ('they pushed us really hard to borrow the money,' complained one woman with a massive mortgage she couldn't afford to pay) and still refuse to accept that they need to spend less ('The man at the bank wanted us to give up our Sky TV subscription so that we could pay the mortgage. Why should we do that? The cheek of it!' said another).

But there are some who may have learned a lesson.

The thrifty have probably learned that it doesn't pay to save. And they should have learned that whereas their responsibilities to their bank are written in stone their bank's responsibilities to them are written in sand. One of the hugely alarming discoveries of 2008 was that bank and investment company guarantees no longer have any value.

But those who created the banking crisis of 2008 have learned nothing. The greedy originators of the mess are still in charge and have neither taken blame for what happened nor learnt from their egregious mistakes. The people who suffered most were the people who worked hardest and who saved hardest. And yet the Government constantly did everything it could to defend the banks instead of defending investors (the people to whom it was responsible). When an insurance scheme was introduced (with great fanfare) it was for banks. A much more effective, and fairer, solution would have been to provide a guaranteed insurance for depositors.

An enormous opportunity to cleanse the system of much toxic waste has been ignored – on both sides of the Atlantic – for the sake of short-term advantage and political expediency.

★ ★ ★

After the demise of the investment banks in the late summer and early autumn of 2008 the remains of these pathetic hulks were bought up by clearing banks (for example, Barclays jumped in and eagerly bought up the remnants of Lehman Brothers).

And Brown et al let them do it!

So, as a result of the mess of 2008, investment banking and commercial banking grew ever closer.

In truth the two have very different aims and purposes, and have clients with conflicting interests. The new super banks, created when commercial banks used the money entrusted to them by retail depositors to purchase parts of failed investment banks (and to pay huge billion dollar bonuses to the bankers whose incompetence and arrogance had led to failure) will increasingly put the requirements, expectations and rights of ordinary investors below the greedy, often extortionate, demands of those working in investment banking.

We often hear criticism of loan sharks who charge up to 5,000% in interest. But small-time loan sharks aren't the only guilty ones.

There are some pretty unpleasant people working in banking. In the year 2000, bankers in London, New York and Buenos Aires charged the country of Argentina a commission fee of £150 million on a loan of £55 billion. The interest rates on the loan brought about a financial crisis in Argentina.

And although lots of them are incredibly greedy, bankers are not as clever as they like to think they are. If there is a way of losing money the bankers will always find it – especially if they can lose billions at a time. But, sadly for the rest of us, they aren't entirely stupid either. It is always our money they lose, and not theirs. The crash of 2008 clearly showed that when banks and investment groups make big profits it is the bankers who make big money but when they make big losses it is the shareholders and the investors and the depositors and the taxpayers who lose out. And so, because they are rich (the sole criterion for judging success in the world of the Labour Government) the bankers are smothered with knighthoods and peerages and important, well-paid positions advising the Government.

★ ★ ★

One banker stated that the problem banks face is that they have responsibilities to employees, customers, regulators, governments, suppliers, pensioners and shareholders – among others. This is not true. The directors of banks, like the directors of all public companies, have real responsibility only to shareholders – who own the company and are their employers. If bank directors took this single responsibility seriously their other responsibilities would be taken care of automatically.

★ ★ ★

The vast majority of bankers are no longer worthy of our trust. Regard your common or garden local High Street banker with the same amount of suspicion as you would regard a man in a mask climbing through your bedroom window.

The world has changed, and as far as the ordinary investor is concerned, it has not changed for the better. It is going to take years for those banks which resist nationalisation to recover from their American subprime debts, their British property debts and the debts they now owe the Government. And the real danger, perhaps, is that people will be so fed up with the greed of the bankers that they will welcome nationalisation and more public sector regulation and more Government involvement in every aspect of our lives. That would be a source of great joy to the EU and the Government; so much, indeed, that in my darkest moments I sometimes wonder if the whole darned credit crunch crisis might not have been engineered to persuade us to accept even more interference in our daily lives. I don't really believe that, of course. They aren't that clever. Are they?

★ ★ ★

Many people who appeared rich at the start of the 21st Century were swimming with no clothes on. They had geared up as much as they possibly could, borrowing against the value of their main home every time it went up and then using the money to buy holiday cottages, cars and boats. In many towns and country villages the people who seemed to have all the money were, in reality, far poorer than their neighbours who appeared to be surviving on the breadline but who did, nevertheless, own a major part of their home and have some very real savings in a deposit account.

The credit crunch crisis will have exposed greedy and reckless consumers just as surely as it exposed the banks and the governments who had borrowed (and spent) too much. British households are the most indebted of any leading economy. In 2007 and 2008 the amount of personal debt in Britain was higher than the entire value of the UK economy. This has never, ever happened before. The figures are truly scary. In the decade or so of Blair and Brown, outstanding mortgage debt rose from £450 billion to £1,200 billion. Consumer debts (credit cards, overdrafts, etc) have risen from £100 billion to nearly £250 billion. The UK population is now the most indebted in Europe. (And would be the most indebted in the world were it not for the Americans – who always like to be biggest and worst at everything.)

During 2008 over four million families used their credit cards to pay their mortgage. And they were, don't forget, paying credit card interest rates of at least 17%. (These debts are also likely to lead to more problems for banks. Many credit card debts were resold as banks sought to make more and more money in the mad, greedy years of the early 21st Century. As people struggle to pay their bills so the banks will face ever greater debts.) The British have become addicted to spending money they don't have. And they will do anything to get what they believe is their due. Before Labour came to power in 1997 Britons spent £7 billion a year gambling. By 2005 it had risen to £53 billion. And, encouraged by the Labour Government, the figure spent on gambling is racing upwards.

Thanks to our communal indebtedness and greed, Britain now officially has the highest living costs in the Western world. (And since there isn't anywhere terribly expensive in the Eastern world, that pretty much means on the planet.) It costs considerably more to live in England than it costs to live in Zurich, Los Angeles or Paris.

But the one thing we can be certain of is that the topsy turvey Government will continue to put the interests of debtors above savers. Those who rely on dividends and interest for an income (because they aren't former public sector workers with huge pensions paid by taxpayers) were devastated by cuts in both in 2008. And many were appalled when the interest paid on National Savings, and used to provide prizes for Premium Bond holders, was slashed after savers, terrified that their bank might go bust, had rushed to put their money into National Savings accounts. It was yet another example of the Government's cynical abuse of the prudent in order to help the imprudent. In early January 2009, the taxman threatened to investigate savers who had switched bank accounts and it was suggested that the Government might introduce a special tax on savings to force those who had been so 'unpatriotic' that they had saved some of their money to spend their savings and therefore help out the 'patriotic' whose enthusiastic work in the shops had pushed them deeper and deeper into debt. And it was suggested that the Government might buy homes from people who had bitten off bigger mortgages than they could chew, and then rent the homes back to the same people at a modest rent.

★ ★ ★

'People who don't work, don't want to work and expect to be looked after by the State demand respect and consideration. Fair enough,' wrote a reader of my books. But, 'I want to live somewhere where people who work hard and support themselves and who save for bad times and their old age are respected just as much. Is that really too much to ask?'

★ ★ ★

The most common cause of relationship-breakdown is not alcohol or drug abuse, sickness, depression or unfaithfulness. It is the sort of money problems that come with debt. Nevertheless, the Labour Government has constantly encouraged people to go into debt. In the same way that the EU creates butter mountains and wine lakes,' the Labour Government has created a debt pit. And the Government has built its own economic framework upon debt. Brown's policy has been to spend too much in the good years. Its policy now is to spend too much in the bad years too. The British Government will soon owe more than it did in the 1970s when James Callaghan's Labour Government had to ask the International Monetary Fund for a handout so that Britain wouldn't go bankrupt.

And the Labour Government's wondrous policy for dealing with the recession has been to encourage consumers to get spending. The Government doesn't want people saving and investing and being sensible with their money. The Government wants us out there in the shops buying stuff we neither need nor particularly want. The Government wants to get money circulating and shops booming. It wants more taxes to pay for all its spending. Politicians know that, unless we spend, the Government's tax income will fall dramatically. Encouraging spending and debt may well be the irresponsible and stupid thing to do, but irresponsible and stupid are the two things the Labour Government does best.

During the Labour Government's reign, leverage (borrowing) at the major British banks has doubled. And now that the banks have gone bust (or almost bust) they have to rebuild their balance sheets. Banks aren't lending to small businesses or potential home owners because they are stuffing every penny they can find under their banking mattresses. (But it seems that banks still seem unable to work out precisely what 'wealth' actually means. In January 2009, Barclays Bank wrote to customers telling them it intended to provide a better service for its 'wealthy' clients. It defined wealthy as having assets of at least 50,000 euros or a home loan of more than 400,000 euros. I find it worrying that the bank still hasn't worked out that there is a difference between assets and debts.)

Few outside the Government can have been surprised when, at the end of 2008, five Anglican bishops questioned the morality of the Government's policies of encouraging people to get into debt. And fewer still can have been surprised by the Archbishop of Canterbury warning that resorting to borrowing is like a drug addict returning for another fix. Brown and his Chancellor and his ministers refuse to recognise that they have created deep-rooted economic problems. Instead they continue to contemplate, design and put into action ever more reckless short-term solutions designed not to solve the problem but to provide short-term political relief. It is impossible not to feel contempt for such people.

It took Britain until the 1980s to repay the huge debts it had accumulated during the Second World War. By 1992 we had dragged ourselves back to being a major player in the world.

Brown has destroyed all that and his massive borrowings and imprudent policies have set us on a straight course to dishonour and impoverishment. When Brown's Government lent more money to the Royal Bank of Scotland he told the bank-with-no-funds that it had to increase its lending by another £6 billion. It's as though a bank manager had called in a customer who couldn't pay his debts and ordered him to solve his problem by borrowing more money.

⋆ ⋆ ⋆

Gearing (the posh word for debt) got out of hand a decade ago. The hedge fund managed by two Nobel prize winners, LTCM, was more than 100 times geared in 1998. The people running it had only to be out by 1% and they would go bust. In the end, the Americans couldn't let LTCM go bust because the scale of the financial bets they had made was so great that the whole of Wall Street might have been brought down. So the Fed bailed them out and created moral hazard.

This was the first time that a company had been deemed too big to fail.

And so suddenly leverage was a good idea. It meant that if you were in trouble but got bigger and bigger eventually you would be considered too big to fail and the Government would bail you out.

In America it has happened with General Motors, AIG, Fannie and Freddie Mac and Citigroup. Huge firms with declining profits all borrowed and grew on debt. They all geared up to absurd levels. And they all either went bust or headed that way.

Debt, gearing, leverage – call it what you will – was the source of our nation's problems. We created a world where speculators used other people's money to grow. And the risks they took eventually exposed the prudent, as well as the reckless, to unbelievable levels of financial danger.

Joseph Schumpeter's great fear was plutocracy – the rule of society by the wealthy. This happened in Germany in the early 1920s, when hyper-inflation blew the wealth of the fortunate few to absurd levels. There was no economic prosperity but huge fortunes were made by a lucky few. This is exactly what happened in Britain and America during the 1990s and the early years of the 21st Century. Investment bankers, private equity managers and hedge fund operatives made fortunes by gambling with other people's money.

People got rich not through producing things or creating wealth. People got wealthy because they bought stuff when stuff was rising in value. And if they borrowed and bought more than they could afford they got very rich. People got very, very rich through the poverty of the people.

Creative destruction, allowing companies to go bust when things go wrong, prevents complacency and absurd levels of leverage. There is risk and so there is some caution.

* * *

Whenever there was talk of having bankers charged with criminal offences for allowing their banks to get into such a mess, commentators spoke out against it. When anyone suggested that bankers be sacked it was widely agreed by politicians and 'experts' that this would be unfair and unhelpful. 'We shouldn't kick people when they're down,' said one well-known commentator, as though kicking them when they are up might be better. 'Criticising bankers is just about vengeance,' moaned another.

I didn't understand any of this.

Criticising bankers had nothing to do with vengeance but it had everything to do with preventing the same thing happening again.

Brown and his Government should have fired every banker in Britain above the level of 'clerk' who was employed by one of the banks which went bust, or which needed Government help in any way.

Britain needs a fair, secure banking system.

And we are never going to get that while the banks are run by greedy, self-serving morons.

But that's probably why the politicians didn't want to do anything.

Greedy, self-serving morons tend to stick together.

* * *

What happened in 2008 will lead to high taxes and massive state involvement. Brown has weakened Britain so much that we are going to be the worst nation in the world in which to try and run a business (or live your life without state interference). The people and the Government spent too much. That was the problem. And the solution was glaringly simple: earn and save to pay off the debts and to put some corn in the barn. But, when you've been used to years of plenty, earning and saving are dull, unattractive solutions.

By the time you finish reading this sentence Britain's national debt will have risen by another £1,500 to £2,000. And that's money which you or your children will have to repay. Read the first sentence in this paragraph again: that's another £1,500 to £2,000.

* * *

When the banks which had been greediest went bust in 2008 the British Government's response was not to say 'Serves you right. You greedy bastards got what you deserve. We will make sure depositors don't lose any money by guaranteeing their deposits. But bankers are toast. And the banks can go bust. In future, banks which take money from ordinary depositors will only be allowed to lend and borrow. None of the fancy stuff.'

That would have been a sensible response, and although investors with shares in the banks would have lost money, careful, prudent depositors wouldn't have lost a penny. The system would have been cleansed.

Instead, the moronic Brown and his advisors decided to bail out the banks so that they could carry on doing what had caused the problems in the first place. And when it didn't work the first time they did it a second time.

Roger Phillips of Evolution Securities wasn't the only expert to be sceptical about the Government's plans. 'We expect the UK Government,' he said, 'to try to solve the obesity crisis next week by nationalising the supermarkets, so that they can then resume the supply of cheap doughnuts to fat people.'

'The scale of stupidity and greed at the big banks defies belief,' wrote Luke Johnson, chairman of Channel 4 and chairman of a private equity firm. 'With few exceptions, the banking breed has brought capitalism into disrepute and massively compounded a brutal downturn. Their story is a tragedy for those of us who believe in free markets and private enterprise. They have smashed the world's confidence in our financial systems and delighted those who would see our way of life destroyed.'

By supporting and protecting the greedy, corrupt system, Brown and Darling & Co ensured that the same problem will happen again. Why did they do it? I suspect that politicians simply didn't understand just how appalling the behaviour of the bankers had been. Politicians themselves behave badly, and with only their interests at heart; they are not worthy of our trust and they offer neither leadership nor inspiration. Why would they understand just how badly the bankers had behaved when to them it probably seemed rational and perfectly normal?

Once this financial crisis is over there will be another one. And another one. And another one. Until some politician, somewhere down the line, is brave enough to let a lot of very rich bankers go bust and lose their yachts and helicopters and race horses and villas and private islands.

Meanwhile, investors face a difficult time.

Just how bad will the recession turn out to be? How long will it last? How much will profits (and dividends) be affected?

No one knows the answers to those questions.

But it seems likely to me that the problems created by the Government and the financial industry aren't going to go away. I suspect that in the future investors are going to be exceedingly wary about putting their savings and their pension money into the stock markets. The risk premium will have to be higher. Share prices will be lower. And the potential for hedge fund managers, bankers and other investment company parasites to gouge billions out of ordinary savers will be somewhat slighter.

In early 2009 there was a popular feeling among British politicians that the problems created by the bank crashes of 2008 would soon be over. Government Ministers talked about a short, sharp recession and a return to 'normal' in 2010 at the latest. There was talk of 'green shoots', though no one seemed able to point to any.

I don't know which planet these Ministers live on but it's not Earth.

Many things are possible, but a return to a spending-fest is not one of them. Britain will, I suspect, recover much more slowly than any other country. The near-collapse of the financial system will lead to a long depression, a serious deterioration in the economies of many countries (especially Britain) and a good deal of social unrest. There will be considerable (delayed) anger at the way politicians and bankers have led us into chaos. There will be political instability, strikes, demonstrations and, I fear, considerable unrest. The Government will use powers it gave itself to deal with terrorism to suppress dissent. That, inevitably, will lead to more unhappiness, more anger and more violence.

The banking problem isn't going to go away in a hurry. The British banks that are in trouble have accumulated $4.4 trillion worth of foreign liabilities. That's $4.4 thousand billion worth of debt. That's a lot of debt. It's twice the size of the entire British economy. And if the banks can't pay it back, and their debts have to be taken on by the nation, then we're in serious trouble because Britain has foreign reserves of less than $61 billion – that's less than Malaysia or Thailand. If Britain defaults on these debts (as it could) our credit rating as a nation will go through the floor. And we'll be down in the financial cellars with those funny little countries which no one can spell or find on the map.

There will, I suspect, also be a return to high inflation.

And before then, bank charges will rise for both private and business customers. In a desperate effort to make some money the banks are already increasing their charges for all kinds of services. This will happen more and more. And it won't matter whether the bank is privately owned or has been nationalised.

★ ★ ★

I've discussed the banking problem in some detail for two reasons.

First, until the bank problem is solved nothing else will be solved.

Second, the bankers running our banks are crooked, stupid and enormously greedy. The ones who weren't directly, personally responsible for the mess must share collective responsibility. Too many of today's bankers believe they are untouchable, and entitled to vast salaries and bonuses. And the Government, blinded by them, cannot see beyond this nonsense. It is now widely accepted that it was the bonus culture, rewarding people who took enormous upside-only risks with other people's money, which helped cause the banking crisis. But the Government has done too little to stop this. So, the result is going to be enduring chaos.

For the future there is only one certainty: everything the Government, the banks and the regulators can do wrong they will do wrong. Everything they can do to make things worse they will do. This is not cynicism. It is prudent thinking born of experience.

Chapter 4

Deflation, Inflation And The Coming Hyperinflation

The Government wants to create inflation to boost the economy. Creating inflation is so easy that even Brown will succeed. But he won't be able to control the inflation he creates. And so that's the next big problem we all face. Hyperinflation will destroy the lives of millions and will prove more devastating than the credit crunch.

As I write this there is much dispute among economists about whether or not we can expect to be overwhelmed by deflation or inflation. Economists are incredibly poor at predicting developments. Even in their own specialised field they tend to get things wrong so often that their recommendations and advice are best regarded as contrarian indicators. (In other words if they say that X is going to happen you can pretty confidently expect the opposite of X to happen.)

We are warned that deflation is coming. And, indeed, it undoubtedly is. Bubbles everywhere have burst. Assets have been liquidated, effectively at gunpoint. Every suggestion is that deflation will destroy our society and is something to be greatly feared. By the beginning of 2009 experts were warning that we were facing a decade of Japanese style inflation – with prices and values falling, falling and falling further. In a real deflationary world the prices of everything falls – houses, shares, salaries, bonds, cars, socks, washing machines and bribes. Only MPs' and civil servants' salaries and expenses remain untouched. And the only thing increasing in value is debt. During a deflation debts get bigger and push the economy into a depression.

There is certainly going to be some deflation.

For one thing, there is a lot of deleveraging going on at the moment.

Bankers who borrowed too much money and then invested it in dodgy investments which failed have to claw together enough money to pay back what they borrowed. Investment companies, venture capitalists and private equity buy-out specialists who borrowed too much money to invest in property or businesses, but who now find themselves holding assets which are worth less than they borrowed, have to sell some of the stuff they bought in order to pay back some of the loans they took out. And home owners and buy-to-let owners who borrowed money to buy property which they believed could only ever go up in value, find themselves in negative equity: their loans are greater than the value of their property. They have to sell something to pay back their loans. If they don't then the banks which lent them the money will do it for them.

That's a lot of deleveraging to be done. And it is going to take a long time. Deleveraging is going to dominate the financial landscape for more than a year or two. Governments will hate it because deleveraging is deflationary. And governments much prefer inflation to deflation.

But although it could last for a while, is deflation really our biggest threat?

Deflation produces falling prices. And the politicians tell us that this is dangerous because once they realise that prices are falling people will hold back on buying the things they need – hoping to be able to buy them cheaper in a few months' time. And thus, they say, deflation will lead to a slowing down in growth and a stagnant economy.

This is nonsense, of course.

Prices of many things have been falling for years. Electrical equipment is cheaper now than it was last year and far cheaper than it was ten years ago. Do people refuse to buy computers or telephone or television sets because they think they might become cheaper? Of course not.

Politicians really dislike deflation for other reasons.

First, when prices fall the effective cost of our existing debts rises. If you have borrowed £500,000 to buy a house and the value of the house falls to £250,000 you still have to pay back £500,000 but you have lost £250,000. Borrowing money becomes expensive in deflationary times. Deflation is bad for the imprudent and spendthrift.

Second, people who have savings tend to do well in deflationary times. If you have £1,000 in the bank and television sets cost £500 each you can only buy two of them. But if deflation pushes the price down to £250 each, you can buy four of them with your £1,000. Deflation is bad for spendthrift people who have big debts but it helps people who have saved and been prudent.

Third, (and this is the real reason why politicians hate deflation with a vengeance) deflation means that tax revenues don't grow as quickly. If wages and salaries fail to rise very quickly then fewer and fewer people move into higher range tax brackets.

Fourth, once deflation gets hold it tends to be self-reinforcing. The problem is that although workers always want a pay rise when prices are inflating they never want to take a pay cut when prices are deflating. And so more and more businesses fail and the number of jobless rises. As the number of unemployed people goes up so demand for stuff goes down. And that results in prices falling and more deflation. And so it goes.

Britain may well be heading for a period of deflation. By the time this book comes out we will probably be in it up to our knees.

But for anyone who didn't get carried away by the enthusiasm for borrowing and spending, a period of deflation may well be quite a good thing.

However, it isn't the deflation we should be worrying about. (Indeed, the cautious and the prudent should, perhaps, welcome it rather than fear it.) What we should be frightened about are the consequences of the way the politicians will tackle the deflation. As is so often the case, the water damage will be more destructive than the fire.

Determined idiots with printing presses will conquer the threat of deflation by what they merrily refer to as 'quantitative easing' (a piece of 'friendly fire' style modern jargon which means printing loads more money so that the value of the existing stuff goes down to match the falling value of the things – such as houses – that it buys). Vast amounts of money will be created so that accumulated debts can be written off more speedily. The deflation will, I believe, then be replaced by the far uglier sister, inflation. The politicians will use inflation to destroy the deflation. The Japanese didn't start printing money until seven years after deflation had first appeared. The British and the Americans, determined to protect the greedy bankers and property buyers who had accumulated unmanageable debts, started before it had begun.

Another reason why deflation isn't going to be as big a problem in Britain as the economists claim is that the value of the British pound is dropping. And, thanks to the bizarre policies of the Labour Government, the British currency is likely to keep on dropping. As the pound falls so imports will become more expensive. And since Britain now has to import virtually everything (from oil to bras) prices will rise – not fall.

It is the rampant hyper-inflation which will follow that will really do the damage.

And you will not be surprised to hear that it's the inflation that Brown is hoping for.

The trouble is that Brown just wants a bit of it.

And we're going to get a lot more than a bit of it.

Deflation may well be a short-term problem but the medium and long-term problems will undoubtedly be raging, uncontrollable hyper-inflation created and fed by governments creating money. Those who saved and were prudent will be massacred. Those who were imprudent and reckless will be saved.

★ ★ ★

Economists pretend that economics is a science. This is balderdash. In real life, economics depends on what people want and do and fear. It depends on greed. Chemistry and physics are true sciences. What people fear or suspect doesn't affect the boiling point of water. But what people think and do and fear affects every aspect of economics. Economics, in short, is not a science and no more reliable than gossip. And economists are a plague on our society. They may sound convincing but they have less idea of the future than the astrologers who write columns for the daily newspapers. We would be better off without economists.

★ ★ ★

Sadly, the vast majority of politicians, economists, senior bankers and commentators don't understand what inflation is. I'm never quite sure whether this is through simple ignorance or a hope that if they say something often enough the general public will believe them.

And so we hear experts warning us that if commodity prices go up then we can expect inflation to hit us soon. This, of course, is utter nonsense. Rising commodity prices don't cause inflation. Rising prices don't cause inflation. Rising prices aren't inflation. Rising prices are a consequence of inflation – not the cause. Today's official dictionary definition of inflation is likely to reflect the popular assumption, and to define inflation as an increase in prices and a fall in the purchasing value of money. But the older, original, proper definition of inflation is an increase in the amount of currency in circulation. And it is the increase in the amount of currency circulating (the inflation) that causes a fall in the value of the currency and, therefore, a rise in prices.

The simple truth is that inflation occurs when the value of money goes down and you can't buy as much with it as you used to be able to. And the value of money goes down when governments print more of it.

If I paint a picture I might be able to persuade a dealer to give me a pound for it. But if I paint the same picture a hundred times the chances are that I will get much less than a pound. By flooding the market I have devalued my pictures.

It's the same with money.

If the Government prints a billion pound notes then a pound may buy you a loaf of bread. But if the Government prints a trillion pound notes then there will be far more notes floating around and so the value of the ones in existence will fall. The baker will want more money for his loaf of bread.

That's inflation.

The term the spin-doctors have thought up to describe the policies espoused in America and Britain is 'quantitative monetary easing'. But this wonderfully obtuse 'friendly fire' style phrase simply means printing more money so that the stuff sloshes around and everyone is knee deep in it. The theory is that by making more money available, the governments are making the economy grow again. It is an insane theory. (Nowhere in the world is inflation currently better illustrated than in Zimbabwe. In January 2009 Zimbabwe produced a hundred trillion dollar banknote. The hundred trillion dollar note was worth about £20. Well, it was worth about £20 for a few minutes. By the time you read this it will probably be worth a fiver. In Zimbabwe, the money supply increased 20 million times between August 2007 and June 2008. Printing money as fast as the presses would go round pushed up inflation to 2,000,000 per cent for a while early in 2008. Still, it didn't stay at that for long. By Christmas 2008 it had soared to 230,000,000 per cent. Now that's inflation. Bizarrely, the Zimbabwean Government limited bank withdrawals to 500,000 Zimbabwe dollars a day. Brilliant. Of course, with a bag of sugar costing a considerable amount more than that, the new rules made shopping tricky. But, hey, you can't please everyone all the time. And it must have been fun to live in a country where you could stand in line at the cash point machine for ever without being able to withdraw enough money to buy a small bottle of water.

The other myth about inflation is that governments dislike it. They don't. Governments love inflation. They adore it. Inflation is the politician's best friend. (Debtors love inflation too. If you borrow £100,000 and the value of money goes down 10% a year then your loan is shrinking faster than you're paying it off.) When inflation pushes up prices and salaries, the government's income (taxes) rises dramatically.

As a result of the depression created by Gordon Brown's disastrous decade as Chancellor, the Government's income will fall dramatically. People will earn less and spend less and so the Government's income will fall. Inflation will push up prices and help the Government enormously. Inflation is the most potent form of taxation there is because it is invisible.

In public the politicians will promise to do everything they can to prevent inflation. In private they will welcome it. When property prices fall the Government's income from stamp duty, inheritance tax and capital gains falls. When inflation pushes up prices then the Government's income rises.

And that's one of the reasons why Brown and Darling want to print more money and to spend their way out of the depression their government has created.

They probably didn't mention that.

(Indeed, they haven't mentioned much. In January 2009 the Government, obsessed with secrecy, abolished an 1844 law which required the Bank of England to publish a weekly account of its balance sheet. Did they do this to hide the extent of their 'quantitative easing'? Don't they realise it is our money they are destroying? Why get rid of a law which has served the nation well for 165 years?)

Inflation is a relatively modern phenomenon but it seems that modern governments have fallen in love with it. Inflation occurs when governments cheapen their currency by spending more than they can afford and printing currency to pay for the spending. Brown, despite his dishonest claims to be a prudent Chancellor, has spent, is spending and intends to spend so much money that the Great British Pound will be destroyed. Hyper-inflation is almost inevitable.

★ ★ ★

The future will be difficult for the West in general and Britain in particular. In addition to the problem of the disappearing oil (as outlined in my book *Oil Apocalypse*) there is the problem that inflation in Asia will mean the end of cheap goods in the West. But it will still be cheaper to manufacture things, and to provide services, in China and India and so unemployment in the West will rise and rise. As the Government's official inflation figure rises (even its manipulated inflation figure will soar) then the Bank of England will be forced to push up interest rates ever further.

And that, in turn, will result in the greatest and deepest depression the modern world has ever seen. The precious metals will, I suspect, be the only investments in the world to hold their value.

The rest of the world will be in much the same condition (though not quite so bad as Britain). Britons will, thanks to Brown, be the paupers of the developed world.

And then the problems created by Peak Oil will really start to hit hard. As China and the rest of Asia develop so demand for the diminishing supplies of oil will rocket and the price of oil, in sterling, will reach unimaginable levels.

Chapter 5

Britain Is Heading For An Energy Crisis

The oil is running out. The gas is running out. Our power stations are near the end of their working lives. The European Union has introduced strict laws controlling energy production. And big, big problems are just a year or two away. Windmills and wave power aren't going to make any difference.

The demand for energy in Britain is constantly rising but a study carried out by Capgemini, a global energy consultancy firm, recently reported that electricity generation has fallen to its lowest level in 10 years. I'm not surprised. Encouraged by the EU, politicians and campaigners insist that we build wind turbines instead of more reliable sources of electricity. Arguments about nuclear power and coal have caused crucial delays in the building of new power stations. Protestors who, nevertheless still want their washing machines, their tumble driers, their televisions and their computers, have delayed the very necessary building of new sources of power. Use wind power, they say, not having the faintest idea what they are talking about. (There is an explanation of the shortcomings of wind power in *Oil Apocalypse*.) About a quarter of Britain's energy plant capacity will close by 2015 as the country struggles to balance its energy needs with the Government's carbon emission targets.

In 2005 Britain became a net importer of gas (the oil and gas in the North Sea passed its 'peak' level some time ago) and by 2010 gas imports will account for 40% of our gas needs. By 2020 Britain will rely on foreign sources (for which, read Russia and the Middle East) for 80-90% of its gas needs. In other words we will rely for our gas supplies on nations with whom, thanks to the Labour Government's support of the American neoconservatives, we can hardly claim to have 'good' relations. And it seems reasonable to remember that Russia has twice stopped gas supplies to the entire nation of Ukraine because of disagreements over payments. The latest stoppage, early in 2009, occurred because Ukraine would not pay a 40% price rise. Numerous other EU countries (including Poland, Bulgaria, Romania, and Hungary) get much or most of their gas from Russia. Indeed, European Union members as a whole rely on Russia for 25% of their natural gas supplies and 80% of that is delivered through Ukraine. Unfortunately, when Russia stops sending gas to Ukraine some of the gas intended for Europe has a tendency to disappear en route, and to find its way into homes in Ukraine.

Britain is, as usual, more at risk from any disruptions than any other European country. Many western European countries have protected themselves against supply disruptions by building and filling huge gas stores. France and Germany, for example, have gas storage capacity of over 20% of their annual consumption. Britain is the world's third largest gas market and extremely reliant on gas imports. So, how much gas do you think Britain stores? It's a measly 4%. And that 4% would last around a fortnight in the summer. In the winter months the amount of gas we have stored would last less than five days.

There are two reasons why Britain has not built gas storage facilities.

First, obtaining planning consent for building essential gas stores takes a long, long time.

Second, no one in Government foresaw the decline in our North Sea gas reserves and our inevitable increasing reliance on gas imports.

The result? There will soon be a huge gas shortage crisis.

Nuclear reactors provide only 20% of our electricity needs. And that is shrinking because the Government has done nothing to replace old reactors. Four ageing nuclear power plants will soon be shut. Within 20 years we will get only six per cent of our electricity from nuclear power. Since it can take at least a decade to build a nuclear power station that problem is not going to be easily or quickly dealt with.

Nine oil and coal-fired British power stations are going to close before 2015 because of an EU directive designed to limit pollution. Recognising that the problem is desperate the Government is considering building one or more new coal-fired power stations. There are two problems with this. First, environmentalists don't like the idea and will campaign loudly against such a plan. And second, building a new coal-fired power station would endanger the UK's commitment to the European Union's target to generate 20% of all electricity from renewable sources by 2020.

China is building one coal-fired power station a day and is planning to build vast numbers of nuclear power stations. It's buying up uranium mines so that it doesn't run out of the raw material for its nuclear power stations. In Britain, however, the most rabid environmentalists seem to disapprove of anything likely to produce energy in reasonable quantities. Coal, nuclear power and oil are all politically unacceptable. The trouble is that between them they produce 99% of our energy and unless we are all content to simply stand still and shiver there isn't much hope for a modern country that doesn't have a good supply of energy.

And our electricity needs are rising. It seems inevitable that Britain's energy needs will far exceed supply long before 2015. That will lead to regular power cuts. Solar panels and little windmills stuck on politicians' houses aren't going to solve this problem. (One of the great ironies of the modern world is that the people who campaign so vociferously against nuclear power – the only practical option – are also enthusiastic users of the Internet. They are as committed to blogging and surfing as they are to opposing nuclear energy. I wonder how many of these misguided idiots realise that using a search engine uses up electricity and generates significant amounts of carbon dioxide. Publishing books is far more energy efficient than writing a Web blog. The bloggers and surfers will have to give up their computers if we are all to rely on solar and wind power.)

* * *

And then there is the oil problem.

When the oil price collapsed in 2008 there were many who declared that it was merely the end of a bubble.

It wasn't.

The price of oil will resume its upward climb very soon. And it will rise faster and further than ever.

There are several reasons for this.

1. Emerging countries (such as China and India) are growing fast. Their growth may have slowed temporarily during the global financial crisis. But the people of those countries won't stop wanting cars and television sets and an endless supply of cheeseburgers. In February 2009 car sales in America fell below car sales in China for the first time (in spite of the fact that manufacturers and dealers in America were offering steep discounts and American taxpayers were supporting their failing car industry). Countries such as China are building huge amounts of infrastructure and will need vast amounts of oil (and other commodities) to continue with this work. China is planning 97 new regional airports. That rather suggests that they might be expecting a modest increase in air traffic. It is absurd to assume that a temporary financial crisis will produce a permanent end to China's development. (China's economic growth is widely said to have stalled. It will, nevertheless, probably grow by 7.5% in 2009, according to the World Bank. That's not a bad rate for a country whose development is supposed to have stalled.)
2. As I showed in my book *Oil Apocalypse*, the oil is running out. No large oil fields have been found for decades. Supplies in existing, mature fields are falling. In 2004, 30 billion barrels of oil were consumed but only 8 billion barrels of oil were discovered. When oil fields are half empty it becomes increasingly difficult to extract the remaining oil, and most of the world's existing giant oil fields are more than half empty. Many established oil producing countries report that their production is declining. Many large companies have had to restate their reserves downwards. Moreover, most of the new supplies are heavy crude oils which are difficult to turn into heating oil, diesel or jet fuel. When my book *Oil Apocalypse* came out, several readers wrote to tell me that someone would either find more oil or an alternative. 'The markets will save us,' I was told. Yes? How? Most people preferred to keep their heads buried in the sand. 'I read the first third of the book,' said a reporter for *The Independent* newspaper,

'but I found it too depressing so I gave up.' Incidentally, when I wrote *Oil Apocalypse* (in the early summer of 2007) I warned: '...if there is a financial crash within the next year or two which has nothing to do with the disappearing oil (as I suspect there could be) then the demand for oil will probably fall and the oil price will probably fall with it. If that happens I will be buying more oil – not selling what I have.'

3. Nations are holding onto their resources with more determination. Russia and Venezuela are now big players in providing oil. They aren't going to roll over and let the Americans grab their oil. (The Americans, who comprise just 4% of the world's population have an enormous thirst for oil. They use 25% of the world's oil supplies and import nearly 70% of the oil they use.)
4. Countries such as the UK have slowed down the search for oil by introducing new, additional taxes on oil companies.
5. The global crisis of 2008 resulted in many companies abandoning investment in new oilfields. This will exacerbate the shortage of supplies in the future. The more the oil companies cut back on their expenditure on research and development the bigger the shortage and the higher the price. In the autumn of 2008, more than four out of five refinery construction projects faced cancellation.
6. The UK is (like the rest of Europe and the USA) dependent on countries with which it does not have a good relationship for its oil and gas supplies. The European Union as a whole imports 50% of its energy needs and that figure will rise to 70% by 2020 at the latest. Russia is by far the EU's biggest supplier of oil and gas. If you're happy to feel dependent on Vladimir Putin's generosity of spirit then this won't worry you. And if you believe that the European countries will behave rationally and sensibly, and work together to forge supply deals with Russia when their oil and gas supplies have run out then you won't find that a worry either. And if you believe that any British Government is capable of forging a warm, loving relationship with Russia then you will remain unworried. But then if you believe all that you probably believe in fairies too, so I doubt if anything much concerns you.

7. By November 2008 oil was costing more to get out of the ground than it was selling for. You don't need a very big brain to realise that such a situation is unsustainable. North Sea development costs were about $40 a barrel but big oil companies are now evaluating projects at $50 a barrel. You don't need to be an economist to work out that this suggests that oil will be selling for considerably more than that.
8. OPEC and the oil producing countries will cut supply to help protect the oil price. I expect Russia to join OPEC in order to join with other oil producing countries in helping to push the oil price up while demand is relatively low. (In July 2008 newspapers ran the headline: 'Brown Warns Iran'. I'm still trying to work out what made Brown feel he was in a position to make threats to Iran. The phrase 'flea warns elephant' springs to mind. Naturally, the Iranians took no notice whatsoever.)
9. Politicians are so desperate to encourage alternative forms of energy (windpower, solar power and wave power, for example) that they will do everything they can to push the price of oil back up. If the price of oil is too low, companies will not be able to make money out of alternative forms of energy. And politicians, who know that the oil is running out, will do everything they can to make alternative forms of energy profitable. Actually, the only thing they can do is to make oil cost more. And so America and the EU will quietly support OPEC's attempts to push the price of oil back up.

★ ★ ★

Reading the press (or listening to TV or radio) in the summer of 2008, when the Russians and the Americans were rattling sabres over Georgia (a place most newspaper and television editors had to look up on the map) you probably wouldn't understand why the Russians and the Americans were squabbling over Georgia so severely. What no one liked to mention is that there are serious oil and gas fields in that region (and two major oil and gas pipelines too). When the Soviet Union broke up, Russia lost control of those fields. It wants them back. They know that oil and gas are scarce and getting scarcer and they are fully aware of the value of these commodities. Naturally, the Americans want control of these oil and gas supplies too and in April 2008 the North Atlantic Treaty Organisation (NATO) said that Georgia would be allowed to join at some time in the future. This was probably a lie but the Russians took it seriously and regarded it as a threat to their national security (not surprisingly, since Georgia is right next door to Russia and look what happened when Russia got friendly with Cuba back in the Kennedy days). The Russians then started improving their ties with separatists in South Ossetia and Abkhazia (two regions which wanted to split from Georgia) and sent peacekeeping troops into the area. (The Americans always call their invading armies 'peacekeeping troops' so it is difficult to complain when the Russians do the same.) Naturally, this annoyed the Georgians, and the Americans got very vocal in support of the Georgians and threatened to do all sorts of nasty things to Russia. But America is so stretched by its oil-inspired adventures in Iraq and Afghanistan that it didn't have the money or the troops to start a war in Georgia or do anything much other than make a lot of diplomatic noise. So Russia could do pretty well what it liked. So it did.

* * *

There is more information about oil, peak oil, biofuels and the alternative possibilities in my book *Oil Apocalypse*. The changes that are going to take place will affect every aspect of our lives. To give a simple example, sporting events will in the future be played out purely for the television cameras. There will be no spectators because people won't be able to afford to get to the venues. People building stadia are wasting their money. And some sports (motorsport for example) will just die.

* * *

Just to make things really, really bad for Britain, Brown has annoyed the OPEC countries and he and his Government have annoyed Russia. Even the wretched, banana-toting Miliband geek, who pretends to be Foreign Secretary, has managed to annoy the Russians. The Russian foreign minister is reported to have become so incensed by what he regarded as Miliband's condescending manner that he is alleged to have barked: 'Who the fuck are you to lecture me?' It was, perhaps, a demand with which many in England might have great sympathy. (Actually Miliband seems to be unusually good at annoying foreign ministers. On a trip to India he caused a diplomatic storm and was described as 'almost condescending' and 'tactless'. His 'attention span' was singled out for criticism and a local Indian newspaper reported that the Indian Prime Minister had written to Gordon Brown to protest about Miliband's behaviour. Everyone later denied the existence of any such letter.)

Annoying Russia hasn't been enormously clever.

Here are two facts you should know. They help to illustrate the Russian way of doing things.

Fact one, Russia has sold Iran a package of missiles and has given Hamas a $10 million a month subsidy to replace the subsidy withdrawn by the European Union. Russia is almost certainly also selling arms to Syria.

Fact two, Russia has also launched a satellite for Israel to enable it to monitor Iran's nuclear activities.

What can you deduce from those two facts?

Could it possibly be that Russia (where the leadership has its roots in the KGB and where there is still much suspicion about America and the UK – suspicion that has recently been rekindled because of America's interference in Georgia) might conceivably be playing some sort of game in the Middle East?

Would you like to take bets that Russia would like to see Israel start a war with Iran?

What would happen if such a war did start?

Well, for one thing America would doubtless get involved in the conflict. That would tie up America at a time when it really cannot afford another war. It would also cause the Muslim world to hate America (and Britain) even more.

And for another thing the supply of oil from Iran and the rest of the Middle East would be disrupted.

That would put up the price of oil.

And Russia has a lot of the world's oil.

And, remember, Putin, the power behind the throne, is a former head of the KGB. You don't get to be head of the KGB by being kind to cats or good at needlework.

Who do you think is the cleverest, meanest and craftiest? Putin or the entire American and British Governments?

It is worth remembering that in times of peace the KGB hung, shot, starved and worked to death more Soviet citizens than the whole number of combatants, on both sides, killed in World War II. And it's worth remembering that the Soviets manufactured 30 tons of smallpox virus for use in biological weapons. (The Americans are, of course, the only people to have actually used chemical, biological and atomic weapons against their enemies.)

And the Russians are tough negotiators. Have you ever wondered why Russians are rarely kidnapped by terrorists? Could it possibly date back to the fact that during Lebanon's civil war four Soviet diplomats were kidnapped by a terrorist group. One diplomat was killed. Two days later the leader of the terrorist group received a box containing his son's testicles and a warning from the Russians 'Don't ever bother our people again'. The three remaining hostages were released unharmed and no more Soviets were kidnapped in Lebanon.

★ ★ ★

Meanwhile, since the Government is aware of the problems peak oil will bring, politicians are doing everything they can to reduce oil consumption and to keep as many cars as possible off the roads. This is why they are covering the country with speed cameras. (These are inaccurately known as 'safety cameras'. The evidence shows that speeding is not a significant cause of road traffic accidents and that speed cameras actually cause more accidents, rather than preventing them.) The Government is now planning to ban drivers with fewer offences. Just two speeding offences and you're off the road. As the oil supply shrinks the Government will do more and more to get drivers off the road. And of course the politicians and the police, who are addicted to the revenues from motorists, will target the remaining motorists ever harder.

The sensible solution would be to improve the quality of public transport. Improving train services, and subsidising train fares, would make good sense. Instead, the Government is rapidly reducing the subsidies it gives to train companies, and railway travel is going to become considerably more expensive in the next few years. Annual train fare rises are doomed to be considerably higher than the rate of inflation for the foreseeable future.

★ ★ ★

The Government claims that it aims to provide 20% of Britain's electricity needs by wind and wave power by 2020. This, however, would require a multi billion pound investment. It would also consume a great deal of energy and, in the case of windpower, put us at the mercy of a very unreliable source of energy. Bizarre and unrealistic attempts to shift to environmentally-friendly methods of electricity production will exacerbate Britain's energy problem.

When will the problems really start? Around 2015 is my best guess. Homes and businesses will often have to cope with no electricity.

And by 2020 we will be in serious trouble.

What can you do about all this?

Well, if you move house then I suggest that you make sure your new home is near to a railway station. As the oil runs out so driving will become increasingly expensive. The rising price will mean that there will be fewer petrol stations. Taxis will be few and far between because the number of people able to afford them will shrink.

And if you don't have a bicycle, then buy one.

If you can't ride one, I suggest that you learn.

Oh, and I suggest that you buy a supply of candles and some warm clothes. And make sure that you have a home with a fireplace which burns logs.

Finally, the price of electricity in Britain tends to be higher than elsewhere in Europe for one very good reason: a good deal of our electricity production depends on oil.

And with the price of oil about to soar, what do you think is going to happen to the price of electricity?

Chapter 6

The Truth About Climate Change, Global Warming and Plastic Bags

Climate change may or may not be a genuine problem. The scientific evidence is contradictory and increasingly unconvincing. Politicians have lied too much in the past for them to be believed now. What is certain is that the evidence has been exaggerated and manipulated in order to satisfy political aims and used to justify a bizarre variety of pieces of oppressive new legislation. The war on global warming has that in common with the war on terrorism.

As custodians of the planet we have screwed up. If we were house sitting we would be fired. And probably find ourselves in court. And we'd deserve it.

Campaigners (a disparate bunch of pop singers and politicians) are making names for themselves by flying around the world in private aeroplanes instructing the rest of us that we must stay at home because flying around the world is damaging the planet. These are usually the same group of multimillionaires who, having made fortunes out of flogging overpriced albums, T-shirts and other tat, have several large, energy-consuming homes and fleets of limousines, live as tax exiles and then make critical remarks about consumerism and capitalism.

Now, I don't know about you but I don't want to take any advice (or be hectored) on any aspect of the environment (or anything else) by self-indulgent divas who have their own jets, employ more than six personal servants and spend more than £10,000 a month on cut flowers. Such people have no right to preach to the rest of the world about world poverty, global warming or anything else without attracting criticism that they are doing it for the publicity.

Almost as bad are politicians who use taxes to try to force the population at large to fly less and then allow Heathrow airport to have a third runway. It's like telling people they can't smoke and then building another cigarette factory.

★ ★ ★

The global warming doomsters want us to cut our carbon emissions by 80% from the 1990 level. The only way we will hit this target is by cutting out Gross Domestic Product by 80% too. That will cost every British household £2,200,000 between now and 2050. And it will mean no central heating, no cars, no television, no computers and no washing machines.

★ ★ ★

One of the most remarkable things is that there are campaigners worrying about global warming (and the food shortage) who still eat meat. This is remarkable for two reasons. First, the increasing demand for meat and meat products is one of the reasons for the world food shortage. (I explained precisely why in my book *Oil Apocalypse.*) Second, animals on farms are responsible for 18% of greenhouse gas emissions. This is more than all forms of transport. This means that raising animals for food generates more greenhouse gases than all the cars and trucks in the world combined. Anyone who professes to be concerned about global warming but does not also campaign for vegetarianism is, I fear, something of a hypocrite.

Nevertheless our vastly optimistic (but inadequate) Kyoto promises are irrelevant. The oil is running out. Amen. Nothing else really matters.

★ ★ ★

How true is the 'evidence' we have been presented with? How honest are the politicians and scientists who claim that our world is heating up because of our behaviour?

I have no idea.

But I would not trust politicians, scientists or journalists to tell us the truth about anything.

Take a subject I know: vivisection.

I know (and can prove) that vivisection is entirely worthless. I know (and can prove in less than a minute) that animal experiments do only harm to the prospects of human patients. The facts show this, quite clearly. I can, for example, name scores of drugs which kill animals but which are sold as safe for human patients. The companies making these products claim that the results are irrelevant because 'animals are different to people'; and so a test which shows that a drug causes cancer in, say, rats is of no consequence. On the other hand, when a drug is shown not to kill animals the results are accepted as proof that the drug is safe.

And yet it is widely believed by the public that vivisection is essential. The old lie about 'I put my child's life above the life of a rat any day' is commonplace. Politicians and scientists have succeeded in establishing a lie as the truth simply because it suits their purposes. Drug companies, academics and politicians all benefit. Journalists sustain the lie because they don't have the courage or the intelligence to expose the lies. (And even if they had the courage and the intelligence their employers would not allow them to do so.)

In an open society the evidence is the only thing that matters. It is upon the evidence that we base our opinions. Without facts and evidence the perceived truth is decided by authority, by money, by power and by violence.

So, I do not believe that we can trust what we are told about global warming. What we are fed are facts that are convenient to the people with the power, the money and the ability to use legalised violence.

★ ★ ★

Here's another example of how they spin the truth.

For some time now politicians and journalists seem to have regarded the plastic bag as the major threat to the planet. Stores have run huge campaigns explaining that they are banning free plastic bags in order to save the environment.

(There is a strong argument that the sole aim of a company is, in fact, to make a profit for its shareholders. It should do so in a responsible manner but that doesn't include making preachy choices which impinge on the freedom of their customers and which are based on bad science. Worrying about the environment is something best left to politicians and lawmakers. Those who feel this way might be comforted by the thought that the 'we are going to charge for plastic bags' campaigns were probably designed to increase corporate profits and were not inspired by any concern for the planet. Am I the only person to be offended by the wild hypocrisy of stores which sell heavily-packaged Easter eggs and then campaign against giving away plastic bags to their customers? The *Daily Mail* ran a ferocious anti-plastic bag campaign. But the paper still wrapped its Saturday magazine (and its inserts) in a plastic bag.) Moreover, in February 2009 the *Daily Mail* produced a booklet entitled "Look after our world". The booklet contained 35 ways to 'go green' and was enclosed with the newspaper. Number 19 on the list in the booklet was entitled "Banish the plastic bags". Sadly, the booklet came inside a plastic bag. The word 'hypocritical' seems painfully relevant.

Politicians have egged them on. Gordon Brown said that if supermarkets didn't ban plastic bags he would bring in legislation to make them do so. Stores, spotting an opportunity to save some money, immediately started charging for plastic bags. (They didn't stop making or using them, you will note, they simply started charging money for them, sometimes promising to give part or all of the profits made from the sale of bags to some worthy charity. Naturally, they didn't offer to give to charity the money they were saving by not handing out free plastic bags.) Newspapers have run excited campaigns telling us all that if we use plastic bags we are threatening our children's future. Important issues (the increasing role of the EU in our lives, the nation's approaching bankruptcy, wars on two continents) have been set aside so that the issue of the plastic bag can be discussed at length.

How true is all this?

Well, actually, it's not very true at all.

1. Paul Fahy reports in an excellent article entitled 'Plastic Bag Propaganda' published in The UK Column that plastic bags are manufactured from a form of plastic derived from a by-product of the oil industry. If the by-product wasn't turned into plastic bags it would have to be burned off – increasing carbon dioxide emissions. So people who use plastic bags are actually helping to save the planet – not destroy it. And, ironically, the oh so self-righteous people who campaign against plastic bags are actually campaigning against the planet's best interests.

2. Fahy reports that the manufacture of plastic bags consumes less energy than the manufacture of paper bags. Plastic bags generate less solid waste than paper bags.
3. Plastic bags are widely reused. Few things are recycled as often or as efficiently or as extensively as plastic bags.
4. Most modern plastic bags are biodegradable.
5. It is not the fault of the plastic bag that some litterbugs throw them around. To ban plastic bags because some of them end up littering the countryside makes as much sense as banning newspapers because some of them end up littering the countryside.
6. It has been claimed that plastic bags are responsible for killing millions of birds every year. And that they kill 100,000 marine animals too. In fact, there is no evidence to support these claims. The original source was a report from 1987 which found that between 1981 and 1984 around 100,000 animals had been killed by discarded plastic fishing nets. This report was subsequently misquoted and the plastic fishing nets became plastic bags. There is not, and never was, any evidence showing that plastic bags kill millions of birds every year. (Just how the bags were supposed to kill the birds was never explained.)
7. Some stores have replaced plastic bags with paper bags. Paper bags may be nice and old-fashioned but they were never very practical. Try carrying one, packed with groceries, in a rainstorm. And you can't usually put handles on paper bags. There is also the problem that you have to chop down trees to make paper bags. This damages the environment and contributes to global warming by reducing the number of trees on the planet.
8. Other stores are selling heavy-duty cloth bags that can be used more than once (just like plastic bags can be used more than once). These bags are usually made of cotton. There is a shortage of cotton. Furthermore, making cotton bags requires a good deal of energy and a lot of water, both of which are in short supply. And in order to grow the profitable extra cotton to make the bags, farmers are growing less food. The result is that people in Africa are starving to death so that nice, liberal do-gooders can wander around carrying their shopping in cotton bags.

9. By charging for plastic bags stores are punishing the poor who cannot afford to buy environmentally unfriendly cotton bags. and who have to buy the plastic bags so that they can carry their shopping home.

Readers who find this material of interest will doubtless also find my analysis of the light bulb nonsense (which appears in *The OFPIS File*) equally illuminating. The facts about the new dangerous, mercury filled light bulbs which we are being forced to use have been distorted in order to support a bizarre nonsense.

★ ★ ★

Whatever the truth may be about climate change (and it is still something of a mystery – we certainly cannot believe what we are told by politicians, journalists, state employed broadcasters or government approved scientists) politicians will continue to use climate change as a reason for cutting the use of oil.

Governments around the world keep signing up to ever more ambitious plans to deal with climate change. None of their promises will be kept, of course. None of their targets will be met.

But it doesn't really matter. And they know it doesn't matter.

The energy shortage created by peak oil will ensure that people will use less and less energy and waste less and less of everything, thereby reducing the problem.

Unless they are stupid beyond even my wildest nightmares politicians must realise this, of course. And, indeed, I strongly suspect that the almost hysterical attempts to warn us of the dangers of global warming, and to persuade us to use less oil and other fuels, are, in reality, merely their way of conserving fuel sources which are disappearing and of getting us accustomed to life without oil.

Why don't they just tell us the truth – that the oil is running out and we have to use it more sparingly?

Well, that might cause even more concern than the chances of half the world flooding.

And it would enable more people to see just why we are fighting wars in Iraq and Afghanistan.

And politicians find lies much easier to tell than the truth.

★ ★ ★

Climate change may or may not be a genuine problem. The

scientific evidence is contradictory and increasingly unconvincing and I am now sceptical about the threat involved. The more politicians become strident about it the less I believe them. Politicians have lied too much in the past for us automatically to believe that they are now telling us the truth. They have cried 'wolf' too often. What is certain, however, is that the evidence has been exaggerated and manipulated in order to satisfy political aims and used to justify a bizarre variety of pieces of oppressive new legislation. The war on global warming has that in common with the war on terrorism.

Chapter 7

Will Interest Rates Stop When They Reach 15%?

In 2009 interest rates in Britain reached an all time low. But how long will it last? By printing money to pay for its reckless spending the Government will force inflation up – and interest rates will rise too.

In January 2009 the Bank of England lowered interest rates to the lowest level since 1694 (when the Bank was founded). This was done to rescue those (including the Government) who had fallen into serious debt. But cutting interest rates to such low levels was a huge mistake. It was also immoral and unfair. It was a huge mistake because it is nigh on impossible to make money when loans are at a modest premium to a bank rate of one or two per cent. And the banks have to start making money to repair their damaged reserves. Three of Britain's banks have to pay the Government 12% a year interest on the preference capital they were given to help them stave off bankruptcy. And how can banks attract depositors if they are offering virtually no interest at all? Putting your money in a sock under the bed suddenly becomes attractive when a bank that might well go bust can only offer 0.1% interest. And without private sector savings what hope do the banks have of building up stronger balance sheets? Cutting interest rates was also unfair and morally wrong because it took money away from people who had been prudent and had put some of their money to one side. Cutting interest rates to rescue debtors reduced the incomes of private sector pensioners dramatically. Would public sector pensioners think it fair if they were told they had to take a cut in their pensions in order to bail out the feckless and the reckless and the stupid and the criminal? I suspect not.

Pushing interest rates down enabled Brown to issue a flood of 50-year Government bonds at a record low cost. It was this cheap money that enabled the Government to spend, spend, spend on hiring new staff. The Government has, in fact, been hiring its way out of bad unemployment figures (turning all those unemployed people into underemployed civil servants). Hang the extra expense.

And yet, in early 2009, with interest rates as close to zero as they could reasonably get, inflation in the UK was still officially 3-4% (and unofficially considerably more than that). This meant that it was virtually impossible for savers to maintain the value of their money.

Property values were falling. Equities were in a serious bear market. Bonds were falling in value. Banks were failing. And the interest paid by banks was considerably less than the rate of inflation.

★ ★ ★

'As a sensible operating rule, central bank rates should be set at 2.5% above inflation (i.e. the real cost of money should be 2.5%). Anything lower leads to misallocation of capital and economic inefficiency for any economy. Fully functioning banking and capital markets are essential for sophisticated developed economies but nothing will be resolved until the real returns on financial assets are substantially in excess of inflation.'

IAN RUSHBROOK

★ ★ ★

When inflation comes back with a vengeance, as Gordon Brown has ensured it will, interest rates will have to go up to try and control the rate at which inflation rises.

To begin with, Brown will welcome inflation. He will know (I expect someone will have explained it to him) that inflation helps eradicate debts. The nation's debts will disappear a little as inflation goes up. And the greedy millions who are still hugely in debt will benefit as inflation rises.

But eventually even Brown (or his successor) will realise that the inflation is getting out of control.

And then interest rates will soar, as they always do when inflation gets out of control

How high will interest rates go?

I wouldn't be the slightest bit surprised to see them go over 15%.

Chapter 8

Immigration, Multiculturalism, Racism And Emigration

Thanks to the European Union and the Labour Government Britain is now one of the most overcrowded countries on the planet. Many Britons feel they have become second-class citizens in their own country. And the natives are getting restless. How long will it be before simmering resentment turns to violence?

The statistics about immigration are startling. In 2007, Poles sent £1.8 billion back to Poland. (So much for the argument that immigrants were enriching Britain.) One Chief Constable blamed 'migration surges' for a 35% rise in violent crime in his county. (No one likes to talk about it in public but there is a widespread belief that immigrants are responsible for more than their fair share of crime in Britain today.) Britain sends £28 million a year in child benefit to 34,000 eastern European children whose parents are living in Britain but who themselves live in eastern Europe. Labour ministers often claim that immigrants are a boon to the British economy but this simply isn't true. Huge numbers of immigrants claim benefits: 81% of immigrants from Somalia aren't working, 39% are claiming income support and 80% are living in social housing paid for by English taxpayers. The figures for immigrants from Turkey, Bangladesh, Pakistan and many other countries are similarly horrifying. One Afghan family (the estranged wife of an asylum seeker and her seven children), living in a £1.2 million home paid for by taxpayers, receives a total of £170,000 a year in benefits and has stuffed their valuable home with hi-tech gadgets including a plasma screen television set. 'Every family here has a plasma TV so it's perfectly normal for us to have one as well,' said the woman. Once an EU foreign national has been working in Britain for a year he and his family become entitled to all UK welfare benefits. Over 80,000 foreign nationals now living in Britain are claiming child benefit. In addition, the British taxpayer is contributing £2.5 billion towards a six year EU programme to treble social security benefits in Romania and Bulgaria.

(Incidentally, failed asylum seekers, who agree to leave Britain voluntarily, are given £6,000 as a 'thank you' for leaving the country without making a fuss. Many failed asylum seekers remain in Britain because airlines refuse to carry potentially rowdy passengers. Asylum seekers who are taken to airports simply have to behave a little anti-socially and they will be refused admittance to a flight.)

The flood of immigrants has changed England enormously. (The rest of Britain has been much less affected. Very few immigrants choose to go to Scotland.) Over six million UK residents were born abroad. Many of them arrived within the last ten years and came from eastern Europe. Millions more aren't counted in the official figures because they claim to be visitors, students or self-employed. Just how many are here illegally is anyone's guess. The Home Office has no idea. Over 450,000 are known about but how can anyone know what the real figure might be? The British Government admitted in 2007 that it didn't investigate illegal immigrants. It is now contemplating a third amnesty – making illegal immigrants legal. Most of those coming to Britain have few or no skills, no knowledge of Britain and little or no understanding of our language. There are an estimated seven million illegal immigrants in the EU. Around 90% of them aren't sufficiently educated to undertake anything resembling 'skilled' work. Most simply become a burden on the taxpayers of the country where they choose to settle. Most want to settle in Britain where the benefits are most generous. (Incidentally, Britain is forbidden by EU rules from expelling non-British nationals jailed for criminal offences. However, Italy is allowed to expel non-Italian EU nationals who commit criminal offences. Curiously, as I write, the European Commissioner responsible for EU immigration policy is Italian.) British taxpayers spend over £1 billion a year on costs such as legal aid required by asylum seekers and illegal immigrants. A relatively small group of lawyers is getting very, very rich.

Only two in three babies born in England are now registered as 'White British'. (Naturally, mothers aren't allowed to register babies as English). The average indigenous British woman has around 1.5 children. The average Muslim woman living in Britain has 5 children. Not surprisingly, the Muslim population is growing much faster than the indigenous population. Leicester is the first city in which indigenous, white Britons will find themselves in the minority. Birmingham will have more immigrants than Britons within a decade.

The Government wants Christmas to be downgraded in order to make Britain a more multicultural country. Muslim medical students have refused to treat patients with alcohol-related and sexually-transmitted diseases. In contrast, Christians in Muslim countries must obey all the local laws. In Saudi Arabia, for example, Islam is the State's religion and Islamic laws are State laws. Christianity is strictly controlled and only tolerated. Immigrants moving into Saudi Arabia must accept and obey all local laws.

A combination of a massive influx of immigrants, and a plethora of EU laws, means that Britishness seems to be almost beyond repair and our social fabric has been very nearly destroyed both in cities and in the country. Law and order is so threatened that gated communities are springing up everywhere – and vast numbers of loyal Britons have already emigrated, having decided that there is no place for them in their own country. Migrants often form their own ghettos, living according to the culture of the country they chose to leave and avoiding those aspects of Britishness which, they claim, attracted them to Britain in the first place.

One third of people living in London were born abroad. Another 10,000 foreigners settle in the English capital every month. Immigrants are given taxpayer-funded translators to help them secure British passports. Thanks to the EU, Britain has to employ, at taxpayers' expense, lawyers and translators to speed up migration. Two and a half million people living in Britain speak a language other than English at home. Many of them don't speak English outside their homes either. And they expect us to accommodate their language problems. Indeed, the Government (and the EU) plan to force employers to pay for English language lessons for migrants. The NHS spends £55 million a year on translation services. (During one day recently a British doctor in a London hospital treated patients from Albania, Algeria, Ecuador, Eritrea, Ethiopia, Germany, Iran, Iraq, Italy, Mexico, Peru and Portugal. He treated just one Englishman. Naturally, it takes hospital staff far longer to treat patients who don't speak English.) The police spend over £30 million a year on translators. Local councils spend £100 million a year on translators. Why should British taxpayers pay for all this? Do other countries provide such an array of publicly funded translation services? Of course, they don't. People who travel to a country are expected to learn to make themselves understood in the local language or pay for their own translator.

In London, a judge agreed to the removal of Jews and Hindus from a jury because the counsel for the Muslim defendants said his clients would not get a fair trial with them on the jury. The Government banned a Dutch member of parliament, and leader of the Party for Freedom, from entering Britain because of his anti-Islamic views (prompting the Dutch Government to protest).

Black politicians and campaigners are now talking about having special schools for black pupils. The 'all black' schools will have only black teachers. Whites will be excluded. Is that really what we want? Segregated schools and buses? There are already 150 Muslim schools in Britain. They teach a Muslim way of life to 100,000 children who were born in Britain. Is that what people mean by 'multiculturalism'?

Some Muslim groups in Britain suggest that Muslims in Britain keep themselves apart from the rest of the country until they become the dominant force. There are recognised to be several thousand Muslim activists in Britain. It is worth remembering that Lebanon used to be a Christian country. Over several decades in the second half of the 20th Century Muslims became the dominant group and took control of the country.

There are now so many Muslims living in the UK that senior members of the Muslim community are demanding that Sharia courts (which already exist in the UK) be given legal authority. Even the Archbishop of Canterbury (whom one might reasonably expect to be concerned with defending English religious and legal traditions) has suggested that Britain should 'constructively accommodate' certain aspects of Sharia law. (I can't help wondering what the response would be in Muslim countries if English residents suggested that English law be given legal authority.) If Sharia law is introduced, Christian churches will be strictly controlled, as they are in Saudi Arabia. Christians and other infidels will be second-class citizens in Britain. Very little is written or broadcast about these prospects for the simple reason that the authorities (i.e. the police) clamp down quickly when such things are discussed in public. It is at best 'politically incorrect' and at worst racist to discuss these issues.

Sharia is the law of the Middle East. Mixed marriages are not tolerated. Many Islamic marriages are arranged between families. Changing faith is punishable by death. Pictures, music and alcohol are banned. Women must wear veils. Censorship is strict. Thieves have their hands cut off. Adulteresses are stoned to death. Homosexuals are beheaded or crucified. In November 2007, a Saudi woman was sentenced to 200 lashes and six months in jail because she had been gang raped. She was regarded as responsible for what had happened because she had been out in public with a man who was not a relative. Shortly afterwards a British woman working in Sudan was threatened with 40 lashes and a jail term because young children in the class she taught named the class teddy bear Muhammed. I wonder how the sanctimonious, politically correct, liberal feminists who are so enthusiastic about the idea of multiculturalism when it is just a theory will feel about it as it becomes a practical reality. Those who fought white men with such venom, and who fought for a multi-cultural society with such enthusiasm, will have a nasty shock when they get what they thought they wanted. I do suspect there may be a few squeals of outrage. Still, they won't be squealing for long. A magistrate who objected when a Muslim woman defendant insisted on wearing a veil, covering her entire face, and who refused to deal with the woman's case while she was wearing the full veil, was formally reprimanded and sent for 'further training'.

Schools in England are now serving only halal meat at school dinners. (Animals are slaughtered by having their throats cut without being stunned first.) Parents who objected to this were described as racist by Muslim parents.

And am I the only one to have noticed that our streets now seem to be filled with eastern European beggars and Big Issue sellers who don't speak a word of English and are clearly immigrants? Is that not proof that we are importing homeless people? Do we really need to import Big Issue sellers, beggars and homeless people? Half the people sleeping rough in central London are Polish. Imagine the pressure this puts on the people and services available for British homeless people. A generation ago we used to have tramps; gentlemen of the road. Today we have beggars. Thousands of them. And many of them have turned begging into a business.

★ ★ ★

The new Oxford Junior Dictionary (edited by someone called Vineeta Gupta who is the head of children's dictionaries at Oxford University Press) is a tribute to the murderer of culture, multiculturalism, and the killer of humanity, political correctness. The 'dictionary' now includes words such as 'blog', 'broadband', 'celebrity', 'dyslexia', 'citizenship', 'biodegradable', 'bungee jumping', 'citizenship', 'euro' and, of course, 'EU'. But gone, apparently dismissed as irrelevant to today's children, are such traditional, and essential, English words as 'blackberry', 'brook', 'buttercup', 'carol', 'conker', 'coronation', 'cracker', 'duke', 'empire', 'holly', 'ivy', 'mistletoe' and 'monarch'. A host of words relating to the English countryside have been banished as irrelevant. Words which relate to the Christian church (such as 'abbey', 'aisle', 'altar', 'bishop', 'chapel', 'christen', 'disciple', 'monk', 'nun', 'parish', 'pew', 'psalm', 'pulpit', 'sainthood' and 'vicar' have gone too (on the grounds that England is now apparently a multifaith country, though this may come as something of a shock to some). So words such as 'Whitsun' and 'Pentecost' have disappeared. Maybe, while she was at it Vineeta Gupta should have removed the word 'Oxford' from the book's title. It's bad enough that newspapers, television and radio now feed us politically correct, multicultural, means-tested rubbish. But it's a bit much when even the dictionaries are edited according to political tastes.

★ ★ ★

Anger is rising as accidents on British roads involving eastern European drivers have soared eight fold in six years. Cars registered in countries like Poland were involved in 933 crashes in 2001. In 2007 they were involved in 7,266 crashes. Accidents caused by foreign drivers on British roads have increased by 47% in the last five years.

Foreign drivers don't bother to pay car tax (their cars are officially registered elsewhere) and they don't bother to pay insurance either. Nor do foreign drivers bother to take a British driving test. After one fatal accident it was found that a Polish bus driver couldn't read road signs. Another fatal crash was caused when a female Polish driver drove the wrong way round a roundabout. In some areas of the country 40% of drink drivers are foreign.

And there is anger at the way that many immigrants complain about British customs and laws – and expect to be treated differently because they are foreign. A Muslim who claimed he did not know that Tesco sold alcohol sued the store for religious discrimination after he was asked to carry crates of alcohol as part of his job.

Soaring food prices and food shortages have resulted in a massive increase in poaching. Most of it is done by immigrants. Fish, chickens, ducks, pheasants and swans are all considered 'fair game' by gangs of modern day rustlers. There is a worry that carp (a popular eating fish among the Poles) will disappear from ornamental ponds. Raids are organised from cities and towns and conducted by people who have guns but little or no knowledge of country ways. Modern poachers aren't characters in scruffy jackets and flat caps who pick up an odd rabbit or pheasant with a snare or some other trick. Modern poachers are criminals who fill their lorries with wildlife – in or out of season. Some use guns. Others use snares, crossbows and other methods. They damage woodlands and crops, leave gates open and terrorise innocents who get in their way. Gamekeepers and landowners are shot. Even farm animals (particularly sheep because they are easier to carry away) are stolen.

This isn't a fantasy. It is happening. Scotland's National Wildlife Crime Unit has recorded 335 incidents of poaching in the last 18 months. And the incidence of poaching is soaring. In parts of England poaching is three times as common as it was a year ago. The modern poachers aren't catching an occasional fish or a few rabbits. They are catching industrial quantities of animals and taking them into towns to sell.

★ ★ ★

The changes are happening all over Europe. In Linz, Austria, Muslims are demanding that all female teachers (whether Muslim or Christian) should wear headscarves in class.

Bat Ye'or revealed in her book *Eurabia* that over thirty years ago the EU guaranteed that Muslim immigrants into Europe would not be compelled to adapt in any way 'to the customs of the host countries'. The EU encourages migration into the EU, it encourages social and political rights throughout the Union for migrants, it encourages 'secure citizenship' for migrants. And it plans to give votes to all migrants into the EU. It expects, not unreasonably, that the people so well protected by the EU will, in return, provide unswerving loyalty to and support for the European Union and its bureaucratic leaders. As I explained in *The OFPIS File*, the EU is introducing a Blue Card visa (rather like the Green Card work permits used in the USA). The Blue Cards will offer permanent residency to workers and their families anywhere in the EU. Over 20 million Asians and Africans are officially expected to apply. The real figure will, of course, be far, far higher than this. No prizes for guessing where most of the 20 million will head for.

It seems that in Europe the new tenants are already in residence and have a right-to-buy agreement. We are taught by our politicians that we should fear China or Russia. But the Chinese have never shown any real inclination to take over the world. And Russia has got its hands full regaining control of its ex-USSR neighbours. The Muslims, however, are in Europe to stay. And they know what they want.

* * *

A report commissioned for the Government and published early in 2009 showed that white families, particularly those on the country's poorest estates, believe that they have been betrayed and abandoned by politicians who favour newly-arrived immigrants. A Government representative admitted that white people 'sometimes just don't feel anyone is listening or speaking up for them' and added that white people should be allowed to talk about their worries 'without fear of being branded a racist'.

'I know of foreign families who have got start-up vouchers to help them with their housing,' said one white woman, 'and I never got that. They all seem to get their houses and have decent places to live.'

'You know we're expected to understand values and backgrounds of other people, but it doesn't seem to be a two-way thing,' said another white woman. 'When it's not a two-way thing, that's what gets people's backs up.'

As people get poorer and find that life gets harder so they will look for someone to blame. As unemployment rises so more and more people will complain about foreigners taking jobs. Battle lines will be drawn. Politicians will struggle to walk the tightrope; reluctantly supporting nationalism and trying to avoid the pitfalls of protectionism and racism. There will be anger at some of the EU legislation which has lain hidden for a decade or so.

Racism will rise. Supporting England and opposing immigration are both regarded by the politically correct as overt signs of racism. And although no minister would ever dare forbid membership of the Scottish National Party, there are many who have spoken out insisting that membership of the British National Party is incompatible with public employment. Immigrants will be the top of the list to hate. Enoch Powell's rivers of blood aren't far away. There will be much racially-inspired violence in Britain.

★ ★ ★

A new equality law has been introduced (originating in Brussels) which now makes it legal for female or black job candidates to be given preference over white men.

That will go down well as unemployment rises.

There is more pressure on political parties to have all-women shortlists. This will ensure that the House of Commons will contain more women. It will not, of course, ensure that the women who are forced upon the electorate are any good at what they do.

It is now pretty well impossible to be found guilty of discriminating against a white, middle class, middle aged or elderly English male. Racism and sexism are institutionalised, legalised and to a certain extent now compulsory. As long as the victims are white males, of course.

'It seems to me that it is now open season on white, middle class, middle aged males,' wrote one reader of mine. 'If any other specific group – such as Jews or blacks – were treated like white males there would be an outcry.'

The Government took 80 public sector jobs from the town of Corby because its residents were deemed to be 'too white and British'. Prison Service jobs were moved from the former steel town, where there was high unemployment, to Leicester where the proportion of white people was considered by the State to be acceptably low. Positive discrimination gives the State power over aggressive and potentially disruptive sections of the community (for example, black men and militant feminists) by providing them with what they want. Positive discrimination also reduces the power of white men and creates anxiety and resentment. This is good for the State because it makes people frightened, unsettled and uncertain.

The simple truth, however, is that whether you try to disguise and sanctify what you're doing by calling it 'affirmative action' or 'positive discrimination' it is, underneath the smart words, nothing more than simple, old-fashioned racism – just as using quotas to ensure that women get particular jobs is sexism. Those who propose this type of social engineering are guilty of bigotry and prejudice. Whatever you call it, whatever labels you use, whatever excuses are dreamt up, racism destroys lives, hopes and ambitions and it is (or should be) repugnant to all thinking humans.

'It's not possible for me to be racist,' said someone accused of racist behaviour. 'I'm black.'

He should, perhaps, look at the way the Cape Coloureds are treated by blacks in South Africa, where a new elite has emerged and where apartheid is now just as rife as it ever was. He should look at the way white families are treated in parts of Britain where over 90% of the population is black or brown or some colour other than white.

★ ★ ★

Anti-Englishness is fashionable, even among many of those born here and those who choose to live here. *The Cricketer* magazine published an article by someone called Dileep Premachandran who, after England won the Ashes (it was some time ago), concluded by saying: 'Though England had been by far the better side, it sickened me to admit it and I can hardly wait for Australia to regain the urn.' I sent a complaint to the Commission for Racial Equality. I should have saved my stamp for something more useful. Replace the name 'England' in the sentence I have quoted with 'India' or 'Pakistan' and imagine the outcry which would have resulted.

★ ★ ★

Because of our fetishes for multiculturalism and political

correctness, racial profiling isn't allowed when the police are searching travellers at airports. In fact, we actually have a negative racial profiling policy – introduced so that no one gets upset or made to think that they are being picked on. And so a high proportion of elderly, white ladies get frisked. Fat lot of good it does, too. How many elderly, white ladies carry guns or bombs? When she was in her 80's my mother used to travel abroad quite often. She was always stopped and searched. And sour-looking people in uniforms confiscated the nailfile and nailclippers which she had forgotten were still in her handbag. She used to buy replacements in the airport shop, just before she boarded.

★ ★ ★

Why is there a Black Police Association? Imagine the fuss there would be if someone proposed setting up a White Police Association. There are, indeed, all sorts of Black Associations. Black doctors, writers and just about every definable group of professionals and tradespeople have a special, racially defined group they can join. In what way are a black policeman's professional interests different to those of a white policeman? I ask because I do not know and cannot imagine. My fear is that by forming themselves into groups these people may be isolating themselves and creating more racist problems than they are solving.

★ ★ ★

Politicians lie, lie and lie again about immigration figures. One week in 2007, the Labour Government told voters that only 800,000 immigrants had arrived in Britain since 1997. A few days later they upped to it 1.1 million. And then, a little later on the figure rose to 1.5 million. What is the real figure? Well, your guess is as good as anyone else's (and probably more honest than anyone in the Government) but the Office of National Statistics is expecting another 11 million within a generation. And another 16 million by 2051. Long before then England will be Europe's most crowded nation. Nearly 85% of the population growth in the UK is a direct result of immigration. Much of the rest comes from migrants who are already here. And it's going to get worse; much worse. The European Commission responsible for immigration as I write is encouraging vast quantities of immigrants to come to the EU from Asia and Africa. Many, if not most, will head for Britain. Astonishingly £7 million of British taxpayers' money is being spent on an information centre on Mali to encourage immigrants. Our politicians claim we need all these immigrants to fill job vacancies. Does anyone really believe that? In 2001 there were 600,000 official job vacancies in the UK. Since then more than a million immigrants have arrived. Unemployment among the British has soared. And the official number of job vacancies was (at the last count) still 600,000. Immigrants have, in reality, created new jobs with their demands on health care, education, housing, transport and translation services. And think of all the new benefits officers that have had to be employed to hand out extra money. And the multicultural officers to ensure that the cultural rights of immigrants are properly respected.

There are a total of eight million economically idle people in Britain. And we are importing more. The majority of the immigrants are a net burden on the State long before they retire: even when they are of working age they take far more out of the economy than they put in. And when they retire they will need pensions.

★ ★ ★

As the immigrants are coming in so the locals are going out. Fed up with what is happening to their country, millions of English born individuals are giving up on their homeland and choosing to live, work and retire abroad. More Britons now live abroad than any other nationality. There are Britons settled permanently in 41 different countries. According to the Institute for Public Policy Research the latest figures show that 5.5 million Britons have left Britain to start new lives abroad. And Britons are leaving faster than ever. Labour party politicians say they don't mind. But they should. The people coming in are, to put it politely, not always coming here to work. The people leaving, on the other hand, are largely hard-working middle-class English families who are taking themselves, their skills and their savings somewhere else. The people leaving vary in age from young to old. Some have money. Others have ambition. All have drive and are the sort of people without whom no country can thrive. They are, almost exclusively, taxpayers. People who migrate tend to be the most educated and motivated.

People aren't leaving in search of sunshine (the common, dismissive argument). They are leaving because they no longer feel welcome in their own country. They are leaving because they are fed up of feeling like second-class citizens in the country of their birth. And, of course, they are leaving because they are fed up of the attitudes of Britain's army of petty bureaucrats.

★ ★ ★

Here are the top reasons people give when asked why they want to leave the country:

1. The high levels of street crime; rampant anti-social behaviour; the fact that it is no longer safe to go out at night.
2. The fact that Britain is being altered beyond recognition by the high levels of immigration. 'I feel like a stranger in my own country,' people say. 'Our culture is changing. There's nothing to keep me here now.'
3. The benefits culture. Living on benefits has become a career choice for millions. Those who prefer to work feel angry at the taxes they pay to support their lazy neighbours.
4. Britain has become a fascist state – with too many laws, too many CCTV cameras, too much scrutiny and too little privacy.
5. Britons are, thanks to the Labour Government, the world's number one terrorist targets.
6. Health care has deteriorated. General practitioners no longer provide a decent service. And hospitals are too dangerous to go into.
7. There has been a deterioration and an increase in the cost of public transport. And our roads are badly maintained, overcrowded and festooned with speed cameras.
8. Britain has become a two-tier society. Public sector workers receive huge salaries, job security, loads of perks and massive, inflation proof pensions. Private sector workers are constantly in fear of losing their jobs and aware that they may have to work until they are 70 or even older.
9. Taxes in Britain are unbearably high and (for small businesses and the self-employed) impossibly complex.

★ ★ ★

You really cannot blame people for going. Indeed, one can only marvel at the fact that not everyone of their ilk has disappeared.

They go to Spain, to South Africa, to New Zealand, to Australia and to Cyprus. They go to Ireland and to Portugal and to anywhere they think they will feel welcome. They go to Malta and they go to Canada. The French Government estimates that there are 600,000 Britons living in France.

There are, of course, many things wrong with France but here, just for fun, are some of the reasons people give for moving to France:

1. There are fewer aggressive people around. The French do not take EU legislation seriously. They certainly don't 'gold plate' it in the way that the British Government does. There is, consequently, far less for the French to complain about. And the French haven't adopted the sort of intrusive legislation which accompanies America's everlasting war on terror.
2. The French have not yet learnt to be proud of ignorance.
3. Everyday culture is less crass and less vulgar. The French allow advertisers to put naked breasts on their hoardings but advertisers are aware that marketing programmes work best if they are witty, smart and designed for intelligent people.
4. Public drunkenness is almost unknown. The French are accustomed to being able to drink all day long and they do not feel the need to become legless at every available opportunity.
5. Football hooliganism is virtually unknown.
6. The French are proud of their homes, their villages, their towns and their cities and local politicians are under pressure to ensure that local parks and streets are kept clean and well presented.
7. French streets are regularly patrolled by policemen on foot, on bicycles or on roller blades. Crime rates in France are much lower than in Britain.
8. Rubbish is collected regularly. In Paris, for example, household rubbish is collected every day.
9. Local politicians involve voters when they are making decisions. The other day we received a letter at our French apartment asking us if we preferred to have our rubbish collected in the evening or if we would prefer to change to the morning.
10. As one writer put it 'the French seem actually to like their

children, with the unsurprising result that their children are more likeable than their British counterparts'. French children tend to look smarter and to be considerably more polite than children in Britain.

11. Small shops do well in French towns and cities where they survive, thanks to the sensible policies of local politicians. Most significantly, small businesses are not forced out of business by high council taxes. On the contrary, small businesses are positively encouraged.
12. The food available in France is considerably better than the food available in Britain. The French will not eat genetically modified food and nor do they eat much junk food. When customers demand good food, the shops will provide it (or go bust). And although they enjoy food the French do not eat vast quantities of it. There is, in consequence, far less obesity.
13. The French are far less dependent on the Russians, the Middle East or the wind for their electricity. Years ago they built a number of efficient nuclear power stations which provide over 70% of their electricity.
14. French public transport is efficient, clean, reliable and relatively cheap.
15. The French have better health care. Patients in French hospitals are far less likely to acquire deadly infections than are patients in British hospitals.
16. The French have managed to retain the idea of living in communities. Those who have emigrated and made an effort to fit in say that living in France is close to living in England in the 1950s or 1960s. It is illegal in France for one citizen not to go to the aid of another who needs help.

The Institute for Public Policy Research has estimated that one in every eight UK citizens over the age of 55 will live overseas by 2010. A retired dentist emigrated to New Zealand at the age of 102. 'When I'm 105,' he said, 'I don't want to be thinking 'I wish I had moved to the other side of the world when I was 102'.'

It is not just the elderly who are going, of course. Over a million British graduates now live and work abroad. No other country has so many of its best-educated citizens living away from home. Since Labour came to power in 1997 the number of Britons leaving the country has increased by 45%. The outflow is now the highest ever recorded. Almost 14 million people with British passports (or qualified to hold them) choose to live outside Britain. In comparison less than 1.5 million Americans choose not to live in the USA.

★ ★ ★

Government Ministers always seem to sneer when they are told the latest emigration figures. Their attitude seems to be that they really don't care, and that they are glad to see white, middle-class English families leaving the country. The official policy, widely shared by journalists, appears to be 'Good Riddance'.

This is, I fear, merely another sign of stupidity among our governing classes.

For the people leaving the country are the people who have been paying for the self-indulgent, patronising, politically correct nonsense which has for years been spouted by politicians who think that the only two things that matter in modern Britain are those failures of modern socialism: means-testing and the creation of a multicultural society. The first has failed because it creates an unfair society. The second has failed because no one wants it.

And as the taxpaying hard-working men and women who have been paying for everything for a generation all leave, taking their skills and their savings with them, so the country they leave behind them becomes permanently and dangerously and increasingly impoverished.

Sadly, the collapse of the British currency at the end of 2008 left many emigrants who were living on pensions in sterling in poverty. Quite a number were trying to sell their homes so that they could return to the UK. If they return, as seems likely, this will, of course, result in a considerable increase in the number of people needing benefits.

★ ★ ★

One author who has claimed that immigration should be welcomed pointed out that in 2005, there were 565,000 migrants coming to Britain, but that 380,000 left. Not much of a problem, he said, just a modest net inflow of 185,000. How dumb. The whole country is changing. The people coming in are Romanians and Poles. The people leaving are Britons. What makes a country? The land or the people?

English society is being transformed at a rate which is without precedent since the Danish and Anglo-Saxon settlements of more than a thousand years ago. (I discussed the responsibility of the EU for England's immigration problem in my book *The OFPIS File*.)

'Ask the American Indians what happens when you don't control immigration,' suggested one reader of mine. Another wanted to know why we had to change our customs to satisfy immigrants when if Britons go abroad they are always expected to obey local customs and laws.

★ ★ ★

The newcomers who have saleable skills (the Polish plumbers) will soon go somewhere else; driven away by the twin problems of fewer jobs and a constantly weak pound. (Which means that the money they send home is worth less in their local currency.) The immigrants who have no skills, no jobs and no ambitions will stay in a country where politicians and bureaucrats throw taxpayers' money around as freely as if it were confetti.

Politicians will doubtless express surprise and outrage when there is rising resentment about immigrants claiming benefits. And politicians will, of course, claim that those expressing unhappiness are racist. That is always the instant response to any concern about immigration levels. Anyone who objects must be a racist.

In fact it is easier to argue that people who support and encourage immigration are racists. Advocates of open immigration policies invariably claim that the people coming into Britain are bringing essential skills. If this were true (the figures show it is not) then it would mean that Britain was deliberating taking trained, skilled workers from poorer countries and therefore preventing poor countries from developing and becoming self-sufficient. And that's racist. In the summer of 2007, 30,000 doctors applied for 20,000 hospital jobs. That meant that 10,000 British trained doctors remained unemployed. At the same time there were 10,000 foreign doctors working in Britain.

★ ★ ★

What Happens Next?

Two thirds of British residents say that the UK has too many immigrants and that they believe that race relations are so poor that tensions are likely to result in violence. Nearly half of Britons want foreigners to be encouraged to leave.

The real problems have been created by the do-gooding, politically correct liberals who have for years campaigned for a multicultural society. It is because of their efforts that some road signs in London are now printed in Polish. It is because of their enthusiasm for multiculturalism that many English cities now contain ghettos where English is never heard and where even schools teach children in another language.

Multicultural societies simply don't work. The people who love the idea of a multicultural society don't live in one, of course. They live in nice, neat white liberal middle class societies where black people and brown people and white people all behave like white people, eat like white people and drive expensive motor cars. Outside these comfortable enclaves, the idea of multiculturalism simply provides an excuse for foreigners to come into our country, take no interest in our culture or our way of life and create ghettos within cities. (I realise that using the phrase 'our country' will be regarded by some as 'racist'. Well bugger them.)

★ ★ ★

Politicians like immigrants because they can be exploited and will accept boring, dull, low-paid work in both public and private sectors. This is important because Britons, represented by over-demanding unions, often expect unreasonably high rewards, if they are prepared to do work that might be regarded as demeaning.

The truth is that the immigrants who work have not come to stay. Most of them don't buy houses or become part of the nation. They come to earn money and to send it 'home'. They plan to go back home eventually.

Immigrants have different aims and ambitions and they often don't think much of our culture. They frequently despise our history and are ready and willing (and soon will be able) to replace our ancient legal system with their own.

This isn't a moan or a criticism. It's merely a statement of fact.

★ ★ ★

Immigrants have failed to integrate despite the fact that we have spent huge amounts of public money adapting our society to their requirements and their cultures in a way that no other country on the planet would consider necessary or appropriate.

Our Government and councils have printed official leaflets in dozens of languages and civil servants of all varieties have bent over backwards, forwards and sideways to avoid any chance of political incorrectness.

Moreover, in becoming the ultimate multicultural society and in abandoning (and apologising for) our history and our own culture we have lost virtually every scrap of dignity and self-respect. The final straw is the fact that many of the immigrants our Government is forcing us to welcome send most of their earnings back to the country they still think of as home. And when they have what they want out of us they go back to whichever part of the European superstate they came from. That is the sad reality of the immigration policy the Government defends because it has been foisted upon us by the EU, and British politicians don't have the balls ever to say no to the European Union.

★ ★ ★

Things are going to get far, far worse. The EU has made arrangements for far more foreigners to move to Britain (and, by and large, that means England because Scotland is too far away and the natives are too hostile).

But why is a multiracial society a good thing? Who wants it? Is it possible? Who benefits?

These are, of course, questions no one asks. Everyone in Government simply assumes that multiculturalism is a good thing. No one ever asked the English if they wanted to live in a multicultural society. It was decided for us by interfering, self-righteous busy bodies who are largely immune to the consequences of their actions.

Can you imagine any other country putting up with all this? I can't think of one.

★ ★ ★

A century ago, explaining what The United States of America expected of immigrants, this is what President Theodore Roosevelt had to say: 'There can be no divided allegiance here. Any man who says he is American, but something else also, isn't American at all.

We have room for but one flag, the Union... we have room for but one language here, and that is the English language...and we have room for but one sole loyalty and that is loyalty to America.'

More recently Australia has made it clear to migrants that they should go home if they are not prepared to adopt the Australian way of life and to answer tough questions demanding a thorough knowledge of English, history, politics, heritage and culture.

Other countries have acted similarly on the grounds that a nation that takes no care to protect its integrity will soon cease to be a nation at all.

★ ★ ★

Multiculturalism doesn't solve problems. It accelerates and amplifies them. It makes things worse. A lot worse. Multiculturalism as perceived by Labour has created unfulfillable expectations and resentment. And now that the country is facing hard times there will be a huge price to pay: re-emergent nationalism will morph into pure, unadulterated racism.

Millions will start asking the same question: 'If they hate Britain and the British so much, why the hell do they insist on coming here and staying here? Why don't they go 'home'?'

★ ★ ★

In February 2009, after a walkout by workers at the Total oil refinery in Lincolnshire (complaining about the use of foreign labour) a spokesman for Total said: 'British workers are considered in the same way as anyone else.'

How kind.

★ ★ ★

Multiculturalism doesn't work. It never has and it never will. The insane policies of the EU, gold plated by our own Government, have resulted in a massive diluting of our national identity.

If the British National Party was even moderately well run (and was not constantly 'monstered' in the press) it would win the next election at a canter. And that should frighten politicians enormously. (I am not a member of, or a supporter of, the British National Party, or any other political party.)

Thanks to the European Union and the Labour Government of Blair and Brown, Britain is now one of the most overcrowded countries on the planet. And it is becoming more crowded by the day. The overcrowding has put enormous pressure on our infrastructure. Our power supplies can't cope. Our water supplies can't cope. Our sewers can't cope. Our hospitals can't cope. Our schools can't cope. Our roads can't cope. The benefits system is pouring money into the pockets of foreigners who have never given anything to Britain, who care nothing for Britain and who send the money to relatives in their own home country. British workers are priced out of work by migrants prepared to live five to a room. Criminal gangs terrorise our cities. Gun and knife crime is endemic. British prisons held 60,000 people in 1997. Today the same prisons are crammed with 80,000 inmates. Most of the difference is made up of immigrants. Official figures show that immigrants are eight times as likely to commit a crime as British people.

The time has come to ask immigrants to choose. If they want to embrace our way of life and our culture then they will be very welcome to stay. They should pass language and citizenship tests. They should swear allegiance, not to the EU, but to the Crown. If they want to live apart, merely taking advantages of our over-stretched infrastructure and our diminishing financial resources, then, like gatecrashers at a party, they should be told to leave. And we should make sure that they go. This policy should be matched by stricter controls on those coming into the country. Visas should only be issued at British consulates abroad. Anyone arriving in Britain without a valid visa should be turned back, and returned to the country from which they came.

Chapter 9

Britain's First And Second-Class Pensioners

Public sector workers have secure, inflation-proofed pensions paid for by taxpayers. They retire at 60 – or even earlier. Many private sector workers have no pensions and are destined to work until they die.

We have created two nations within a nation. On the one hand are the public sector workers, highly paid, unstressed, not exposed to the danger of unemployment, entitled to all the holidays and perks you can imagine and secure in the knowledge that at the end of a relatively short lifetime's work there will be an index-linked pension to ensure a luxurious retirement. On the other hand are the private sector workers, the employed and the self-employed, who are much less well-paid, stressed to the point of illness but too frightened to take time off work lest their work disappears, constantly exposed to the hazard of unemployment and knowing that at the end of it all they may well be reduced to living in cold and hungry poverty. It is hardly surprising that the brightest and best brains, the people upon whom any country depends for its future, are choosing to work for the State. And when that happens it should surprise no-one when the State (which depends for its prosperity on people who make a contribution to society rather than enjoying a parasitic existence) goes into a long and steady decline.

★ ★ ★

Private sector pensions are shrinking and, in many cases, disappearing entirely. Poor investments, huge management fees, and gross incompetence have decimated private sector pension funds and dramatically reduced the size of pensions that can be paid. In 2012, new rules to be brought in by the European Union, will cut annuity payments to pensioners by up 20%. (Private sector pension holders are forced by law to buy annuities with their savings.)

Armies of retired people whose pensions put them slightly above means-testing limits but slightly below what they need to pay their council taxes and their utility bills already need to supplement their meagre, and diminishing, pensions by working. Many know they will need to work until they drop – simply to carry on eating, keeping their homes tolerably warm and paying their council tax.

Retired public sector workers, whose pensions are generous and paid by taxpayers, frequently take on post-retirement jobs simply because they want a little something to stave off the boredom. Because they don't need the money they are willing to work for very low wages – or even for no wage at all. Those who try to earn money by writing or photography, or other previous hobbies, are prepared to sell their work for a pittance. Inevitably, this all means that there will be fewer jobs and less money available for those genuinely in need. Retired public sector workers should not be allowed to work in any capacity while receiving pensions. They take work and money from people with private sector pensions who have inadequate pensions and genuinely need the money.

I've always been keen on pensions. I started my first pension plan when I was a medical student (using money from my writing and my stock market adventures to pay the premiums). I'm not at all sure that I could recommend that young people start pension plans these days. The tax benefits hardly seem to compensate for the charges made and the rules and regulations which govern pension plans these days.

But public sector pensions, paid for by taxpayers out of current taxes, are more generous than ever. We have created a two-tier world.

Public sector employees are parasites. Whether they are bureaucrats, policemen, road-sweepers, nurses or teachers they do not produce anything. They are there to make society more comfortable for the rest of us. They are a 'cost'.

Public sector employees have enormous job security. It is almost impossible to fire a public sector employee. The average public sector worker gets paid more than the average private sector worker. And nearly 20,000 public sector workers have already retired with individual pension schemes worth over £1,000,000. That means a pension of about £57,000 a year. Top civil servants, policemen, judges, politicians and doctors can receive far greater pensions. Sir Ian Blair, who resigned as boss of the Metropolitan Police, has an annual pension estimated at around £160,000. Public sector pensioners (former Ministers, civil servants, policemen, etc) can receive virtually unlimited pensions whereas private pensions are subject to a 55% tax if they get anywhere near the sort of level enjoyed by the most highly paid public sector workers.

The average public sector worker has a yearly pension of £17,091 in addition to the State 'old age' pension. In contrast, the average private sector worker has a pension of around £1,700 a year.

Public sector employees pay very little towards their own pension. Public sector pensions are paid out of current taxes and cost around £21 billion a year. That's £700 a year for every working person. Private sector workers pay £14 billion a year into their own retirement funds but £21 billion a year for the pensions of retired public sector workers.

★ ★ ★

Workers who have their pension with the company they work for are protected by the Pension Protection Fund (PPF). The PPF opened for business in April 2005. It was set up by the Government to deal with the political problem of people losing their company pensions and then making a fuss about it. The idea is that companies pay a levy on their pension schemes and the money collected is then doled out to unfortunate pensioners whose companies have gone bust. A sort of pension insurance scheme.

The problem is that as more and more companies go bust so the strain on the PPF increases. By the end of January 2009 the scheme was already heavily in debt itself. And 89% of the company schemes covered by the PPF were either in debt or barely able to cover their financial responsibilities.

And then Nortel Networks UK (a sponsor of the London 2012 Olympics) went bust. Or, rather, the Canadian parent company went bust. This meant that the Nortel UK Pension Plan, with 43,000 members entered the Pension Protection Fund.

And the PPF fell further into debt.

How much further was something of a mystery. Because the parent company is Canadian, getting hold of the pension funds remaining with the company will involve insolvency proceedings with Canadian and American courts involved. American courts tend not to look terribly kindly on British claimants and I suspect it might be possible that they will ensure that as much money as possible remains in North America for the protection of North American pensioners and taxpayers.

The result could be a massive hit on the PPF.

In March 2008, the PPF's reported deficit was already £500 million. It had £6 billion worth of liabilities and £5.5 billion in assets.

The Nortel problem will probably double that deficit.

And, of course, other companies are going bust daily.

Some will undoubtedly have American parents.

What will happen to the pensioners whose companies go bust when the PPF can no longer pay up? How many American companies will use the British scheme to enable them to slide into bankruptcy or administration at minimal cost?

Will the British taxpayer be forced to find the money to refill the PPF's empty coffers?

Whatever happens it will be another financial disaster.

And there will be a great deal of worry for British pensioners and for those approaching pension age.

★ ★ ★

One huge problem for companies with pension schemes is that new legislation has given pension fund trustees enormous powers. As a result of these powers trustees can now force companies to make additional contributions to the pension funds they run if there is any shortfall. This sounds fine in theory (and probably sounded fine to the highly paid and very secure bureaucrats sitting in air-conditioned offices in Brussels who thought it up) but the calls for cash are likely to come just when companies are at their weakest and least able to put money into their pension fund. Some companies will doubtless go bust because they cannot find the money to satisfy the requirements of their pension fund trustees. Others will have to cut the dividends they pay. This won't just affect private shareholders who rely on those dividends it will also affect other pension funds which hold shares in the companies which cut their dividends. And so the whole vicious circle of debt will grow ever tighter. Some of Britain's biggest and best-known companies are vulnerable because their pension funds are inadequately financed.

★ ★ ★

Dividends have always been a solid reason for investing; they make up the best part of an investor's return. And they are an essential part of any pension fund's income.

But dividends will fall as companies realise that they need to conserve money just to stay in business, to pay pensions to retired staff members and to continue to pay into pension funds for current workers.

Nearly nine million pensioners in Britain rely on modest investment incomes to supplement their State income. They are going to be devastated as dividends are cut.

If dividends are cut by just 20% on average that will result in a £10 billion cut in the dividends paid.

That could make £1,000 a year less for each pensioner who relies on dividend income.

★ ★ ★

As the nation divides into two – those who work for private companies or themselves on the one hand and those who work for the State in its many manifestations on the other – so resentment among the former about the latter will increase.

I was the first to draw attention to this massive problem but it is a problem which has continued to grow bigger as Gordon Brown has overseen a massive enlargement in the public sector workforce – the number of people who are entitled to travel First Class when it comes to pensions.

Public sector workers enjoy higher salaries than private sector workers, they get longer holidays, better sick pay terms and are officially protected from unemployment by every piece of legislation going. They work nowhere near as hard as private sector workers and, as a breed, they suffer far less from employment stress. Most important of all, perhaps, they receive index-linked, inflation proof pensions paid not by money they themselves have contributed but by future generations of taxpayers. And while private sector employees can see their pensions disappear if their former employer goes bust or if their pension company makes poor investments, public sector worker pensions are guaranteed by the Government.

* * *

In February 2009, it was reported that a council worker who quit after just seven years in his job as chief executive of Northamptonshire County Council received a lump sum payment of £291,000 and a guaranteed index-linked pension of £97,000 a year. The council worker was 54-years-old at the time so local council tax payers will, presumably, be paying out around £100,000 a year for some time to come. It was estimated that a private sector worker would have needed a pension fund of at least £4,500,000 to provide that sort of pension. And a private pension fund of that size would have attracted huge tax penalties.

* * *

One big problem for private sector workers is that Gordon Brown ruined private pensions in 1997 when he scrapped the tax credit on dividend income. At the stroke of a pen he removed around £17,000 from every private-sector worker's retirement fund, about £175 billion in total. At the time I remember screaming about the damage this was going to do. But no one else seemed to think it mattered much. And so Brown got away with it. And now it's too late.

Anger and resentment about this two-tone nation will rise. But eventually, there won't be enough money available to pay public sector pensions. The Government simply won't be able to raise taxes high enough to keep paying existing or future pensions.

* * *

The problem has got out of control because, under the Labour Government, public sector employment has rocketed. The Centre for Economics and Business Research has pointed out that public-sector employment rose by 23.5% between 1998 and 2006, compared to 3.3% outside the public sector. Today there are six million workers in Britain set to retire at 60 with gold-plated final salary pensions. The 21 million who are outside the public sector will have to pay for those public sector pensions. And they will be lucky if they can retire at 70. The total cost of servicing public sector pensions is so great that the Government hasn't produced an estimate for three years. But the CBI reckons that the total public sector pensions liability is around £1,000,0000,000,000. Whenever a politician murmurs about the impossibility of paying for this huge Ponzi scheme the unions threaten strikes. And since it is the money from the unions which keeps the Labour Party from bankruptcy, nothing is done.

★ ★ ★

How will the Government pay for the pensions of public sector workers when taxes no longer cover the costs?

There are two options.

The first is that they will pay them by confiscating money from private pension funds. And that, believe it or not, is an option. Democrats in the USA have already discussed confiscating workers' personal retirement accounts so that the Government can have access to the money in order to pay public sector pensions. I explained in my book *England Our England* that politicians and bureaucrats elsewhere in the EU have for some years cast envious eyes at British private pension funds. And before you dismiss this as nonsense let me point out that this has already been done in Argentina where the Government took $26 billion worth of private pension fund money into protective custody. The second option is that public sector pensions won't be paid at all. And the millions who smugly believe that they will retire in luxury won't get the big fat pension after all.

Government employees with taxpayer-funded pensions may think they are sitting pretty. And they are for now. But what will those promised pensions be worth in ten, fifteen or twenty years?

The Government has promised to pay its employees their pensions but it has no money to pay for them. More and more private sector workers will get fed up with rising taxes and will leave Britain. As they go so the Government will be forced to keep raising taxes, thereby making the situation worse.

Many private sector workers saw their pensions destroyed during 2008 and an increasing number are aware that their future earnings will be taxed heavily to pay for gold-plated, index-linked public sector pensions – paid out to workers retiring at 55 or 60. They will slowly become aware that even if they can rebuild their pensions there will be a risk that the Government will confiscate them to help pay for public sector pensions. And then the number of people emigrating will rocket.

This will leave a huge multi-million member army of public sector workers entitled to pensions from a desperately underfunded Government. You can't take more than 100% tax from workers and eventually even that won't be enough. So public sector pensions simply won't be paid. And millions of people who thought they were going to travel First Class as far as pensions are concerned will discover, I'm afraid, that they will be back in steerage with everyone else.

★ ★ ★

It was always a lunatic idea to put the onus for providing pensions onto public organisations and private companies. Companies exist to make money for their shareholders. That's their sole purpose. They should, of course, do so in a decent and ethical manner. They should provide good value for their customers and fair pay and working conditions to their employees. But providing pensions for employees is a hang over from another age; an era when feudal landlords allowed aged employees to stay in their cottages on the grand estate.

As the rules and regulations about running corporate pensions become ever more complex and onerous (and a consistent and growing drag on corporate profits) an increasing number of employers are giving up; closing their pension schemes and leaving employees to make their own pension arrangements. An increasing number of company bosses are fed up with constantly having to pour money into pension schemes to keep them topped up. Such contributions are a drag on profits and a punishment for shareholders (and, ironically, for pension funds which hold shares). The regulations are having the opposite effect to the one intended: they are resulting in the closure, rather than the improvement, of pension funds.

It is, by the same token, just as crazy for the State to offer to pay its former workers a salary. Where is the sense in it? And where is the fairness?

Public sector unions scream and shout whenever it is suggested that the wildly over-generous public sector pension schemes be brought more in line with the sort of pensions paid to other employees. But this cannot last for long. Public sector pensions have to end soon.

Chapter 10

On The Streets Where You Live

Changes are coming to towns and cities. And they aren't going to be pleasant changes. Local councils everywhere are going to charge more and provide less. Our cities, towns and villages are going to change more in the next few years than they've changed in centuries. And then, just as we've got used to the way they look, they'll change again.

Wherever you live, two things are certain to happen.

First, the tax you pay to your local council will continue to rise – at a rate above the rate of inflation. (In his Pre Budget Report in November 2008 the Chancellor detailed council tax rises much higher than inflation. Council taxes have risen around 100% since 1997. Naturally, however, council taxes are excluded from the Government's inflation figures.). But things will get far worse if Labour wins the next election. The Labour Party plans to revalue the council tax bands of all properties – taking into account any positive features (such as conservatories, greenhouses, tree houses, pleasant gardens or pretty views) and putting up the council tax accordingly. This process goes one way, of course, and so naturally, council taxes are not expected to fall if the council builds a refuse tip across the road. A database of nearly every property in the country has already been created in order to ensure that this process goes smoothly. (There has already been a council tax revaluation in Wales. Unsurprisingly, a huge number of homes moved up a band.) Since more than half of pensioners already pay more than 10% of their income in council tax any further rises will lead to increasing poverty among the aged who will have to choose between heating their homes or going to prison for non-payment of council tax. Many, I suspect, will choose not to pay their council tax on the grounds that in prison they will at least be kept warm and given something to eat.

And, second, the services provided by your council will deteriorate, though there will be money available for politically correct projects. Councils always seem to find more money to hire more unwanted but politically correct advisers and consultants (as recommended by the European Union). Local councils now pay enormous salaries to people whose sole job is to go shopping for or with people who have chosen to live off the State. Taxpayers actually provide companions for people whose joblessness has made them feel lonely. Untrained idiots are paid huge salaries and given grand titles and smart offices to undertake bizarre non-jobs. Your local council almost certainly has a squad of Specialist Stop Smoking Support Advisers In Pregnancy. What for? Doctors and nurses tell women it's bad to smoke when they're pregnant. Actually, there are warnings printed on the packet. Those who want to give up smoking can attend classes any day of the week. (Does it ever occur to anyone that if society didn't throw so much money at people who sit around all day eating and smoking they wouldn't be able to afford as many packets of fags?) Wadebridge Council spent £3,000 on a wall for graffiti artists to practise on. (Sadly, before the wall's official opening someone sneaked past security and painted the slogan 'I paid my tax and all I got was this lousy wall' on it.) And councils everywhere will continue to spend a good chunk of your money producing glossy leaflets and magazines, packed with photographs of council employees and eulogies about the services they are offering. In the middle of the credit crunch crisis Croydon Council was reported to be spending £250,000 of taxpayers' money on a new newspaper. I bet the local taxpayers cheered. (There's a danger that free newspapers produced by local councils will put independent newspapers out of business. That certainly won't help democracy.) And councils will spend a fortune hiring rainmakers – experts able to advise them on new ways to make money out of charging for services that are already paid for (and fining people who don't do what they're told to do by the people hired by the people who were elected to govern the community). Finally, at the end of each financial year councils will continue to spend their remaining cash on utterly pointless projects designed simply to use up the money and avoid having to return a surplus. (You may have noticed that in the months of February and March council workmen everywhere can be seen digging up and replacing kerbstones and perfectly satisfactory stretches of pavement. It's known as National Kerb Week, though it lasts for longer than a week.)

* * *

The one thing everyone expects the council to do is to collect their rubbish. But thanks to EU regulations your council will collect your rubbish at ever-increasing intervals and will make ever more complex rules defining precisely how and where and when rubbish must be prepared for collection. The rules get dafter by the week. An 85-year-old man was told that he had to drag his rubbish 100 yards up an unpaved lane if he expected it to be collected. If you leave your bin out on the wrong day they will fine you up to £5,000. If you leave out too much they will sulk and they won't take any of it away. Bin men (who almost certainly prefer to be known by some far grander name) have now been given authority to rummage through your bin to make sure you haven't mixed your whites with your coloureds. The unscrupulous bin men will doubtless help themselves to your old gas bills and bank statements and then help themselves to the content of your bank account.

One of the daftest notions was the idea of 'pay as you throw'. The idea (which probably originated with central Government) was that householders would be charged by the number of rubbish sacks they put out to be collected. The council would charge 50 pence or £1 per black bag. The idea was, of course, utterly absurd. Apart from the disputes between householders and councils ('you charged me for nine bags last month but I only put out eight') there would, of course, be much moving around of bags in the nights before collections. Householders would be shuffling around at dawn dragging their bags down the street and putting them outside the home of a less wide awake neighbour. Only bureaucrats with both feet on the clouds could have possibly dreamt up such a scheme. I suspect that everyone else in the country saw the problems the minute the proposal was aired.

Labour Ministers were warned by their own scientists from the

Department for Environment Food and Rural Affairs in January 2006 that abolishing weekly rubbish collections would spread disease and encourage rats and other vermin. The number of fungal spores and bacteria rises dramatically too. The breeding rats may well bring back the plague. For many of us it is like living through a permanent dustmen's strike.

Despite all this, ministers have campaigned to pressure town halls to cut back on bin rounds still more. (Actually, this has nothing to do with the Government. The rules come from Brussels. We pay them billions to be members of the EU and then they tell us how often we can have our bins emptied. Councils like the rules, however, because it cuts their costs and leaves more money for those insatiable pension funds.)

★ ★ ★

There's been a massive increase in the amount of flytipping since councils stopped collecting rubbish. My wife and I used to own a small woodland. We wanted to turn it into a small wildlife sanctuary. Unfortunately, the woodland bordered a quiet road. And every week the part of the woodland nearest to the road was waist high in domestic refuse. In the end we sold the woodland. We couldn't cope with the rubbish.

★ ★ ★

We live in a quiet street. Very early one morning I heard a noise outside. I looked out of the window. The refuse lorry was parked outside. Backed up to it was another lorry. The bin men and the men from the other lorry were busy moving broken bits and pieces of furniture from the other lorry into the machinery at the back of the refuse lorry. A whole lorry load. It took them an hour. For a moment I couldn't understand what was happening. And then I got it. The bin men were earning a little extra by taking delivery of some unwanted rubbish.

This will happen more and more now.

★ ★ ★

There are plans to stop collecting household rubbish completely. When this happens councils will simply put a large rubbish skip at the end of each street (what a pleasant sight that will be) and then empty it once a week, once a month or whenever there is a full moon. This has already started in some parts of the country.

Each superbin will be expected to cope with the rubbish from 50 households. Some families will have to carry all their rubbish 150 yards or more. Families living close to the bins will have to cope with the spilt litter, awful smells and rats. The potential for fighting and inter-street warfare should be vast.

They will lie, of course, and tell you that all this is being done to save the planet. If you fail to do what they tell you to do then they will punish you with a hefty fine. They may even refuse to take away your rubbish again. With staggering (and dishonest) sanctimoniousness they will insist that they are trying to force residents to do more to prevent global warming.

It isn't anything to do with saving the planet in general or the local environment in particular. It is to satisfy EU regulations and to avoid being fined by bureaucrats in Brussels. And to cut costs. If councils cared tuppence about global warming and the environment they wouldn't waste a fortune printing leaflets telling you how wonderful they are. And they wouldn't waste energy buying and installing spy cameras.

Incidentally, more than half of councils admit that they use anti-terror laws to spy on families suspected of putting their rubbish out on the wrong day. Councils are recruiting 'environment volunteers' to snoop on their neighbours and report those who fail to sort their rubbish properly. And councils are employing people to tear open refuse sacks in search of the wrong sort of plastic so that they can prosecute confused old ladies. In some areas residents have to sort their rubbish into seven different containers. There is, unbelievably, a quango called the Local Authority Recycling Advisory Committee.

All council employees involved in dealing with rubbish should be doing one thing only: heaving sacks of refuse into the back of council dustcarts. Meanwhile, as rubbish lies uncollected in our streets and back gardens, Britain's rat population is soaring to record levels. And rats spread potentially fatal diseases.

★ ★ ★

The irony is that while limiting the amount of rubbish which we can dump, the Government – in the form of the Post Office – relentlessly pours increasing amounts of real junk mail through our letterboxes. Theoretically this can be stopped. In practice it can't.

★ ★ ★

Recycling is a sick joke.

It's a sick joke for many reasons.

Here are two.

First, as I have explained in previous books, recycling makes global warming worse. People who think they are saving the planet are, in reality, destroying it. The collection, transportation and processing of recyclable materials increases greenhouse gases. Thousands of tons of recyclables are shipped out to China because there is insufficient capacity and demand for dealing with the stuff in Britain. Hundreds of thousands of tons of carefully sorted recyclable waste is simply dumped. The truth, of course, is that councils use 'recycling' to justify the scrapping of weekly rubbish collections. And they want to scrap weekly rubbish collections because they cannot afford them because of the huge sums they are paying out in pensions to former employees.

Second, the bottom fell out of the waste paper market a long time ago and all over the EU there are now mountains of recycling material waiting to be recycled. Godot will arrive sooner. The stuff that is stored incurs massive storage charges. And because the recycling isn't being done (because it can't be done because no one wants the damned stuff) British taxpayers have to pay fines to the European Union for failure to meet EU recycling targets. (You couldn't make this up.) Of course, we could use the waste paper as fuel. We could burn it and turn it into heat and power. That's what other EU countries do with their waste paper. You will note the words 'other EU countries'.

Why, then, don't we burn our waste paper and turn it into something useful?

We can't burn our rubbish because the Department for the Environment, Food and Rural Affairs (known to its enemies as Defra – it hasn't got any friends to know it as anything) made a gigantic cock-up and classed waste paper as 'waste' instead of classifying it as 'biomass' as other EU countries did. And you can't burn stuff classified as 'waste' without hugely expensive equipment designed to comply with the Waste Incineration Directive of the European Union.

If Defra had understood EU law properly we could burn the 12.5 million tons of waste paper and cardboard that we produce every year. We could generate more than 10% of our electricity from our rubbish. This would reduce our dependency on foreign imports of gas and oil. It would go a long way towards meeting our renewables target. And it would get us £2 billion a year in subsidies from the EU under the Renewables Obligation.

But Defra screwed up.

So council taxes will have to rise still higher to pay for storing all the waste paper until someone decides what the hell to do with it.

(If you think this is bad, you should read about 'gold plating'. There is more about this in my book *The OFPIS File*.)

★ ★ ★

Public lavatories everywhere are closing. The trick is always the same. The council allows the public lavatories to deteriorate. No repairs are done. Little or no cleaning is done. When the lavatories are in a sorry state, the council announces that it has to close them on health and safety grounds. 'They are too dilapidated to keep open,' says a local spokesman. Since the public lavatories near to public car parks are often the first to go the result is that shoppers who get back to their car find themselves a mile or more from the nearest convenience.

★ ★ ★

More and more councils are turning off street and motorway lights late at night to save money. '(Let's turn off the lights when it gets dark.' 'Great idea.') This ignores evidence showing that ordinary street lighting can be four times more effective in cutting crime than costly security cameras. Turning off the lights will, of course, result in more accidents and more crime. You don't need a degree in street lighting to see that.

★ ★ ★

Council taxes will continue to rise, at a rate well above the level of inflation, until they stop because there is rioting in the streets. But never again will services be as good as they used to be. They will not, indeed, be as good as they are today. (And given the poor services provided by most councils that is pretty scary.) From this day on you will always be looking back on this as the 'good old days'.

Local roads and pavements will be left unmended. Road repairs take months when they should take weeks and weeks when they should take days. Pavement enhancing schemes (to satisfy EU rules) cost millions and add nothing, especially when the pavements are installed in parts of the countryside where no one ever walks. Unnecessary road delays cost billions of pounds in wasted time and petrol. (And do endless damage to the environment because of all the fuel burned unnecessarily.) During the snow flurry in February 2009, councils everywhere said they either didn't have enough salt to de-ice the roads, or they couldn't afford to buy any more. And so buses, lorries and cars ground to a halt. As for the pavements? I don't know of a single council in England or Wales which put salt down on icy pavements. The result was a huge increase in the workload for hospitals and ambulance services as people with fractured arms and legs were treated. The money councils saved could be measured in thousands. The cost to the nation could be measured in billions.

Back in the 1960s, I remember forecasting that our roads would never again be as good as they were then. As the number of cars and lorries grew and grew, and as the idiotic Dr Beeching tore up our railway system, so the pressure on our roads was bound to result in potholes and traffic jams. Today we are lucky if we can get into the car and be somewhere else within an hour.

* * *

The salaries paid by local councils have been rocketing for years. The average salary of the average council chief executive has doubled to £150,000 since Labour became the Government. They are still the same dandruff stained, lazy incompetents that they were. But now they are rich. Some take home over £200,000. Today, your local council has many employees who are paid more like rock stars than council employees. And, unlike rock stars, your council bosses get massive benefits – including wonderful inflation-proofed pensions that are paid for by the local ratepayers and which are, of course directly related to those massive salaries.

* * *

I've been pointing out for years that council pension liabilities are a ticking economic time bomb. More than a quarter of council tax receipts are now needed to fund public sector pension costs. This proportion is rising rapidly as the number of council workers increases and the pay they give one another rockets.

What can you do about it?

Nothing.

Of course, if you're a council employee you can smile, lie back and enjoy it.

And you can even learn to like yourself.

Sandwell metropolitan council sent its head, Alison Fraser, on a course to enable her to 'like herself' better. The life-awareness programme took Ms Fraser to Germany and Florida on courses.

★ ★ ★

Finally, there is some bad news for home owners. The Labour Government plans to base council tax bills on the social background of the taxpayer. People who own their own homes will be penalised. The Government will use its database to inform council tax inspectors of the 'social background' of residents. As if that wasn't bad enough the Government also plans to force all public bodies to consider sexual background, race, age, gender, disability and sexuality when providing taxpayer-funded public services.

★ ★ ★

At the beginning of this chapter I said that two things are going to happen to towns and cities in Britain: there's going to be an increase in local taxes and there is going to be a reduction in services.

But there's actually a third thing that is going to happen on and around the street where you live: town centres are going to change dramatically in appearance and nature.

Traditional town centres, full of interesting passageways, curious buildings and fascinating small shops are being destroyed by a collection of factors. Just a generation or so ago every town and city in the country had at least one good second-hand bookshop, a row of excellent junk shops and a variety of locally owned specialist shops: an ironmonger, a pharmacy or two, a book shop, a draper, a high-class jeweller, a toy shop, a milliner, a traditional gent's outfitter and so on. For as long as I can remember every small town also had a locally owned department store (usually selling such apparently unconnected essentials as gloves, bras, umbrellas, towels and luggage). Zola claimed that the department store was the cathedral of modern business. Well the cathedrals are on their way out. And few people seem to care. Civic duty and civic pride are now alive only in the fading memories of those of pensionable age. And no one listens to old people any more.

High Street shopping centres are dying fast. Within ten to fifteen years even well-known retail chains will have disappeared, to be replaced by tedious rows of boarded-up stores and charity shops.

Town centre shopping will die for nine, specific reasons.

First, planning officers have, since the 1960s, been determined to create open plan towns and to destroy anything of historical significance. The motor vehicle has been given precedence over the pedestrian, with the result that most town centres are designed for driving through rather than enjoying.

Second, greedy local councils with huge staff pension bills to pay have done enormous damage by making small, often barely profitable, businesses, pay unsustainable amounts of tax. Retail store owners have, simply, crumbled under the burden of taxes they can't afford to pay. (Cities outside the UK have thrived because retailers are given reasonable tax bills to pay.) They push commercial rates on business properties up and up because it just isn't politically acceptable to push up taxes on residential properties (particularly when services are declining rapidly).

Third, supermarkets have destroyed small shops. To begin with, they got rid of small grocers by offering cut-price food. Small garages, unable to compete with low petrol prices were next to go – leaving huge areas of the country without any petrol pumps. Then the supermarkets helped get rid of small bookshops by selling top 'bestsellers' at low prices. Bookshops, struggling to offer a large stock of books, could not survive without the sale of 'bestsellers'. As the supermarkets have increased the range of products sold (to include clothing, ironmongery and electrical goods) so the range of shops destroyed by them has been increased. In most areas supermarkets were situated outside towns, where space was available at a lower rent. These destroyed town centres by attracting shoppers who might otherwise have gone into the town. Supermarkets situated within towns destroyed town centres by selling all the stuff that used to be sold by small shops. The recent introduction of small town centre shops managed by supermarket chains has destroyed the remaining small private shops. Supermarkets can use their purchasing muscle to demand low prices from suppliers – and their small satellite shops benefit from this. The big supermarket buyers can pressure suppliers (including farmers) and get low prices. Attracted by the bargains more and more shoppers will do their spending at supermarkets.

Fourth, more and more consumers will do their shopping on the Internet – having their products delivered by e-mail or by one of the big carrier services. (The Post Office, grotesquely inefficient, will take only a tiny part of this booming industry.) The Internet has helped destroy many small shops. The availability of price comparison websites has enabled shoppers to buy things on the basis of price alone (rather than on a combination of things – including service). Today, many shoppers stay at home, buy on the Web and have their chosen items delivered to them through the post. Bookshops were the first to really suffer from the power of the Internet. It became possible to find a book within minutes, instead of spending wonderful hours browsing in musty bookshops, and, in many cases, to buy books for pennies instead of pounds (with the seller making his profit by charging more for postage and packing than it really cost). Many of the people selling on the Internet are amateurs (often not paying tax). Too many of the 'professional' Internet businesses in existence have never made a profit.

Fifth, charity shops have destroyed a whole range of shops. Charity shops get their stock free, much of their labour is provided at little or no charge and many of their costs are much lower than those of their commercial competitors. (Ironically, the prices that charity shops charge are often higher than the stores selling new merchandise. The argument that charity shops serve the community by providing cheap clothes, books and videos has long since disappeared.) Small, privately owned clothing shops, junk shops (a source of so much joy to so many) and bookshops have been hit hard by the growth in the number of charity shops (which have, overall, consequently done far more harm than good). We will know the economy is in a really bad way when the charity shops start closing down. Meanwhile, it would make sense if charity shops, and indeed all charitable ventures, were prevented from using voluntary labour and were forced to pay minimum wage. Struggling small businesses would stand a much better chance of surviving and there would be more jobs for those in need of work.

Sixth, spending on non-essential items will decline with the deterioration in Britain's general economy. People are never again going to be as rich as they thought they were at the end of the 20th Century and the beginning of the 21st Century. Many large and small retail stores will collapse and disappear. And thousands of small, family owned stores will die too.

Seventh, the rise in commercial property prices has pushed up rents. Family owned businesses, which had bought their premises a generation or two previously, survived because they had no rent bill to pay. Eventually, many gave up – choosing to take a huge profit on their property instead of struggling to run a business being 'attacked' on all sides.

Eighth, a remorseless increase in the number of laws governing the running of shops, and the employment of staff, has hit small businesses particularly hard. Large supermarket chains have been much better placed to deal with the regulations. Many have, for example, protected themselves by choosing to employ staff on a temporary contract basis. Most of the new laws have, of course, come from the European Union and help neither customers nor employees.

Ninth, town centres have been destroyed by the absence of patrolling policemen and a proliferation in the number of feral youths wandering around. This used to be a problem at night. In many areas it is becoming a problem during the daytime. Drug users and alcoholics congregate on street corners making town centres inhospitable places. The sale of alcohol at low prices (it is not uncommon for supermarkets to sell beer and lager cheaper than water) has contributed to the problem. The smaller supermarkets now opening in town centres and suburban shopping precincts are making things steadily worse.

All things considered there isn't going to be much point in heading for the town centre to do a little shopping for quite a while to come. Oh, and the spaces won't be taken up by estate agents either. Most of the estate agents will have gone long before the next housing boom arrives.

In the short and medium term things will deteriorate further. The credit crunch will result in more and more boarded up shops. National chains of shops will close. Small, family run shops which had struggled on making very little profit will give up the struggle. And town centres will die. Villages are going to fare even worse, I fear. The EU is already forcing village post offices, village schools and village pubs to close. (Why do people not realise where all this legislation comes from?) When the village post office goes the village shop usually goes with it. The result is that villages will become small dormitories for nearby towns and anyone who wants to buy a loaf of bread or a stamp will have to travel miles to do so.

And then, by around 2020, the oil shortage will really start to hit hard. And people will no longer be able to afford to drive their cars to the supermarket. Indeed, in time supermarkets themselves will fail. Their method of operation (involving the transport of goods over vast distances) will prove unsustainable. Millions won't be able to afford cars at all. And town centres will, once again, have a purpose. Growing numbers of people will move into town centre accommodation. Others will use public transport or bicycles to visit smaller, more local shops (often selling items which have been grown or manufactured locally). Small privately run junk shops will thrive. Town centres which had died will be revived. They will be full of shops selling locally grown fruit and vegetables. There won't be many shops selling exotic fruits or flowers flown in from foreign parts.

Town centre properties (particularly those near to railway stations) will in the long-term rise in value. Properties in villages and outlying suburbs will fall in value. Just as pawnbrokers are enjoying a revival now, so repair shops will reappear. When the oil really starts to run out there will be a dramatic growth in the number of people offering to repair household items which have broken. Simple, old-fashioned equipment which can be repaired with a screwdriver and a can of oil will become popular again. There will also be a growth in the number of shops selling second-hand and reconditioned goods. Such shops will survive and thrive despite the existence of more and more charity shops.

But there will be a growth in such services and shops long before 2020.

The shortage of money resulting from the banking crisis of 2008 will mean that increasing numbers of people will need to buy reliable second-hand equipment. There won't be so much money available for buying new models.

So the bottom line is that town centres will die.

But they will come alive again.

And they will look very different.

Instead of being full of chain store branches they will contain a good variety of small shops run by local businessmen and entrepreneurs.

And, I'm delighted to say that junk shops and second-hand bookshops will make a return.

Chapter 11

The Remains Of Our Privacy Will Disappear And Identity Card Fraud Will Grow

It's difficult to believe that surveillance could become more intrusive than it already is: but it will. Millions believe the lies about 'protecting us from terrorism'. Calmly and without protest they are walking into the world that Orwell warned us about. The words 'Why should you object if you have nothing to hide?' will be their last.

We are constantly being warned about the danger of allowing our private information to fall into the wrong hands. But, it's impossible to do anything these days without producing reams of private information (passport, gas bills, birth certificate, driving licence, etc) and sharing it with strangers – bank clerks, solicitors, accountants, even estate agents. The people who demand the information claim that they need to do this in order to protect us. They insist on making copies which they promise they will place 'securely' in a filing cabinet. They tell us that the law forces them to take copies of our documents. They tell us that it is being done to prevent terrorism and money laundering. There is much talk of compliance officers and legal responsibilities and such nonsense.

They are lying, of course.

When I say that they are lying what I mean is that they aren't doing it to protect you, it won't prevent terrorism or money laundering, and there is no law requiring you to hand over copies of your private documents. Indeed, all the evidence shows that handing over copies of private documents increases the chances of them being lost or stolen and a crook being able to steal your identity. Most private information is lost not by careless individuals but by careless banks (and other institutions) and careless Government departments.

* * *

The people of Britain are now officially the most spied upon people on earth. (If you exclude places where people are executed for chewing gum we are also the most regulated, monitored and punished population on the planet.) Britain has more CCTV cameras than any other country. Actually, there are more CCTV cameras in Britain than there are in all European cities combined. (At the last count there were 21 million CCTV cameras in the world and nearly a quarter of them were in Britain.) There is one CCTV camera for every 14 people in Britain. Some police forces are now using remote controlled helicopters fitted with cameras. The average person has their image captured on a CCTV camera 300 times a day. Every day. Who are the peeping Toms (and Tomasinas) who spend their lives watching these damned cameras? How many of them are perverts who train their remote controlled cameras onto bedroom windows and park benches in the summertime? Some CCTV cameras are now used to issue verbal warnings as well as to spy on us. Travellers are scanned and searched. (Though there is no evidence to show that forcing travellers through the X-ray scanners is safe. Nor, incidentally, have I been able to find any evidence to show that iris recognition technology is safe to use. How many passengers will develop cancer or go blind? How many of the operatives using this equipment will be made ill? No one knows and your guess is as good as mine or anyone else's.)

We are surveyed endlessly (and often without an opt out clause).

- The police have accumulated over 4 million DNA profiles. Three quarters have had a conviction, a caution or a warning but a quarter of those whose DNA is stored are entirely innocent. There are already 40,000 children on the DNA database. And, although they are all entirely innocent they will stay there for life. The nation's DNA database is growing by 2,000 every day.

Innocent people who try to have their DNA removed from the system are ignored. One police chief has suggested that badly behaved children as young as five should be recorded on the national DNA database. He says that naughty children should be targeted because future offenders can often be picked out at a young age. Police refused to remove an MP's genetic details from their records even though he had done nothing wrong and had helped police merely so that they could eliminate him from their enquiries. The MP said afterwards: 'It seems to me that the Home Office and police are building up a national, universal DNA database by stealth. They are trying to get all 60 million of us on it by hook or by crook.' (Good news for the elderly, by the way, is that it is apparently difficult to get decent finger prints from the over 75s.) The MP is right, of course. And I'm surprised he didn't know. The plan is to record the DNA of every British citizen. Britain already has the biggest DNA database in the world. The eventual aim is to take a DNA sample from babies at birth. Then we will all be criminals. And Big Brother will be happy. Well, happier.

- There is a Government plan to keep the medical records of 50 million patients on computer (with a wide range of public sector employees having access to the data).
- Councils are using anti-terrorism powers in a variety of ways. They use them to check out what you put in your dustbin. Some actually put microchips into dustbins. And they use them to check that people aren't lying about where they live so that they can get their child into a school where one or two of the pupils are actually taught to read and write. Three quarters of local authorities have used powers granted under the Regulation of Investigatory Powers Act (brought in to protect the nation from terrorists) to spy on residents suspected of putting their bins out on the wrong day or breaking school catchment area rules.
- The Government is introducing a Spy in the Sky system to facilitate plans for a national road pricing system. This will enable the Government to charge us for using the roads that they built with our taxes. It will also enable the Government to know where you are at any time.

- Government inspectors now have the right to enter your home and to take photographs of every room and its contents. And Government inspectors are now conducting an annual Integrated Household Survey in which more than half a million people are being asked about their past and present sexual partners and what contraception they use. The inspectors also want to know about monthly earnings, including second jobs. If they haven't been round to your house yet, don't worry. They'll be with you soon.
- At school, pupils as young as 10 are asked if they smoke, how often they drink alcohol, how 'safe or unsafe' they feel at home, whether they receive free school meals and whether their mothers are in paid work. The survey is for Ofsted, the education watchdog, which is compiling a database on children's lifestyle, health and happiness. Children do not need to ask their parents' permission before taking part.
- The Government, the banks, the supermarkets (and anyone else who wants to buy the information) already know what credit cards you have, what library books you have borrowed recently, where you've been, where you stayed and when you returned home, where you live, how much tax you pay, what you've bought recently, what illnesses you suffer from, what pills you take, your job (and your job history), your criminal record, your earnings, your financial assets, your hobbies and peccadilloes, your special dietary requirements, the clubs you're in, the magazines and newspapers you read, the people you telephone (and what you say to them), the people you e-mail (and what you say), the possessions you own, how much alcohol you use and what educational establishments you attended. None of this is private. If a mail order company wants to buy a list of left handed vegetarian women who wear 38DD bras, play golf and enjoy skiing, needlework and bell ringing then they can. If your worst enemy wants to know all this stuff then they can buy it too. Nothing is private now.

⋆ ⋆ ⋆

There is absolutely no evidence that demands for information (copies of passports, bank statements and utility bills) has prevented any money laundering or terrorism. On the contrary, the evidence suggests that collecting and storing all this information makes life infinitely easier for terrorists and criminals. Once you've gone through the pointless rigmarole of providing copies of your driving licence, shotgun licence and gas bill and have managed to open an account, the average bank's idea of security is to ask for your birthday and postcode. It is difficult to think of two pieces of information which are more readily available and which are, therefore, of less value in establishing your identity.

There is, however, plenty of evidence that these demands have led to the serious loss of much private information and to an increase in the problem of identity theft. When I tried to sell a house I was told by the estate agent that because of money laundering regulations I had to provide a copy of my passport and a home utility bill. When I told him he was wrong he told me, very firmly, that he was right and I was wrong. He told me it was the law and I had to do what he said. It was clear from his tone that if I did not comply there would be consequences. There was none of that nonsense about the customer being right. He raised his voice and, if we hadn't been talking on the telephone, I suspect he might have poked a finger in my chest.

The estate agent was, of course, talking utter gibberish. For one thing there is no legal requirement for anyone to allow banks, lawyers, estate agents or anyone else to make copies of private documents. And for another, estate agents do not handle money and giving them copies of private documents cannot prevent money laundering – though it can, of course, contribute to identity loss. What alarmed me most about this was not that an estate agent should demand access to confidential information but that other house sellers should be prepared to provide it. What next? Will supermarkets demand a copy of shoppers' passports before they are allowed to purchase a loaf of bread? It would make just as much sense. When I protested, the manager told me that I would be accepted if I had an entry in the telephone directory. As it happens I don't have an entry in the telephone book or anywhere else but I found it amusing that the security check had been downgraded from a copy of my passport to an entry in a telephone directory.

I told the estate agent to go away and ask his compliance officer to check the legislation. He did, rang me back and then admitted that I did not need to provide copies of anything. He did not, of course, apologise. He wasn't even shamefaced. But, I suspect that he will continue to demand these valuable items from other clients. And that other people will hand them over.

(Where, incidentally, do all these 'compliance officers' come from? Who are they? Are they human? Where are they trained? I suspect they are the sort of people who were milk monitors at school, or would have been if schools still gave out bottles of milk to their pupils. Come to think of it the compliance officers probably come from the same source as the HIP inspectors, the TV licensing Gestapo and the people the council are sending round to photograph our bedrooms.)

★ ★ ★

The Labour Government insists (at the EU's behest) that in future we must all carry ID cards at all times. (Even the homeless will have to carry ID cards. They will be able to give their home address as a bench, bus stop or park. Honest.) The Government intends to create a vast Government database of all Internet and telephone communications. Under the 2000 Regulation of Investigatory Powers Act, agencies and public-sector organisations are already entitled to keep tabs on whom we telephone or e-mail. The Act gives 800 organisations the right to conduct surveillance and access communication records. If one of your neighbours, friends or relatives works for a public-sector organisation (such as the local council) there is a good chance that he or she will have access to far more information about you than you would, perhaps, want them to know.

★ ★ ★

Council tax snoopers are storing information about what you eat, if you use a dating agency, where you go on holiday, if you have a pet, who you vote for and so on. A list of 287 intimate facts will be collected as part of the council tax rebanding. Councils will collect information from supermarket loyalty schemes, the national census, and banks and store it all on a computer together with photos taken by the snoopers. Oh, and they'll also include details about your pension plans, political memberships, illnesses, hobbies, charity donations, eating habits (e.g. if you are vegetarian), central heating and which newspaper you buy.

★ ★ ★

Social workers set up a CCTV camera in the bedroom of a couple with learning difficulties in order to monitor their behaviour. Council staff allegedly spied on the young parents to see if they were fit to look after their baby (who was sleeping in another room).

Not surprisingly the couple were distressed by the fact that they were being filmed in bed at night but it wasn't until the young couple (the ones with learning difficulties you will remember) quoted the Human Rights Act that social services agreed to switch off the surveillance camera while the pair were in bed together.

(Have you noticed that whenever public sector workers, and this applies particularly to social workers, are reprimanded for any activity they instantly whinge about the unfairness of a 'blame culture' and seem to have acquired the curious ability to put aside completely the concept of responsibility.)

★ ★ ★

Blair and Brown have between them given the Government powers that would, just a few years ago, have seemed impossible to comprehend. They can now lock you up for 42 days without bothering to try you. They can torture you to obtain information. And there are 266 separate provisions allowing various authorities to enter your home without your permission.

★ ★ ★

The cost of the surveillance society to taxpayers is around £20 billion a year. That's around £800 per household. Whatever happened to the idea that we pay the Government money to look after us? They are, instead, doing rather a lot of sneaking and peeping. Amazingly, 500 million identity checks are carried out every day in the UK alone. The police are expanding a car surveillance operation that will allow them to record and store details of millions of daily journeys for up to five years. Roadside cameras are able to read 50 million licence plates a day, enabling the police to reconstruct the journeys of motorists. Teams of peeping Toms constantly stare at screens showing them what private citizens are doing in Britain. Curiously, the information obtained hardly ever seems to be used in preventing crime or arresting criminals. In London, for example,

CCTV cameras only help to solve 3% of London's street crimes. And, officially, they don't have much of a preventative effect. Why? Well, according to Scotland Yard, the footage is too grainy to count as evidence in court and 'it's hard work looking through all those images'. It is not surprising that criminals just don't take any notice of the CCTV cameras. CCTV cameras don't prevent crime and don't help catch criminals. The bottom line is that CCTV cameras simply record criminal activities so that the police can sell the film to television companies. Maybe that's why the police are so keen on CCTV cameras.

Raytheon, an American defence company (which is the polite way of saying an American arms company), is the lead contractor on a new project that will log the details of everybody moving into and out of Britain. Under the contract signed with the UK Border Agency, the American company will collect and analyse data on everyone who enters and leaves Britain by air, sea and rail and check them against Government databases before they travel. Permission to enter Britain could be denied before a traveller leaves foreign soil. The contract, which lasts for ten years, is costing taxpayers £750 million. Now that the Government and private companies are storing this information burglars who hack into the system will, of course, be able to see precisely when UK residents are away from home. Amazingly, this programme has upset the European Union which seems worried that the scheme is 'repressive'. The EU, which now controls Britain, can, indeed, prohibit some uses of the data. Maybe the problem is that the EU likes to keep control and doesn't like the idea of individual governments taking the initiative. After all, under an agreement negotiated between the EU and the American Government, agencies in the USA (including the Central Intelligence Agency) are allowed to view details of all your personal details (including your bank accounts, travel plans and the sites you visit on the Internet.) If, as seems likely, an American company is in future hired to conduct a population census, the personal information gathered could be subject to the USA Patriot Act and be made available to the American authorities. All of it.

★ ★ ★

The Government does not take much care of the information it demands. In June 2008, more than 140,000 workers were put at risk when tax forms were sent out with national insurance numbers visible alongside the recipients' names and addresses. A poll conducted in October 2008 showed that the Government came second in the top ten bodies least trusted to keep our details secret. (Gambling companies came top.) This was, in fact, hardly surprising. In November 2007, HM Revenue and Customs lost computer disks containing the personal details of 25 million people. In December 2007, after losing 25 million lots of confidential information, HMRC confessed to seven other incidents of 'some significance'. The chief executive of HMRC quit. But he didn't disappear in shame to hide away and gnaw at his fingernails. Instead he tottered over to the Cabinet Office where he led a project on 'developing civil servant skills'. And he managed to negotiate a retirement package which included a £400,000 pay off. As one MP said: 'Instead of falling on his sword, he's fallen on a feather bed.'

In December 2007, the details of three million candidates for the UK driving theory test (including names, addresses and telephone numbers) went missing in America. (No one explained what the information was doing in America.) And, of course, civil servants continue to leave laptops on trains and in cars as though trying to get rid of them. In January 2008, it was announced that a Navy employee left a laptop overnight in his car. It was, predictably, stolen. The laptop contained the passport numbers, national insurance numbers and bank details of 600,000 people who had joined or applied to join the Navy, Royal Marines and RAF. In April 2008, an army captain's laptop was taken from under his chair as he ate in a McDonald's, near the Ministry of Defence's headquarters in London. In June 2008, a senior intelligence officer from the Cabinet Office left top secret documents about the Al Queda threat on the seat of a commuter train. In July 2008, the Ministry of Defence admitted that 747 of its laptops and 121 of its computer memory sticks had been stolen. (This was 400 more than they had originally thought.)

As I predicted some years ago the new, more expensive, more intrusive microchipped passports can be cloned and manipulated in minutes. Incidentally, the passport office has been renamed the Identity and Passport Service and in future citizens who want a passport will have to go for an interview and be photographed and fingerprinted. Applicants will be grilled and have to give up 200 pieces of different personal information. Those who fail to persuade a bureaucrat they deserve a passport will be denied one or will face a full investigation by anti-fraud experts. There is no appeal process. Anyone who refuses to have an ID card won't be allowed to have a passport, driving licence, national insurance number, pension or health care.

The latest biometric UK passports have an RFID chip in them that can be cheaply and simply read from a distance by criminals. (You can now buy a foil pouch to contain your passport to protect against this risk.) The National Audit Office has revealed that new passports which are supposedly valid for 10 years have chips inside that are guaranteed for two days. The National Audit Office said: 'The full security benefit of e-passports (sic) will not be realised until UK border control readers are fully upgraded, and it is only then that we will know the impact of this new technology on travellers.' Just about every other piece of IT commissioned by the Government has failed to work properly. More than four million e-passports were issued in the first year.

The Government's claim that these passports (and ID cards) are a protection against identify theft, money laundering and terrorism is clearly a blatant lie. One security expert attacked the so-called secure chip by injecting a malicious code into it so that when the passport was scanned it crashed the scanning device. Another cloned the microchip on a British passport and then implanted digital images of Osama bin Laden into the passport.

★ ★ ★

Even when they don't lose it, the information all these civil servants collect is not treated confidentially. Our most private information is vulnerable to terrorist and criminal hackers and fraudsters. Identify fraud is the fastest growing crime in Britain. State employees are required to pass on confidential information they obtain. Doctors, teachers and social workers are to be told to act as informers to identify potential violent offenders for monitoring by the police and other agencies. So much for patient confidentiality. Another 1,000 official bugging operations start every day. If you are an object of such an operation the buggers will tap your phone, intercept your e-mails and open your post.

The information that is stored on official computers isn't even always correct. One in five entries on the Government's driver registration database is wrong. (In other words the DVLA holds the wrong personal data for 7.8 million drivers.) And these days much of the information stored is described as 'soft intelligence'. This means that there is no proof that the information stored is accurate. It is, in fact, no more than rumour and gossip. But it is stored on computers, to be accessed by millions of public sector workers.

The security of the online computer system used by more than three million people to file tax returns was put in doubt when HM Revenue and Customs admitted that the site was not secure enough to be used by MPs, celebrities and the Royal Family. (Thousands of 'high profile' individuals have been secretly barred from using the online tax return system because of concerns that their confidential data would be put at risk.)

* * *

If you want to complain about unreasonable official snooping I suggest that you think twice before wasting your time. The Investigatory Powers Tribunal (and I bet you didn't know that one existed) deals with public complaints about unreasonable official snooping. In its first seven and a half years of existence the Tribunal received just 600 complaints and upheld just one of them. The Tribunal does not make its rulings public and does not tell unsuccessful complainants why their claims were rejected. Even the ruling made in the case of the one successful claim remains secret.

* * *

Companies are now enthusiastic snoopers and peepers too. Financial institutions (and even stores offering cards) want customers to fill in a mass of personal details. One I saw recently asked for (among other things) name, address, bank account details, security password, date of birth and passport number. The institution claimed that it wanted this information to protect its customers from fraud. This is nonsense. (As is the claim that all this information is required by law). If you give this much information to any institution you will be exposed to fraud and, in particular, to identity theft. If any institution demands this much information from you tell them that their demands are a threat to your personal security and that you are taking your custom elsewhere. If enough people refuse to comply with these absurdly intrusive demands then the institutions concerned will stop asking for them.

★ ★ ★

Google, the American search engine (surely one of the most evil companies on the planet, in my view outscoring even Monsanto and BAE in any 'nasty company' competition) has made it possible for anyone to type in a UK postcode and instantly see a clear picture of buildings, cars and people. The level of details in the photographs is remarkable.

The US based Ponemon Institute, a privacy research group, found that some marketing managers are prepared to give out key private customer data, such as sexual orientation, political affiliation and credit card details to third parties in an attempt to increase sales. None of this is particularly surprising, of course. After all, local councils readily sell electoral roll information to private companies; the Government has admitted that it will sell all the information on ID cards, and British courts allow the sale of names and addresses of people owing money to debt collection agencies and anyone else who wants them.

★ ★ ★

If you want to buy someone else's identity you can do so online. A UK credit card costs $2 and access to someone else's online bank account costs $300, according to an American Internet security company. Spammers can buy a list of 29,000 e-mail addresses for $5. Details of a computer that has been hacked into and can be controlled from outside costs $6. (It will not have escaped your notice that all these prices are in dollars. Americans who hack into your accounts will be quite safe from prosecution in their own country. The Americans don't care what happens to Britons.)

★ ★ ★

Credit card fraud will continue to grow. And the problem is almost entirely due to America.

Credit card fraud involving UK retailers fell by two thirds from 2004 to 2007, thanks to the introduction of chip and pin technology (which had, incidentally, been used in France for years before it was introduced in the UK).

But credit card fraud involving the misuse of UK cards abroad more than doubled in the same period.

Before chip and pin technology was finally brought to Britain, fraudsters used to be able to copy credit cards using information contained within the magnetic strip on the cards. It is, however, much more difficult to counterfeit cards which contain chips requiring a personal identification number.

The problem is that some poorly developed countries haven't yet changed to the new system. And the primary offender is the USA.

European countries will have all introduced chip and pin technology by 2010. Canada will soon follow suit. And countries in Asia and South America are also introducing chip and pin technology.

But American banks can't be bothered and so credit card fraudsters are now concentrating on cards which are used in America. In 2007, there was a 50% jump in fraud committed on UK cards in the USA.

The answer: don't use a credit card if you travel to America.

And use credit and debit cards as little as possible elsewhere.

The safest way to pay? Cash, of course.

★ ★ ★

Two thirds of marketing professionals surveyed admitted that consumer information had been lost or stolen in the previous two years. (Curiously, impersonation of the dead is now Britain's top form of identity theft. Almost a quarter of a million dead Britons had their identity stolen in 2007.)

Jonathan Bamford, the UK's assistant information commissioner (no, I didn't know we had an information commissioner, let alone one with an assistant) said in November 2008 that technology used by companies and public authorities made data security breaches an accident waiting to happen.

Mr Bamford said that too many institutions failed to ensure that they had the electronic tools to protect the confidential details they held. He added that embarrassing data losses by companies and government organisations were part of the price institutions were paying for bolting data security safeguards on as an afterthought rather than designing systems with them in mind.

'It was,' he said, 'obviously a bit of an accident waiting to happen. They are all things where people have messed up rather than acted in a malevolent way, which says a lot about what the safeguards were in the technology itself.'

During the year to October 2008, a total of 277 data security breaches were reported to the Information Commissioner's Office. Of these 80 were by private companies and 75 by the National Health Service and other health care providers. In all of these instances vast amounts of information was 'lost', 'mislaid' or 'stolen' through a mixture of incompetence, rank stupidity or dishonesty. In just one incident, the Revenue and Customs lost details relating to 25 million people. None of these bodies seem to learn anything from their mistakes. A year after HM Revenue and Customs (HMRC) had been publicly castigated for losing the personal data of half the country, it wrote to some taxpayers telling them that it would pass on their names and details to a market research company – unless told not to do so before next Tuesday. It seemed an arrogant way to mark the first anniversary of Britain's biggest ever data breach. One accountant said that he thought that for HMRC to pass information onto a third party might be a criminal offence. Government departments in general seemed to learn nothing from HMRC's loss.

Government agencies and private bodies seem to be still living in a pre-computer age. They demand information which they don't really need and then, seemingly unaware of the risks and hazards that identity theft can pose, treat that information quite carelessly. Many don't seem to realise just how vulnerable computers can be. 'The only system that is truly secure,' says Eugene H. Spafford, a professor of computer science and a leading security expert, 'is one that is switched off and unplugged, locked in a titanium safe, buried in a concrete vault on the bottom of the sea and surrounded by very highly paid armed guards. Even then I wouldn't bet on it.'

★ ★ ★

All fascist societies encourage citizens to spy on one another. It aids the state not just by suppressing defiance and increasing the number of people who can be arrested but also by spreading fear and causing suspicion and distrust. Thanks to official encouragement we have become a nation of sneaks. In a single year recently over 200,000 people telephoned a tax snitch line. Eight-year-old children are recruited by councils to spy on neighbours and to make sure they aren't putting too much of the wrong sort of rubbish in the wrong sort of bin on the wrong day of the week.

Snitching and sneaking isn't just encouraged by the people working for HMRC or the morally incontinent tyrants employed by your local council. Naturally, the Government uses the ever present threat of 'terrorism' as a reason to encourage us to put our loyalty to the State above our loyalty to friends and neighbours: we are all encouraged to snitch on people who might be terrorists. Some of the snitching is done out of 'duty'. Much of it is done because the Government doles out chunks of taxpayers' money to those who provide 'information leading to a conviction'.

There is no doubt that people are snooping and reporting one another with unprecedented enthusiasm. When I wrote a national newspaper column I received a letter from a reader who told me that her neighbour had taken delivery of a computer. 'Do you think I should report him to the police?' she asked. 'He might be a paedophile.' Another reader wrote to let me know that the washing her neighbour hung out on her line included underwear that was too big for her. 'I think her husband may be a transvestite,' wrote the reader. 'Should I inform the council?'

Nurses are encouraged to snitch on doctors if they don't approve of their prescriptions. Computer companies check out the hard drives of computers they repair – and if they spot anything of which they disapprove they telephone 'the authorities'. Lawyers and accountants and their staff are told (on pain of imprisonment) that they have to snitch on their clients if they suspect they might be doing something illegal. Banks snitch on their customers if they can't show where their money came from. Neighbours, friends and relatives are told to ring the appropriate authorities if they suspect that someone they know is claiming social security benefits to which they are not entitled. People operating photocopiers are often encouraged to snitch if they suspect that someone is copying something they shouldn't be copying. (The Formula One team Ferrari were alerted to the fact that one of their dossiers had been copied when they were alerted by an employee at a photo copy shop.)

The argument, of course, is that the end justifies the means. And that if a tax cheat or a social security cheat or a paedophile can be caught then we should all be prepared to share all our suspicions with the authorities. Encouraging people to grass on one another (and, indeed, receive a financial reward) might sound like good sense but in fact it is destructive. It creates fear and suspicion among the public, it damages communities enormously and it strengthens the power of the fascist state. No one objects to benefit cheats more than I do. But encouraging neighbours to sneak on one another is not the way to deal with this, or any other, problem.

How long will it before, like the old-time Venetians, our streets are festooned with special letterboxes wherein citizens can place accusations (founded or unfounded) about neighbours or relatives or people they just don't like and want to see destroyed.

This is not a society progressing; it is a society destroying itself; it is a society whose members are allowing the forces of evil to destroy everything noble and valuable with distrust and well-placed paranoia.

⋆ ⋆ ⋆

Sadly, and worryingly, most people don't seem in the slightest bit concerned by the way their privacy is disappearing. 'Why should I worry,' they say. 'I've got nothing to hide.' And if they have hair they doubtless toss it back with a self-satisfied and very superior sniff.

If you don't mind sharing your financial, health and personal secrets with the rest of the world I suppose that's fine. Assuming that you don't mind if some of the information is wrong and is used to decide whether or not you can travel, hold a bank account, own a house or have a vital operation then it doesn't matter. And assuming that you don't ever have any conversations that you would rather keep private then it doesn't matter.

Maybe those people will sit up and take notice when the authorities decide that we should all have numbers tattooed on our arms or have brands marked on our bums with a hot branding iron.

Actually, the tattoos and the branding irons will not be necessary.

There is already a plan to put microchips in newborn babies in Europe and America. The technology is ready.

'A good idea,' I can hear the idiots saying. 'If your baby gets mislaid you'll be able to find it in a trice.'

⋆ ⋆ ⋆

All this is going to get much, much worse. But there are a number of things you can do to protect your identity.

First, if a bank or other institution demands to see your passport, driving licence, birth certificate or gas bill then you should do exactly that: let them see it. And then take it away again. Here it is. See it? Whoosh. Now it's gone. Don't let them take a copy. I have done this many times. When a bank or solicitor (or whoever) demands to see private information (such as your passport, driving licence or latest gas bill) then you should do exactly that: let them see it. Allow them to see it but not to keep it. There is no legislation requiring you to hand over documents or copies of documents. There are rules requiring institutions and individuals to make sure that you are who you say you are. But that's all.

I have, on numerous occasions, allowed people to view documents but not to take copies. It's up to you whether you take my advice or not, of course, but if you are not wary about this then within a few years there will be dozens of copies of your valuable identity documents floating around out of your control. You may think that worrying about this is slightly paranoid but identity theft is now the fastest growing criminal activity in the country.

Second, if you need to post a copy of a private document (such as a bank statement or a gas bill or your driving licence) then write on the copy you are sending, the date and the fact that the copy is to be used solely by XY and Z (whoever it is to whom you are sending it). Then, even if the document is discarded carelessly, it will be of little use to anyone else.

Third, insist that any private documents which you are required to send in the post are returned to you by special delivery. It may help if you tell the person at the other end that they will be responsible if the documents are lost. Do this, for example, if you have to send your driving licence to a police force to be endorsed.

Fourth, never hand out visiting cards without first writing the date and your name on them. This prevents other people from using them and pretending to be you.

Fifth, never work or do private stuff on a computer you use for Internet access. Store valuable information on disks, not on hard drive, and put copies in safe places.

Sixth, never send anything by e-mail that you wouldn't be happy to see painted on a wall near your home. If you want to say something private, say it in a letter, put the letter in an envelope, put a stamp on the envelope and post it. It may be a little slower, but it is still by far the most secure way to communicate. Always use an e-mail address with your own name so that you will remember that it is not even private let alone secret.

Seventh, do not always sign trivial forms with the same signature as you use for legal documents or cheques. Do not use accurate information for trivial enquiries where it is not legally required.

Eighth, never use your passport for anything except passing through customs. If asked for ID, use a gas bill or tax form in preference to something more personal.

Ninth, always use a Post Office box for mail. This reduces the number of people who have access to your address. If anyone questions this (and they sometimes do) point out that banks and HM Revenue and Customs all accept a PO Box address.

Chapter 12

Public Trust And Faith In The Police Will Continue To Diminish

The relationship between the police and the public has deteriorated rapidly in recent years. Arrogance, conceit, an over-close relationship with politicians (who have damaged the police with their emphasis on targets) and a failure at high levels to understand the very purpose of the police has led to a crisis that seems destined to deteriorate still further.

The police were invented to protect the public. We paid them, they looked after us; that was the deal. Today, taxpayers still pay their wages but the police seem to think they exist to protect the State and its institutions the State's employees from the electorate. Taxpayers are simply the mugs who pay the bills (and are always good for a little extra in the form of speeding fines.) Sadly, ordinary, decent, law-abiding citizens are now more likely to see the police as a threat than a comfort

★ ★ ★

When the jury in the inquest into the death of Jean Charles de Menezes decided that a catalogue of police failings had contributed to the Brazilian's death they were merely confirming what every citizen in the country knew, and every politician and jurist seemed to want to deny: the public no longer have faith in the police or the courts.

The jury made it clear, with their verdict, that they believed the evidence offered by 17 members of the public who had witnessed the killing of de Menezes (who was shot seven times in the head, at point blank range, by officers using special bullets which have been banned for over a century) rather than the different evidence offered by the policemen involved.

(The 17 civilian witnesses were interviewed immediately and individually after the shooting so that they could not confer and influence one another. The policemen involved were allowed to prepare their statements together, conferring when they knew that the man they shot had been identified as innocent.)

The police bungled, bungled and bungled again and in a decent, free society there is no doubt that all the police officers involved would have been standing in a courtroom defending themselves on charges of murder.

I have little doubt that if the coroner hadn't banned the jury from bringing in a verdict of unlawful killing that is exactly the verdict they would have reached. (The coroner said that a verdict of 'unlawful killing' was not justified, though I would have thought that that was precisely what the jury was there to decide.) When two police marksmen shoot an entirely innocent man in the head at point blank range, when they already have him under control, it is difficult to see why in a free country the policemen involved, and their superiors, should not be charged with murder or manslaughter.

The policewoman in charge of the operation, Cressida Dick, was said to have overseen a chaotic and confused control room and there seems little doubt that numerous mistakes were made. But far from being censured Ms Dick was actually promoted.

* * *

The notion that the police should be allowed to shoot suspected (and that word is important) suicide bombers is terrifying. This is rampant, practical fascism.

How did Britain become a country where anyone thinks it is acceptable for the police to shoot an innocent man seven times in the head? And to then lie about what happened in an attempt to disguise the awfulness of what was done. (Let's not bother with words like 'spin' which somehow make it all sound rather less heinous than it is. Let's be blunt and call a lie a lie.)

An innocent bloke who gets on a tube train is slaughtered. No one resigns. No one is fired. No one takes responsibility. Nothing happens. There may have been an apology but if there was I missed it. The trigger-happy gunman who shot the electrician is presumably still wandering around London with a gun strapped to his waist.

Like most tax paying citizens, I want grovelling. I want policemen in prison for decades. I want them breaking rocks with their teeth and sewing mail bags until their fingers bleed.

We should never forget the simple facts: with guns and cars the police in Britain have killed more innocent people than terrorists have.

★ ★ ★

I have never understood why the shooting of a policeman should be regarded as more serious than the shooting of a member of the public. Or why the shooting of a member of the public by a policeman should be regarded by the authorities with such equanimity. It is difficult to avoid the conclusion that the establishment doesn't think much of the value of ordinary citizens but feels that the police, hired these days to protect the establishment and often regarded as representatives not of the community but the establishment, must be protected from unruly citizens at all costs.

Two robbers who killed a policewoman were, in December 2006, sentenced to at least 35 years each for her murder. They would not, of course, have received a quarter of that if they had killed a member of the public rather than a police officer. But the police are paid to take risks. Murderers of policemen and policewomen should, if there is to be a difference, receive less punishment not more. Harry Roberts served 40 years for shooting three plain clothes policemen. Would he have spent that long inside (and been kept in jail after his sentence ended) for killing three shopkeepers? Of course he wouldn't.

We send our soldiers to illegal wars and they die by the thousand without much public concern. But our police, who are paid far better and who are far less at risk, are also paid to risk their lives for us. They are well-paid not to patronise us or ignore us but to protect us and to take risks on our behalf. And it is absurd that we should regard a crime against a policeman as more serious than a crime against a citizen.

★ ★ ★

Sir Ian Blair who 'resigned' from his job as Chief of the Metropolitan Police in what some people might, in the past, have described as 'disgrace' was paid £253,000 a year (considerably more than the Prime Minister) and was expected to receive a pay-out of almost £300,000 – what he would have earned if he'd kept working until early 2010. In other words, his pay-out would add up to pretty much what he would have received if he'd stayed in his job. In 2010 he will receive an index-linked pension worth £168,000 a year.

★ ★ ★

The divide between the police and the public seems to be growing ever wider. Police officers are routinely breaking the speed limit with little prospect of being fined. According to statistics released under the Freedom of Information Act only 0.1% of policemen caught by speed cameras are fined. Very few of the cases where policemen are caught speeding involve emergencies.

Even more amazing is the fact that police officers with convictions for gun crimes, benefit fraud and violent attacks are still serving in the police force. Many of the crimes for which the policemen were convicted took place while the officers concerned were working, and supposedly protecting the public. These policemen should all be in prison. Instead, they are sitting in expensive cars parked on motorway bridges.

A lawyer I know told me that most policemen are crooks without the guts or initiative to be crooks. It seems that he was right.

And yet while policemen get away (often literally) with murder, the service provided for the public continues to deteriorate. Many police stations are now closed at night and weekends. If you want a policeman you have to telephone and speak to an operator who may be hundreds of miles away and knows nothing about your locality. This saves the State money but does nothing to help the individual. There are 143,000 policemen in Britain of whom 81,877 are paid to patrol (the rest are presumably too important to dirty their hands by coming into contact with the public or, heaven forbid, criminals). Most of the patrolling is, of course, done in cars these days. But, at any one time, only 2,400 of the policemen supposedly patrolling are actually outside their police station doing anything that could be described as patrolling. Most of the rest are off sick, undergoing extensive counselling to help them deal with the traumas of doing their work or busy with endless paperwork.

★ ★ ★

We spent one hour walking in Paris. We counted 17 policemen. We spent one hour walking in London. We didn't see any policemen at all.

★ ★ ★

In January 2008, the Home Secretary, Jacqui Smith, admitted that she would not feel safe walking the streets after dark. Three days earlier a judge attacked the do-gooder obsession with rights that has left Britain bedevilled by feral youths. In July 2008, the Mayor of London, blond twit Boris Johnson, told Londoners that he would tell his own children to look after themselves first rather than help a victim in distress. The reason? Simple. The risk from violent crime in London is now so high that people are advised to walk away if they see someone else in trouble – in case they end up losing their own life. Johnson's comments followed the knife murder of a 16-year-old who tried to break up an argument outside a bar.

Just before Christmas 2008, it was quietly revealed (in the way that these things are at times when no one will notice them much) that the police ignore four out of ten crimes because 'they are hard to crack'. (Reliable and specific statistics about crime are impossible to find. Politicians and civil servants are so debonair with the truth that no one with more than 10% of a brain trusts what politicians, Home Office officials or the police say any more.)

The police did, however, manage to arrest a 14-year-old girl for assault after she 'pinged' a classmate's bra. A grandmother was fined £80 after her 20-month-old granddaughter dropped a crisp packet on the pavement. The grandmother had picked up the packet, which the toddler had dropped, but had failed to notice that two crisps had fallen out and were lying, naked and dangerous, on the pavement. The authorities swooped and gave grannie an on-the-spot fine. Grampian police have wasted £170,000 repeatedly arresting a stripper for impersonating a policeman. The man, one of whose costumes is a police uniform, has so far been arrested 23 times. As yet none of his arrests has led to a conviction. And a 12-year-old boy was sent to court for assaulting a man with a sausage.

★ ★ ★

A shopkeeper who made a citizen's arrest of a thug who smashed his shop window was charged with kidnapping. He was taken to court and faced a maximum sentence of life in jail.

★ ★ ★

The ferry across the river Teign in Devon has been running since the 11th Century. It will now not operate after 9 p.m. because of the anti-social behaviour of drunken yobs on board the ferry.

★ ★ ★

Taxpayers would like the police to walk around our streets. This would make our cities, towns and villages much safer to live in. But the State prefers policemen to spend their time concentrating on surveillance and on gathering money. It is more profitable for the State if policemen concentrate on catching errant motorists than it is for them to spend their time preventing crime and ensuring that the world is as safe as it can be.

The relationship between taxpayers and the police has deteriorated dramatically and is clearly going to continue to deteriorate. The police have developed some very nasty habits. They shoot innocent people (and have earned the reputation of being trigger-happy) and they drive dangerously and cause far more than their fair share of accidents. When damages are paid it is taxpayers, not the guilty policemen, who have to find the money. The police rarely, if ever, apologise for their stupidity, arrogance, brutality and loutishness and are always defended and protected by politicians and the courts.

★ ★ ★

In late 2008, politicians had a taste of the world they have created when the police entered the House of Commons and arrested a Conservative MP, Damian Green, who was believed to have embarrassed the Government by producing evidence which showed that there was a gap between the Government's statements on immigration and its policy. Police tape recorded the arrest without bothering to obtain permission. (It occurs to me that if the police are going to start arresting people whenever it is shown that the Government has lied then we will need to start building a lot more prisons.) Ironically, the same politicians who have given the police extensive powers over ordinary people clearly found the arrest of Mr Green rather alarming. They also found it disturbing that the police were apparently allowed to enter the House of Commons without anyone asking to see a warrant. Even the *Daily Mail*, a great and usually loyal supporter of Gordon Brown was shocked and published this comment on its front page: 'To say this was an act of political intimidation, executed by a police force rapidly becoming an arm of the State, is no exaggeration. The Damian Green saga shows chief constables, civil servants and politicians can't be trusted with the totalitarian powers Labour has spent ten years introducing.'

Of course, some commentators dismissed the whole episode as irrelevant and insignificant, particularly at a time when many people were worrying about losing their jobs. But in reality the Green saga was important for if no one dares share the truth there is no democracy. Once truth is suppressed, that's it until the revolution.

The Labour Government didn't seem worried. The man said to have been ultimately responsible for the arrest of Mr Green was later appointed the new Metropolitan Police commissioner.

★ ★ ★

The incidence of youth crime is growing at a scary rate. This letter recently appeared in the *Daily Telegraph*: 'A couple I know were recently walking home when they were set on by eight youths, who proceeded to beat up both of them and leave them in a pool of blood. Nothing was stolen – they had mobiles and money – and the youths were not known to them. It appeared to just be violence for fun. This behaviour is new.'

The behaviour may be new to Britain but the concept isn't as anyone who has read *Clockwork Orange* (book by Anthony Burgess, film by Stanley Kubrich) will know. Burgess realised that without structure, discipline and purpose young people will always seek some replacement. And violence, for its own sake, is an easy solution.

★ ★ ★

The targets the police set themselves are revealing.

Here are the target figures published for one police force (though I believe these are roughly appropriate for most police forces in England):

- Target for detection rate of all crime: 28%
- Target for detection of domestic burglary: 20%
- Target for robbery detection: 24%
- Target for detecting hate crime: 40%

- Target for satisfaction with information available on local policing: 38%
- Target for satisfaction on overall service provided by the police: 85%

These unambitious and woeful targets hardly need comment, apart from to point out that the target for detecting 'hate' crime is precisely twice that for detecting robberies.

The detection rate is not helped by the fact that huge amounts of public money are now spent on the utterly pointless Community Support Officers who parade our streets, masquerading as 'bobbies on the beat' but, sadly, fooling no one. The average Blunkett Bobby (these rather sad and scruffy nonentities are named after the disastrous Home Secretary who introduced them in 2002) detects less than one crime every four years. Boy scouts equipped with whistles could probably do better.

* * *

The one 'criminal' all police forces are keen to target is the errant motorist. Catching speeding motorists is much easier (and considerably more profitable) than catching murderers, rapists and burglars. And it is the largely legal motorist who is targeted by the police.

The laws apply only to those who agree to be oppressed. There are two million unlicensed, untaxed, uninsured drivers in Britain. They escape speeding fines, congestion charges and parking tickets. Instead of going after these motorists the authorities simply concentrate on those law-abiding citizens who play by the rules. It is, of course, much easier to target the law-abiding citizen going about his daily work than it is to target the potentially dangerous criminal or the immigrant who claims to speak no English and who will demand the services of an expensive translator.

The number of speeding tickets issued has trebled since Labour came to power. (There are other ways to make money out of motorists. Putting cameras on traffic lights is another good source of income. Authorities have found that if they shorten the time for which the amber light shows they will catch far more motorists going through the red light.)

One result of this policy will be that the number of accidents on our roads will increase. The number of people killed on the roads will inevitably also increase.

For some years now the police have been putting more and more effort into operating speed cameras (which are designed and installed solely to make money) rather than preventing accidents. This tendency will increase as the Government and local authorities find themselves searching for ways to make more and more money.

The number of road traffic accidents could be cut fairly dramatically if the police concentrated on catching motorists who drive when drunk or drugged (the biggest problem is motorists who drive when taking sleeping tablets, anti-depressants or tranquillisers) or on removing from the roads motorists (including many immigrants) who have never taken a driving test or who have been banned from driving.

But the police won't do this. They will carry on with their moneymaking activities.

Our roads will also become more dangerous as the number of ambulances falls (partly because the authorities who run them don't have the money to provide a decent service and partly because the people who crew the ambulances demand better working conditions and shorter working hours). And the absence of money for mending roads or improving signage will also contribute to the number of accidents.

★ ★ ★

There are, officially, a million violent crimes a year in Britain, but fewer than half are solved by the police. (The number of violent crimes is undoubtedly far more than a million. Many people no longer bother to report crimes to the police at all – complaining that even when the police are informed no policeman turns up to investigate.) Yobs and hooligans roam our streets unpunished. Members of the public who dare to protest or stand up to the yobs are the ones the police arrest. It is, after all, far easier to arrest a law-abiding middle aged man or woman than it is to chase after a fleet-footed hooligan who might be carrying a knife.

In the same way that the Americans haven't attacked North Korea because it has got big bombs, so the police won't chase after hoodies because they have knives. Both prefer to bully the weak and easily conquered.

Even when thugs are arrested they have a good chance of avoiding any sort of serious punishment. More than half of all violent or repeat offenders escape a prison term. The Institute for the Study of Civil Study found that 60% of offenders convicted on more than 15 previous occasions are not sent to prison after being found guilty of a serious, indictable offence in a Crown Court. And they also found that more than 70% of criminals convicted of 'violence against the person' in 2007 were not jailed. The number of robbers sent to prison has fallen from 72% in 2002 to 54% in 2007. Altogether, less than a quarter of serious offenders are sent to prison. Why do we have policemen, courts, judges and prisons? We might as well dump the lot and save the money. If we shared out the money saved, every law-abiding citizen could build a wall around their home, buy a gun and protect themselves, their families and their property.

★ ★ ★

Even photographing thugs is now apparently against the law. When a law-abiding citizen took photographs of a gang who were terrorising his neighbourhood he was told by a Police Community Support Officer that he could be charged with assault for taking the photos. And when passengers on a train organised a whip-round to help buy a ticket for a pensioner who had, on the instructions of train staff, boarded the wrong train the guard threatened to call the police and have the organiser of the whip-round arrested. It seems that in modern Britain no good deed will go unpunished.

Meanwhile, the police seem far more concerned with attempting to use spin to protect their image. In 2007 British police forces spent £39,400,000 on public relations. The money would have paid for the salaries of 1,400 new policemen. (The police are so keen on public relations that it is not uncommon for them to be accompanied by press photographers when they arrest prominent citizens.)

The police now shoot more innocent people than are shot by burglars. One man was shot by the police because they thought that the chair leg he was carrying was a gun.

And, of course, the police have the right to stop and interrogate anyone, even if no crime is suspected.

All this is going to get worse. I see no end to the rise in police powers or the rise in crime in Britain.

Chapter 13

The Coming Decline Of Sterling, The Euro And The Dollar

Faith in currencies depends upon belief and trust more than anything else. The world has lost trust in Britain and its currency. The Europeans have lost trust in the euro. And the world knows that America is up to the Canadian border in debt.

Shares and Government bonds don't have any objective value. They are just bits of paper. Like currency. A twenty pound note is only worth twenty pounds if you believe that the Government which has issued the note is honest and honourable and has the wealth to back up the 'promise' behind its currency. A bond certificate is only worth what you pay for it if you believe that the issuer of the certificate is honest and honourable. People buy bonds and shares (and oil paintings) because they believe that these items have a value. They can be sold to other people and, if necessary, exchanged for goods. If you have a twenty pound note you can swap it for a basketful of groceries.

Faith in currencies and bonds and shares (and everything else) depends upon belief and trust. If people lose faith in a company which has issued shares then the value of the shares will fall. If people lose faith in a nation which has issued a currency then the value of the currency will fall. It was Nikolai Lenin, founder of the Soviet Union, who said that the best way to destroy the capitalist system is to debase the currency.

The value of currency depends on trust. People who hold

currency (whether it is pounds, dollars or euros) have to trust the banks which issue it and the countries behind it. They have to trust because there is no longer anything behind the currency. In the good old days governments only issued currency if they had gold in their vaults to back up their promises. Today, the promises are all you get.

Predicting short-term currency movements is impossible. Lots of people try it. And many of them lose a lot of money.

But I'm prepared to make guesses about long-term changes.

1. The long-term future for the euro is glum. During the financial crisis of 2008 individual nations all did their own thing. There was little sign of unity among the various euro nations. I have for years, believed that the euro will not survive.
2. When the USA Government (or, indeed, any other government) spends more money than it takes in, it meets the deficit by printing more bonds. The printing presses enable the Government (and the people) to keep spending. The interest on America's debt is now running at $406 billion a year. That's a staggering $1.38 billion a day. China, Japan and the oil-producing nations in the Middle East, each hold hundreds of billions in dollars. The only way to finance this sort of ongoing debt is through inflation – in other words by depreciating the value of the dollar. America's gross national debt is now $8,883,212,488,519. (Well, it was when I started this sentence. Now that I've finished writing that sentence it is, of course, considerably greater. And now that you're reading this sentence the debt total is much, much greater.) When George W. Bush fiddled his way into the presidency, America's national debt was $5.7 trillion.

   All the figures relating to America are horrifying. The USA trade deficit is more than three quarters of a trillion dollars a year. The dollar is America's IOU to the world. There are effectively trillions of them stuffed in vaults, wallets and boxes under the bed all over the world. Companies and governments have got them too. They all think that dollars are a paper equivalent of gold. But the more dollars the Americans print the fewer the assets behind them. The Americans long, long ago failed to have enough gold to cover all the paper they've issued.

   Americans have for years enjoyed a huge advantage from the fact that the USA dollar is the world's currency. America's bankers have been able to speed up the printing presses and just create more money. It really is a huge confidence trick. De Gaulle complained about the way the Americans used the dollar. It is, he said, an 'exorbitant advantage...that the Americans can pay the rest of the world with a currency whose value they control'.

Other countries have been forced to increase their supply of their own currencies in order to keep up with the rapidly increasing number of dollars in print. The link between currencies and gold has long since been forgotten. The world has for several decades now enjoyed a wild, dream-like and unprecedented period of madness

The dollar is the international currency and the American Government also controls the World Bank. The system therefore favours America to the detriment of all other nations. What irony it is that while the rest of the world is subject to the market discipline dictated by Washington, the USA is exempt. The unfairness of the system is illustrated by the fact that the subprime crisis which led to the crash of 2008 originated in the USA and yet did far more damage to the rest of the world than it did to America.

At the end of 2008, the American dollar strengthened not because people believed in America or wanted to support or encourage America but partly because so many nations and investors were so deeply committed to the dollar that they could not escape its hold and partly because the dollar was still regarded as a safe haven currency protected to a large extent by a bullying and entirely self-serving Government.

★ ★ ★

The Americans, who tell everyone they are the world's richest people, save almost nothing and depend entirely for their wealth upon the hard work and thrift of the citizens of other nations. The Americans have borrowed billions of dollars from the poor. Rich, overweight Americans driving around in petrol guzzling, air-conditioned, planet-destroying SUVs are doing so on tick. Contrary to their belief, their wealth is not created by their own hard work, or by their nation's natural resources, but by their Government's determination to keep the printing presses running, churning out a constant supply of increasingly worthless dollars. Foreigners who put their earnings and their savings into dollar based investments (such as USA Treasury bonds) are subsidising the American way of life.

The world now depends upon the dollar. The Chinese (holders of billions of US dollars) are willing to defend the value of the American currency so that they can continue to trade with America. But the dollar is now built on debt. And the end is nigh.

As long as oil is bought and sold in dollars the world's central banks are forced to stockpile American dollars regardless of their value. The world has to buy and use dollars to purchase oil because that is how oil is valued and how it's sold.

In order to remain solvent – and a superpower – America has to continue to control the global economic system by preserving the relationship between oil and the dollar. And in order to preserve that relationship America has to control the oil.

Middle Eastern nations have made no secret of the fact that they would like oil to be bought and sold in another currency – probably euros. They are getting rid of the link between their own currencies and the dollar.

The Americans cannot possibly allow that to happen.

That, above all else, is why they have to own the oil.

And that is why they had to start their illegal war in Iraq.

★ ★ ★

Kuwait has already abandoned the direct link between its currency and the American dollar. Other middle eastern countries are considering doing likewise. China only maintains a loose link because of the trading advantages. (China has, however, in the summer of 2007 announced that it will pull out of investing in American Treasury bills and invest instead in American companies and property. Washington was able to steal China's money by simple printing more currency. It will not be able to deal with this development quite so easily.)

★ ★ ★

The poor around the world (and in America) subsidise rich Americans. The Americans save nothing and spend more than they earn. Where does their money come from? It comes from poor people in Africa and Asia who earn very little but who save great percentages of their earnings and whose governments put their money into buying dollars. This keeps the dollar strong and enable the Americans to keep buying television sets made in China and cars made in Korea.

★ ★ ★

The world is currently playing poker.

Or, perhaps more accurately, a huge game of pass the parcel.

No one wants the game to stop.

Everyone knows that once the dollar starts to collapse it won't stop going down.

The Chinese, the Japanese and the rest don't want to be the first to dump their dollars.

But they don't want to be last either.

Everyone knows that whoever is left holding the dollars when they really start collapsing will be in deep, deep trouble. Foreign banks don't want to dump their dollars because they know they might be starting a crash which will not only destroy their holdings but also destroy their future business.

When the crash comes everything will change. America will no longer have a powerful role in the world.

A few years ago President Clinton set up a commission to look into America's balance of trade problem. The commission concluded that the American people had to start saving and that America as a nation had to stop spending more than it was genuinely earning.

The commission's report was ignored. It is still being ignored.

Lester Thurow, who was a member of the Clinton commission, concluded that no one would believe that America's balance of trade problem could produce a crisis until it happened.

Then they'll believe it.

★ ★ ★

The American dollar will probably rise in the short-term (because it is still regarded as something of a safe haven) but it will eventually decline against just about every currency in the world. America will be destroyed not by terrorists but by greed and debt. The Americans have been printing dollars as fast as they can for as long as they have been able to. The USA dollar increases in quantity at a speed up to ten times faster than GDP growth. USA dollar denominated derivative contracts now have a nominal value equal to 12 times the total output of the entire world.

★ ★ ★

The rise in the dollar which occurred in 2008 was partly a technical consequence of deleveraging. As American investment companies and hedge funds sold their assets abroad (to pay off their debts) they took the money back to America, pushing up the dollar. As the world's only reserve currency the American dollar also benefited from a reputation as a safe harbour in a crisis. In truth, the American dollar was a broken currency before the credit crunch hit. By the beginning of 2009, America was effectively bankrupt, totally indebted to foreigners. In the medium to long-term the dollar does not look like a safe haven unless the American economy suddenly starts to soar. It's difficult to see that happening. European governments want the euro to be the world's new No 1 currency. China wants the renminbi to be the No 1. And Russia wants the rouble to be No 1.

There are wonderful advantages to being No 1. Other countries have to hold your currency because it is used for international trade. And when other countries have to hold your currency you control the world. It is because their currency has been the unchallenged No 1 for so long that America is now global top dog. Things will soon change.

3. The Great British Pound is now surely the weakest currency in the world. Its prospect is absolutely dire. Thanks to Gordon Brown's policies, sterling will become steadily weaker. The collapse in sterling, which occurred at the end of 2008, was a clear sign that Brown's policies were regarded as typically moronic. The *Wall Street Journal* noted that Brown's plans to cut taxes by further borrowing were unlikely to stimulate anything except perhaps his approval ratings. Brown's policies destroyed the currency but they also built up huge debt burdens for future

generations to pay. Exporters (the few remaining) will benefit, of course. They will be able to bring back foreign currencies and enjoy improved profits. And tourists coming to the UK will enjoy cheaper prices in hotels and restaurants. (I have a suspicion that the only people buying houses will be foreigners attracted by the weak pound. They will be the only people able to afford houses.) But everyone else will lose out. Britain imports far more stuff than it exports. And now that our oil has darned near run out we have to export huge amounts of oil too. The Government will find that foreign investors will be unwilling to lend such a hugely indebted country any money without receiving a higher rate of interest. The Americans have, for years, dealt with such problems by simply printing more money. But the dollar has for years now been the world's reserve currency. The GBP is not a reserve currency these days. And if the Government prints more money the value will simply go down even faster. Brown's inexplicable and indefensible policy of trying to solve a problem caused by too much borrowing and too much spending of money we didn't have by borrowing more and spending more may make sense on a planet somewhere else in the galaxy but on this one it doesn't. In the end it is quite likely that Britain will have to beg the International Monetary Fund for a hand out to avoid bankruptcy. In 1992 (before he became Chancellor) Gordon Brown said: 'A weak currency arises from a weak economy, which in turn is a result of a weak government.' For once in his life he was right.

4. The Chinese have a strong incentive to devalue their currency as their economy slows. This would help their economy but it would be pretty disastrous for the rest of the world. I can't see the Chinese worrying too much about the rest of the global economy. The Americans have, for years, set an example of national selfishness.

Chapter 14

Commodities In General Will Surge In Price

All valuable commodities are running out. The big developing countries (particularly China, India, Brazil and Russia) need vast amounts of everything. The world will recover from the coming slump but Britain won't. And so the rise in commodity prices will hit Britain hard (and will contribute to the inflation problem.)

Thanks to Gordon Brown and his bunch of half-witted Scottish pals, Britain will be buggered for a decade or more. But the rest of the world will recover much sooner. And once the rest of the world has dealt with the current economic mess things will start to recover quite quickly. China and India will start building roads, bridges, factories, skyscrapers and airports again. And they will need vast quantities of steel, concrete, copper and all the other stuff you need to build things.

At the end of 2008 and the beginning of 2009, miners were cutting supply as quickly as they could. As commodity prices fell they abandoned new projects and shut down the mines that could be shut down. Lower prices meant that many mines simply weren't viable financially.

This inevitably means that if demand goes back up again there will be a dramatic shortage of commodities such as zinc, nickel and aluminium.

In addition, many developing countries have become more conscious of the value of their mineral rights. They are charging companies more to extract essential and valuable minerals. And they are introducing comprehensive health and safety legislation which makes mining far more expensive. And the rising cost of oil will mean that extracting materials from the earth becomes ever more expensive. Finally, in South Africa it has become clear that the electricity supply is inadequate to provide for the needs of the mines.

And so commodity prices will eventually soar.

The big demand for commodities now comes not from the West (which is bloated and failing fast) but from the East. The commodities boom which ended in 2008 was driven by demands from China and India. The analysts, economists and commentators who say that the commodity boom was a bubble are clearly convinced that China and India will now stop growing. They obviously believe that the massive (and rapidly growing) populations of the new superpowers are going to be happy with the progress they've made.

I don't believe that for an instant.

China and India are soon going to be growing again.

And as a result the prices of metals such as nickel, aluminium, steel and copper will soar.

Metals will, of course, become more expensive for Britain too.

And since, thanks to Gordon Brown, Britain is now impoverished, and the currency weakened, these essential metals are going to seem very expensive for anyone left living in Britain.

When commodity prices rise they will, inevitably, add to the rising inflation which is going to be Britain's biggest future problem.

* * *

Just about every major country in the world except France and Britain is building masses of nuclear power stations. France isn't building loads of new nuclear power stations because it did this decades ago. Britain isn't building nuclear power stations because the country has, for a generation or more, been run by complete idiots who seem to have put their faith in the hope that someone will invent a perpetual motion machine.

But while Britain shivers and begs the Russians to let us have a little fuel, the rest of the world will be hunting for uranium supplies.

And everyone in the world except Gordon Brown and Alistair Darling can tell you what happens when a lot of people want to buy something that is available only in relatively limited quantities.

The price will go up.

This will be bad for a lot of countries who will have to fork out the higher prices.

But it will be good for Canada and Australia which have vast amounts of uranium to sell to the rest of the world. Those two countries will become rich. Their currencies may appreciate. And I have a strong suspicion that people who have invested in uranium mines will get rich too.

Since I'm not Canadian or Australian I can only think of two ways that I can share in this boom.

I'm buying uranium. And I'll be buying shares in mines that dig the stuff out of the ground.

★ ★ ★

It may seem strange to refer to water as a commodity. But that's what it is.

And, believe it or believe it not, the stuff is running out just as surely as the oil is running out.

Here's a quote from my book *Food for Thought* (1994): 'The world's freshwater shortage is being made worse by animal farmers. And meat producers are the biggest polluters of water. It takes 2,500 gallons of water to produce one pound of meat. If the meat industry in America wasn't supported by the taxpayer paying a large proportion of its water costs then hamburger meat would cost $35 a pound.'

The world is running out of water. And, unlike oil, there is no possible substitute. Heavy subsidies in many parts of the world mean that clean, uncontaminated water (something of a rarity in many countries) is often grossly underpriced. The result is that, like anything cheap, it is squandered.

The five big food and beverage giants (Nestle, Unilever, Coca-Cola, Anheuser-Busch and Danone) directly consume almost 575 billion litres of water a year. And that is enough to satisfy the daily needs of every person on the planet. Their products also consume vast quantities of water when they are growing.

Similarly, clothing firms which rely on cotton need enormous amounts of water to produce their goods.

A water shortage would not only be catastrophic for individuals, it would also result in many industries grinding to a halt.

★ ★ ★

I think the price of precious metals (gold, platinum and silver) will continue to rise erratically but purposefully. As inflation begins to soar and paper currencies crumble so more and more investors will turn to gold.

Chapter 15

Food Prices Will Soar Again

The Chinese people have discovered the joy of eating hamburgers. And everything else you might have heard about agriculture is irrelevant. Neither genetic engineering nor controlling the weather will prevent food prices from soaring.

There's a general feeling among analysts, economists and financial commentators that the food price rises that ended in 2008 were a bubble rather than a secular change. Many claim to have been surprised by what happened. The director of Friends of the Earth was quoted as having claimed that no one could have predicted the coincidence (of high oil prices, poor harvests, rising food demand and high biofuel production) that has caused the food price rise.

I think the analysts, economists and commentators are all wrong. (And, for the record, I predicted the food price rise that seemed to surprise so many.)

Moreover, I think the price of food will soon start rising again.

My reasons are simple.

1. The world's population is growing.
2. The amount of good agricultural land available is diminishing. Farmers have worked their soil too hard over recent decades. Many farms, particularly in the USA and Europe, are now trying to grow crops on very poor soil. It is, of course, possible to solve part of the problem by dumping vast quantities of fertiliser onto the ground. But to make fertiliser you need oil. And the price of oil, having taken a breather in the second half of 2008, is about to start soaring upwards again.

3. The people of China (and the rest of Asia) are no longer going to be content to live on a bowl of rice a day. They want meat. At least once a day. They want the sort of balanced diet enjoyed by Americans: a cheeseburger in each hand. And that's the key. If China's urbanisation continues and the country imports just 5% more of its grain, the entire world's grain exports will be swallowed up. And it is likely that China will import a lot more than 5% because urban developments are encroaching on previously rich farmland. Another problem is that quality land is being used for high profit crops such as vegetables and flowers.
4. According to a report from the United Nations' Food and Agriculture Organisation the financial crisis of 2008 will adversely affect agricultural sectors in many developing countries with plantings and output being reduced so much that a food crisis develops. The report notes that most of the extra production that has occurred recently took place in developed countries where farmers were in a better position to respond to high prices.
5. The rise in food prices which took place in 2007/8 increased the number of undernourished people in the world to an estimated 938 million.
6. The oppressive effect of the Common Agricultural Policy (which has, in the past, resulted in the EU intermittently dumping unwanted food in developing countries) is responsible for the failure of developing countries to acquire decent home-grown food. Subsidies in America and the EU mean that the production costs of many foods are kept falsely low. Prices have been kept below production costs and have held back the development of commercially viable farming in developing countries.
7. The shortage of suitable land, the shortage of water and the failure to invest in rural infrastructure have held back the production of food in countries where it is needed. Financial problems in developed countries mean that very little money will be made available for improvements in this area. America, the world's richest country, is the world's meanest country and has always refused to contribute much of its wealth to help developing countries.

8. American companies which have patented seeds, and made it illegal for farmers to grow crops which they have been growing for centuries, will contribute to the problem. If a serious problem arises with genetically manipulated foods then we will all be in big trouble. What's the likelihood of that happening? Somewhere between 'quite high' and 'inevitable'.
9. Governments, including the EU and the USA, are still committed to using food as fuel. Despite the evidence showing that this is an absurd and inefficient practice, vast amounts of food simply ends up in fuel tanks. Around 34 billion litres of ethanol is added to American petrol every year. Barack Obama is a firm advocate of ethanol. Mr Obama also just happens to have been a senator in Illinois, the corn-growing state. The politically correct and politically expedient enthusiasm for biofuels means that around 20% of America's corn crop goes into petrol tanks rather than hungry stomachs. Such madness must inevitably mean that food prices will rise.

* * *

In 1994, in my book *Food for Thought* I wrote: 'Half the rainforests in the world have been destroyed to clear ground to graze cattle to make beefburgers. The burning of the forests contributes 20% of all greenhouse gases. Roughly 1,000 species a year become extinct because of the destruction of the rain forests. Approximately 260 million acres of US forest have been cleared to grow crops to feed cattle so that people can eat meat. Every year 440 million tons of grain are fed to livestock – so that the world's rich can eat meat. At the same time 500 million people in poor countries are starving to death. All those lives could be saved (because those people could eat the grain used to fatten cattle and other farm animals) if Americans ate 10% less meat. One hundred acres of land will produce enough beef for 20 people but enough wheat to feed 240 people.'

One thing has changed since I wrote that: several hundred million Chinese have started eating meat.

Of course, if you believe that the Chinese will be content to go back to living as impoverished peasants then food prices won't rise.

* * *

What Happens Next?

At the end of 2008, after the most fantastic harvest the world had ever had, the world's stockpiles of food were at their third lowest level since World War II.

★ ★ ★

When food prices fell during 2008, Gordon Brown claimed that he was responsible. It seems such an absurd claim that I now think I might have imagined him saying it. I rather lost count of the things that Gordon was claiming credit for just as I rather lost count of the things he was saying weren't his fault.

Not that it matters much.

The thing that matters is that food prices are soon going to start rising again.

The world's population has tripled in a remarkably short time. We have managed to continue to feed most of these new additions to the population by using oil to improve our agricultural techniques. But now the oil is running out fast. And although the demand for food is rocketing the supply is diminishing rapidly. Why would the cost not go up?

As food prices rise there will be a revival of protectionism in major food growing nations such as the USA and the nations of the EU. Export bans will be introduced and speculators (still in business because their banks have been bailed out by the American and British governments) will doubtless drive up the price of what food there is. There are also likely to be riots as hungry people protest about the lack of food – and the price of what is available.

If you have the opportunity I suggest that you start growing your own food. And, if you eat meat and care for the world's plight, you might like to think about turning vegetarian.

Chapter 16

Resentment Against Scroungers Will Rise

Britain, once a great nation of writers, artists, explorers, adventurers and traders, has become a nation dominated by, ruled by and best known for its scroungers.

It is right and proper that a nation should support those among it who cannot support themselves. The elderly, the genuinely disabled, the mentally handicapped – all need to be cared for and provided for. It's an expensive business but it is an essential responsibility of a civilised society.

But the problem is that many of the people now demanding to be supported are not genuinely in need of care and support. They want to be provided for but they don't *need* to be provided for. They are, in short, scroungers and layabouts. Millions claim benefits as though it is a god-given right; a genuine alternative to work and self-reliance. Thirty per cent of all households receive half or more of their income from the State.

A huge proportion of Britain's population do no work. Many have never done any work. Moreover they do not intend to do any work. But millions who claim benefits are perfectly capable of working. They choose to stay at home because it's a better option than bothering to go out to work. There are now whole families in Britain for whom 'State benefits' of one sort or another are a career option. Successive Governments have allowed this to happen. And since 1997 the Labour Government has positively encouraged it. Since Labour came to power in 1997 there has been a 60% rise in the number of those under 25 claiming benefit. One in five children in the UK now live in households dependent on benefits. Around 3.5 million people in Britain have been claiming benefits for more than two years.

Around 150,000 families in Britain receive over £20,000 a year each in benefits. That's more than the average household income. You'd have to be insane to work for a living and not feel resentful about whole townfuls of perfectly healthy, able bodied people slumped in front of the television set every afternoon with a six pack and a packet of fags when you're working and worrying about paying the mortgage. (I'm hardly exaggerating by talking about whole townfuls of people living on benefits. Out of the 4,500 residents of Falinge, Rochdale only 300 work – despite hundreds of jobs being available. Most of the rest are 'on the sick'. It pays better than simply being out of work. In Merthyr Tydfil, South Wales, one in five residents has been claiming benefits for more than two years. There are, all over Britain, families where no one has worked for three generations. The words that describe them best are: defiant, aggressive, demanding, grasping, work-shy and self-pitying. I know of one family where unemployed family members berated, belittled and ostracised a daughter who married a man with a job.)

Resentment about Britain's vast army of lazy, taxpayer-funded scroungers is bound to explode. Why wouldn't it? Many of the scroungers are immigrants and asylum seekers who have arrived in England (only rarely in Scotland), had families and now live off the State. It is an unsustainable situation. While taxpayers support an endless stream of foreigners, genuinely disabled Englishmen and women die of cold and hunger. Disabled Englishmen and women cannot get the help they need to sustain even basic needs. English taxpayers who have worked hard for years have to wait months for life-saving surgery.

There is also anger about the number of people claiming benefits who earn extra money by moonlighting. Part-time fiddling, 'ducking and diving', doing a bit of 'dealing' or performing odd jobs, might be quite funny on television situation comedies but it is not so funny in real life. The elderly are ripped off by fly-by-night workmen and honest, tax paying tradesmen are put out of business because they cannot compete with the prices charged by people who have no overheads, obey no rules and pay no tax.

The cost of supporting all these scroungers has to be measured in tens of billions of pounds a year. And lavish welfare states of this kind are simply unsustainable when most of the people accepting benefits are doing so not because they are needy but because they are wanty. Never before in the history of mankind (and nowhere else in the world) has a nation supported so many lazy cheats.

Every year or two a Government will stamp its feet and say that something must be done about this. There will be much talk of encouraging people to go to work. New schemes will be set up (at vast expense). Armies of advisers and consultants will be hired (again at vast expense).

But the Labour Government doesn't want to solve this problem. They know that they can stay in power with little more than the votes of the scroungers. And the scroungers (worried that the rules might be tightened up if a Conservative Government gets into power) are always going to vote Labour.

The few extra votes the Government needs to stay in power come from its own employees. (Civil servants, worried that a different Government might cut the public payroll, will vote for the politicians who gave them their jobs.)

All this means that Britain is now controlled by people who don't do any work and who contribute nothing whatsoever to the nation's prosperity.

★ ★ ★

The Government's programme of welfare support means that increasing numbers of people are now content to lie back and let their nation look after them. Instead of encouraging and rewarding self-sufficiency the Government is encouraging dependence. This is not going to be easy to cure.

There are millions of citizens in Britain today who genuinely believe that the State owes them a living. They seem to assume that the State has a duty to provide them with money and services and they never seem to question the origin of either. Their dependence on the State is the reason for their loyalty to the State. They will keep voting for the fascist State because it cares for them.

And there seems to be no end to people's expectations. For example, some women now claim that they should be given a salary for having babies. Apart from being unaffordable this would be disastrous; encouraging the feckless fecund and penalising (with extra taxes) the conscientious and prudent. (So it would have probably happened if Brown hadn't destroyed the economy.)

★ ★ ★

The genuinely needy (the mentally handicapped and the elderly for example) are deprived of the money and support they need because the scroungers know how to work the system. And once the scroungers have taken what they want there is very little left for the people who need but can't or won't demand on their own behalf.

Britain has an annual 'social protection' budget of £169 billion. That's what we spend on supporting the unemployed and the millions who have chosen to live their lives claiming sickness benefits in preference to working. Nearly six million Britons are on 'out of work' benefits. This number (like the number of public sector workers) has risen at an astronomical rate during Labour's tenure in government. How long will it be before the number of people gorging themselves off taxpayers is greater than the number of people doing real work and paying tax? The utterly mad system of tax credits, combined with the wider enthusiasm for means-testing, has helped to create and strengthen generations of dependant scroungers. There are thousands of children now growing up in families where their parents and grandparents have never worked. Children are taught to take advantage of the benefits system. There is no sense of responsibility. Children are taught to take rather than to give.

★ ★ ★

My wife spoke to a beggar the other day. She told me that he was concerned about (and depressed by) the state of the nation's economy. He said he had been offered a job but didn't want to take it in case the company went bust and he was left high and dry. He was, it seems, enjoying a comfortable living from the benefits he received from the State and the additional contributions he received from pedestrians who walked past his pitch in the street. He happily admitted that if he got a job he would lose his benefits and his pitch.

It isn't widely recognised but many of the beggars on our streets are people already receiving social security payments but seeking to supplement their income with additional money.

★ ★ ★

Parents who earn less than £50,000 a year would be better off splitting up because of the fact that tax and benefit systems are designed to favour lone parents. What sort of madness is that? Government figures show there are officially 1.9 million single parents in the UK. But there are 2.1 million sole parents claiming benefits or tax credits. This must mean that around 200,000 are cheating. Lone parents are five times as likely to be receiving benefits as couples. Government policy discourages marriage and encourages fraud.

Our town and city streets are dominated by young, single mothers pushing expensive two-seater pushchairs. Having illegitimate children has become a career option for thousands of young women. The more you have the richer you become. The Government rewards irresponsibility. Providing extra benefits to single mothers (so that they would have the same financial resources as families) meant a rise in fatherlessness and welfare dependency and a rise in the number of teenage girls deliberately getting pregnant as a career move as well as a badge of honour.

★ ★ ★

Back in 1993, Gordon Brown didn't seem keen on means-testing. It is even possible that he thought it unfair. He certainly promised the end of the means-testing for the elderly. But he's a politician and so since 1997 he has fallen in love with, and massively extended, means-testing. Means-testing undermines the incentive to work, punishes the thrifty and discourages people from getting married. It has become one of Gordon Brown's basic tenets.

It has sometimes seemed as though the Government has deliberately chosen policies which will encourage people to avoid work. (It is perhaps worth remembering that Lo Scroccone – the scrounger – was the name given to Tony Blair by the Italian media because of his fondness for freebie holidays.) For example, the system of tax credits introduced by the Government means that the poorest people in Britain pay up to 90% of their earnings in tax if they work hard and attempt to escape from their poverty. Where is the incentive to pull yourself out of poverty if the Government taxes you at a rate of 90%? The Labour Government's means-tested benefits, and higher taxes, have reduced the incentive to work.

Incidentally, even fines are now means-tested. When ID cards are introduced (and it becomes compulsory to carry them at all times) the Government plans to fine people for non-compliance. If you are found in the street without your ID card you will be fined. If you fail to inform the authorities about any change in your personal details you will be fined. But, says the Government, 'some people may find it easier to pay a penalty for non-compliance than others' and so, guess what, if you are a scrounger living on benefits your non-compliance fine will be far less onerous than if you are working and pay tax.

And charities now often only provide help for people who are on benefits. This extension of the means-testing philosophy is cruel. It means that the hard-working poor are constantly discriminated against and disadvantaged. It also means that people are discouraged from getting work because they know that if they accept work they will lose even more benefits. Too many people are better off, in every sense, by choosing not to work. Charities which apply means-testing rules are doing more harm than good.

The Government has even threatened to use means testing to decide who gets (and doesn't get) compensation payments. One million pensioners who together lost £5 billion in the Equitable Life debacle have been fighting for years to get compensation from the Government. The official Ombudsman (appointed by the Government) found the Government guilty of 'a decade of regulatory failure' in the lead up to the darkest days in Equitable Life's history. The Ombudsman found the Government guilty of maladministration on 10 occasions. But when the Government at last apologised and agreed that it might pay some compensation (naturally, there was no question of anyone being sacked, censured, fined, sent to prison or put into the stocks so that penniless Equitable Life policyholders could throw rotten vegetables at them) it let it be known that the compensation payments would be decided after another enquiry (lasting another two years, during which many more policyholders will die) and after 'means-testing' the people who had lost their money.

Previously, while delaying the whole process so that the number of pensioners still living would be reduced, the Government had dismissed the claimants as 'middle class' (and therefore, by implication, of no importance).

Now, after a decade of prevarication and denial, the Government is planning to pay compensation only to poor people. Anyone who still has two pennies to rub together won't receive the compensation they are entitled to. In whose world is that fair?

★ ★ ★

The cost of supporting the people who falsely claim benefits is approximately the same as the money the nation spends on the NHS.

So, if we took back the money spent on people who are pretending to be ill we could double the amount of money spent on people who are genuinely ill.

The people who are cheating, and pretending to be sick when they are not, aren't cheating the politicians or the civil servants. It isn't their money they are taking. They are cheating the sick and the genuinely needy.

★ ★ ★

When the nation was relatively rich, the scroungers didn't arouse too much feeling among taxpayers.

But that is changing rapidly.

I recently visited a provincial English town in the West Country. The whole place seemed depressed. Many of the high street shops had already shut. Some, of course, had been replaced by charity shops. To my surprise, however, I found three smart and not inexpensive cafes. They were all full. Looking around, something occurred to me about the clientele. I thought I knew what it was but I wanted to be sure so I popped into a local stationery store and bought a clipboard. I then conducted a quick job survey. (Ostensibly I was trying to find out what sort of employment the cafe customers had.)

I was not in the slightest surprised to find that over 85% of the clients sitting enjoying good coffee (and, in some cases, sandwiches or pastries) did not have jobs. They were all receiving incapacity benefits, though I didn't see many signs of incapacity.

Personally, I feel that anyone who can sit in a pub or café, play football, cut grass, watch a football match, play golf (a surprising number of scroungers are regular golfers) or eat a meal out is fit to work. Anyone receiving benefits who is seen doing any of these things is cheating society in general and, in particular, the most vulnerable and needy (i.e. the elderly, the genuinely ill and those needing health care). They should be stripped of the right to all future benefits. (Why send them to prison where they will be supplied with free food and television?)

★ ★ ★

I recently made a very rare appearance on a BBC radio station. I was invited onto a programme to discuss the accusation in my book *Why Everything Is Going To Get Worse Before It Gets Better* that many of the people claiming sickness benefit are perfectly fit and healthy and are capable of doing a normal day's work.

I may be wrong but I got the impression that I had been invited onto the programme because someone at the BBC felt that my comments were unfair and inaccurate.

But when listeners were invited to call in it quickly became very clear that no one believed I was being cruel and harsh in suggesting that some people who claim sickness benefit are perfectly well enough to work.

Every caller I spoke to (and there were a lot of them) agreed with me. Many were extremely angry and resentful about the way people pretend to be sick, claim benefits and then lounge around all day watching television or sitting in the pub. (It is hardly surprising that obesity is much commoner among those without jobs. They have too much time for sitting and eating.) Benefits have soared way past subsistence. If you do no work you have lots of free time and these people expect to be given money to buy expensive computer games and plenty of fags. Produce a couple of kids and it's relatively easy to pick up £400 a week in benefits. The hardworking soul round the corner works hard, pays tax and worries about the mortgage. He and his wife can't afford any children because they are too busy paying for the parasites.

One outraged caller (a taxpayer) made it extremely clear that he was fed up with his own relatives sponging on the State.

★ ★ ★

There are, at the moment, around three million people claiming incapacity benefit. I doubt if more than a tiny proportion of those three million are genuinely disabled or incapable of work. The vast majority, as we all know, are lazy scroungers; shameless layabouts who are, with the connivance and support and encouragement of crooked, gutless, mendacious politicians leeching off taxpayers. Few, if any, ever ask themselves what they can do to help the community which supports them so generously. Most charitable work is done by private sector workers who do their charity work in addition to earning a living.

The 19th Century virtues of self-help have been devoured by the something-for-nothing culture. Morally bankrupt parasites now run the country, in every sense. There are the best part of three million people in Britain who believe that the nation owes them a good life. Their votes, together with the votes of the parasites whose pay cheques come from the Government, have kept Blair and Brown in power for over a decade.

In 2002, Social Security cost the country £115 billion. The following year Social Security was renamed Social Protection and it has never looked back. In 2007, Social Protection cost the country £169 billion. That's a hell of an increase. And £169 billion just happens to be £9 billion more than total income tax receipts. To describe such nonsense as unsustainable is an insult to anyone's intelligence.

* * *

It is sometimes said, by apologists for those who are long-term unemployed and long-term sickness claimants, that people are driven to this lifestyle by lack of opportunity. This is rubbish, of course. There is plenty of work available. The question no one likes to ask is why so many of the poor are unwilling to work when there is work available. Some have argued that they are demoralised and don't bother to work, so the argument goes, because they have given up hope. They are overwhelmed by a sense of defeatism.

This is nonsense.

People who aren't genuinely ill claim incapacity benefits of one sort or another because they are lazy and it is a darned sight easier to live off the State than it is to earn a living the traditional way.

I know of whole families who have been brought up to regard the State as an easy and justifiable target. One generation after another learns to regard work as something other people do. Very few are ever caught. And even those who are caught rarely seem to be punished. When a benefit fraudster was shown to have claimed more than £100,000 by pretending he was disabled when he wasn't the judge warned him that 'a custodial sentence could not be ruled out'. A custodial sentence could not be ruled out? What sort of planet is the judge living on? If I steal £100,000 from a bank I will go to prison. This piece of human detritus steals £100,000 from taxpayers and the judge says he can't rule out a custodial sentence!

Providing the unemployed with 'dole' money provided a floor for earnings. Obviously, very few people will be prepared to work for less money than they can get for sitting at home and doing nothing. And if you offer people extra money if, in addition to not having work they claim they are too sick to work, you will create a huge underclass of citizens who, through 'stress', 'backache' or other vague maladies, are permanently sick (or, in most cases, pretending to be permanently sick).

Millions have become institutionally dependent – rejecting work and finding ways to maximise their income by masquerading as sick. Whole families, communities and villages have grown up deliberately choosing to follow a life of benefits. And the basic reason – which is constantly repeated – is that the money received on benefits is more than, or at the very least equal to, the amount that the individual could expect to earn if they were working. Brown's means-testing has made it irrational for those people who have grown up without work experience, without a work ethic and without any family history of working, to look for work. They see themselves as cleverly cheating the system (rather than cheating taxpayers). Millions have now grown up thinking there is nothing wrong with not working. On the contrary, there is something to be applauded in finding ways to extract as much money as possible from the system. If you're not going to work for a living then it makes sense to not go to work for as much money as possible. Thanks to a sequence of weak and dishonest politicians (none weaker or more dishonest than Brown) Britain now has second generation scroungers in the same way that there used to be second generation miners or second generation dockers. 'It's what my Dad did,' has become the watchword of the false sick. Many have moved to pleasant seaside towns where life is gentle, the air is good and there is plenty of cheap accommodation available. (And, most crucially, there is not much work available.)

Britain has a greater percentage of fake sick than any other country in the world. And until politicians find the courage to be ruthless in forcing people back to work when they are fit for work it's going to get worse.

Resentment will rise against the lazy unemployed, the shirkers and the fake sick. Resentment will rise about the fact that the scroungers (the people who have no savings, job or house to lose, and who are entirely dependent upon the generosity of hard working taxpayers) always carry on their lives unchanged.

In my book *The Health Scandal* (published in 1988) I forecast that by the year 2020 the number of disabled, unemployed, pensioners and sickness benefit recipients would exceed the number of working taxpayers. I predicted that at that point our society would collapse as taxes rose so much that no one was prepared to work at all.

If we are looking at how society is funded we have to add all public sector workers to the total number of disabled, pensioners, unemployed and sickness benefit recipients. Civil servants may or may not contribute to the quality of our lives. But they do not contribute to the wealth of the nation. On the contrary, they are an expense, a burden.

Thanks to Gordon Brown we are already perilously close to the point where the cost of supporting all the people who receive their income from society (aka taxpayers) exceeds the money available from people and companies who make and sell 'things' or 'services'.

Such a society will, of course, be unsustainable. The credit crunch and peak oil will bring forward that turning point. And when it is reached the number of genuine beggars on our streets will rocket. As will the amount of crime. The scroungers will become beggars and thieves.

Chapter 17

The Number of Laws Will Continue To Rise, And So Will Civil Lawsuits Designed To Win Compensation

It has become impossible to keep up with all the new laws being introduced. Most new legislation comes from the European Union and is often inappropriate for Britain. But laws created to oppress aren't the only problem we all face. Civil litigation has also become a major headache for everyone, but particularly for those in business.

I believe that it is almost impossible for anyone who lives a normal life to get through a day without breaking a law. And I firmly believe that it is quite impossible for anyone running a small company to do so. There are now so many new laws coming out that even specialist lawyers find it impossible to keep up with new legislation in their own area of expertise. It is, perhaps, hardly surprising that respect for the law is diminishing faster than at any time since the signing of Magna Carta. It has become ridiculously easy to break the law. To the Government and the police we are all criminals (or potential criminals).

Since 1997, Labour has passed 365 acts of parliament and 32,000 statutory instruments (rules and regulations with the force of law). They fill 114,000 pages. Most of these new laws originated in Brussels and were sent to us by the European Union where bureaucrats clearly believe that it is always possible to hold someone responsible and that every problem will be solved with a new law.

The 2009 edition of Archbold, the leading criminal law text, used by advocates and judges, contains a preface: 'It has been a recurring theme of the preface to this work that there is far too much criminal legislation. The willingness of the Labour Government to continue its practice of legislating by trial and error has shown no signs of abating even in its eleventh year in office...The state of the criminal statute book is a disgrace. The Criminal Justice and Immigration Act 2008 is the usual hotchpotch of measures, with no theme, with much of the detail tucked away from close scrutiny in the schedules, and consisting in large part of textual amendment to earlier legislation. Much of the amendment is by way of undoing this Government's earlier legislation.'

The new edition of *Halsbury's Laws of England*, the encyclopaedia of the country's laws, has grown to 102 volumes. Since 1987, the EU and successive governments have added tens of thousands of new pieces of legislation. When there are so many laws to obey it is absurd that ignorance of the law is not allowed as a defence. Laws governing employment have quadrupled (thanks to the EU) as have laws governing schools and universities (ditto). During his first year as Prime Minister, Gordon Brown brought in 2,823 new laws.

All these figures are, of course, subject to constant change. By the time you read this there will be many more new laws.

★ ★ ★

The result of all these new laws is that today we are all liable – except the politicians, the bureaucrats, the police and the criminals.

If a burglar trips up or hurts himself while climbing into your home then you are liable. He can sue you. It makes burgling a million times easier. Don't steal anything. Just fall over.

If another driver steals your numberplate and then drives around with it fastened to his car you are responsible for his fines.

An Englishman's home used to be his castle. Today there are 266 laws under which state officials can raid your home. These include: 'inspection of high hedges', 'checking for foreign bees' and 'checking for offences related to stage hypnotism'. If the authorities want to get into your home, they will get in.

The Terrorism Act 2000, sections 43 and 44, allows the police to stop and search anyone they believe might be a terrorist, or to look for articles which could be used for terrorism. The police can do this regardless of whether or not they believe that a crime has been or may be committed.

And the police do use their powers. For example, in the year to September 2008, the Metropolitan police stopped and searched 157,000 people in London.

When conducting a 'stop and search' the police may even photograph and fingerprint members of the public. And they may ask for a DNA sample too. (I would refuse to be photographed or fingerprinted unless I was arrested. And I would refuse to give a DNA sample too. If I was arrested and I felt the arrest inappropriate I would inform the officer that I would sue for wrongful arrest. And I would remind the police that the Human Rights Act provides citizens with some legal protection.)

These are strange and difficult times.

★ ★ ★

When British soldiers beat an innocent Iraqi hotel worker to death there was no conviction. When British policemen shot and killed an innocent Brazilian electrician there were no charges. But when two British civil servants leaked the text of a discussion between Bush and Blair both were jailed.

★ ★ ★

A convicted drug dealer refused to leave his prison cell for a court appearance. He refused to go because he liked his comfortable cell and thought he might lose it to another inmate if he shuffled off to court. He quoted the Human Rights Act and said he could not be made to go to court against his will. His lawyer told the judge that his client 'refused to leave his cell this morning because he is comfortable there and doesn't want to lose it.' Prison staff had no choice but to leave him in his cell.

★ ★ ★

In the aftermath of the attack on America known as 11/9, the British Government (like the American Government) gave itself far-reaching powers over ordinary citizens. The powers were taken (and sold to the electorate) as essential to defend both nations against a cruel, unseen enemy.

The truth, of course, is that any new dangers to Britain would never have occurred if Britain hadn't joined America's illegal war against Iraq. And, even so, the new powers never had anything to do with terrorism – the so-called 'war on terrorism' was merely an excuse to introduce new laws oppressing ordinary people and suppressing any dissent.

It is now possible to be sent to prison in Britain for writing factually correct articles and for speaking out in public. You can be put in prison for making critical remarks about the Government. You can be put in prison without a trial. And the Government may arrange for you to be tortured while you are there. That's Britain in the 21st Century under a Labour Government.

The new laws were, I believe, also introduced ready to deal with the public disorder that the Government knows will come when the oil really starts to run out.

Since 1997, the Labour Government has introduced, on average, one new criminal offence for every day they have been in power. Not even Hitler or Stalin managed so much oppressive legislation. There are twice as many things for which you can be put in prison today as there were when Blair entered Downing Street on a carefully stage managed wave of glory.

The Labour Government gave itself the same powers which Hitler helped himself to. Both used the same excuse: the threat of terrorism. It is now known that Hitler faked the threat.

Since Labour came into power in 1997, we have lost most of our freedom. And there has been very little fuss about its loss.

The Labour Government has introduced an endless variety of laws (many of them emanating from Brussels) which have taken away our civil liberties. The laws against incitement to religious hatred. The laws endorsing racist attitudes against whites. And, of course, a whole library of laws allegedly introduced to combat terrorism but widely used to combat any sort of public protest. The police can now stop and search people as and when they wish. The Government can lock people up with a trial. And the Government has approved, and legalised, the torture of suspects and people 'who might know something'. The Government has even announced its intention to take control of citizens' bodies – the last refuge, you might think. In the past, organ donation has always been voluntary. The Labour Government has announced its intention to make organ donation compulsory. How long will it be before they don't wait until you've died before taking what they want, to replace the organ requirements of some Labour Party apparachik?

We don't have a free country. There are many subjects which cannot be discussed openly. There is suppression, oppression and censorship. Believe me, I have had much first hand experience of this.

When did you last see a television programme truly questioning the purpose and methods of the European Union or Britain's three party system? When did you last see a commercial television programme investigating the BBC in depth? Censorship is done quietly and subtly, according to the prejudices of the establishment. But it is nevertheless censorship.

Today the Government is the biggest source of terrorism in our lives; we endure the terrorism of state control, the erosion of all our traditional values and their replacement with oppressive laws allegedly designed to protect us from violence but in practice designed to impose a reign of terror similar to that which followed the French revolution. We live in a police state. Publicly expressed opinions can now be against the law. Discussing of what is or might be illegal can itself be illegal. People can be and are arrested and put in prison for things they think of and might do.

★ ★ ★

When the bloodless revolution comes, all legislation relating to political correctness, race, multiculturalism, performance targets, means-testing and other social engineering will be repealed.

Meanwhile, we must be wary.

★ ★ ★

Laws created to oppress aren't the only problem we all face. Civil litigation has also become a major headache for everyone, but particularly for those in business in any way. The American enthusiasm for litigation has spread to Britain with increasingly disastrous consequences. EU legislation and American-style lawyers have proved to be socially destructive and expensive; enriching the legal profession and allowing the penniless but well-represented to join the greed generation.

★ ★ ★

A lesbian soldier won £200,000 for 'hurt feelings' after a male colleague had sent her text messages saying 'You don't know what you're missing.'

That, of course, is considerably more compensation than most soldiers get when they return from combat missing bits and pieces of body.

A London commuter who hurt his back after slipping on a single flower petal (outside a flower stall in Marylebone Station) sued for £1.5 million in damages. The judge agreed with him on the grounds that the presence of petals (or, in this case, a single petal) presented a foreseeable hazard of slipping and should, therefore, have been prevented. A woman received £30,000 for slipping on a grape.

A woman sued her employer for sexual harassment when a fellow employee complimented her on her dress. She won, of course.

The compensation culture will hit ever harder as increasing numbers of people find a little light litigation is easier than work and offers better odds than the lottery. The number of absurd lawsuits brought (with staggering success) has been well-documented but what is of particular concern are the number of litigants who seem to plan their campaigning with total scepticism and great greed. There was, for example, a woman who repeatedly applied for jobs and then sued the potential employers who hadn't offered her work, on the grounds of age discrimination. If she'd worked as hard at a job she would have been an asset to any firm. And then there was the Asian youth who accessed hundreds of jokes on a commercial phone 'joke' line until he found one that he considered to be racially offensive. As the recession deepens and cheap money becomes a thing of the past more and more people will resort to such tactics. Anyone with a little money (or a small business) should beware. Somewhere, out there, is a litigant planning to sue you too. How unlikely is it that two people in search of some easy money might strike a deal? He makes a remark about her breasts. She sues the boss for sexual harassment. They share the half a million winnings.

This new, nastier than ever, turn to the compensation culture means that fewer and fewer people will be prepared to set up businesses; it means that more and more people with a little money will emigrate and it means that company profits will be forced down as firms spend a bigger and bigger chunk of their earnings on protecting themselves from these leeches (and paying out legal fees and compensation payments).

★ ★ ★

A teenager with a criminal record fell through a warehouse roof (on which he was trespassing) and received £567,000 in compensation.

Burglars tried to break into a public house. They couldn't get through the door or the windows so they tried to get in through the roof. They fell and sued. It cost the landlord £5,000 to repair the damage to his roof. He didn't bother to claim on his insurance because he knew the company would put up the premium. 'Now what do I do?' asked the landlord. 'Do I put up barbed wire to stop people getting on the roof and falling through? If they catch their clothes on it they will probably sue me. (He's right to worry. Burglars have sued for that.) Do I put up a sign telling people not to climb on the roof (which will doubtless encourage them to do so)? Or do I put netting underneath the roof in case burglars fall through?'

★ ★ ★

Two doctors were sued for leaving a scar when they performed a tracheotomy on a man who had collapsed in the street. A woman who was told that she would live for five months sued her doctors when she lived for twelve months. A man jumped under a train, was injured and sued the train company. A child sued because he became fat after eating too many burgers. A man sued the manufacturer when he had an accident while drunk in charge of a golf cart. A woman sued the gun manufacturer after her husband shot himself. A teacher was sued for £175,000 by a parent for shaking hands too hard (or was it the other way round?). A shoplifter was given $3.2 million in damages for the trauma of being handcuffed in front of her children. A female lawyer sought £19 million in damages for what she described as 'bullying and harassment' that lasted 18 months.

Thirty years after they were divorced a former wife sued her former husband. He had given his former wife a house and some money. She had spent it all and wanted more. She had never had a job and admitted that she had spent the money rashly. But it had gone and she wanted more. She won. The judge said her husband was rich enough to be able to afford to give her more. And so she got more.

New laws now allow lawyers to initiate lawsuits on a contingency basis and class action lawsuits (in which a lawyer, or a firm of lawyers, represent a huge number of plaintiffs) are destroying shareholder value in many companies.

★ ★ ★

The prospect of litigation has resulted in some wonderfully bizarre warnings appearing on products now being sold. Here are just some of the (genuine) ones I've collected recently:

- 'Wearing of this garment does not enable you to fly.' (On a child's superman costume.)
- 'Instructions – open packet, eat nuts.' (Instructions printed on a packet of nuts provided on American Airlines.)
- 'Warning – Keep out of children.' (On a kitchen knife.)
- 'Do not iron clothes on body.' (On the packaging for a Rowenta iron.)
- 'Allergy advice – contains eggs'. (On the outside of a six pack egg carton.)
- 'For indoor or outdoor use only.' (On a string of Christmas lights.)
- 'Warning – may cause drowsiness.' (On a packet of sleeping tablets.)
- 'Warning – contains nuts.' (On a packet of peanuts sold by Sainsbury's.)
- 'Do not drive car or operate machinery.' (On a children's cough medicine sold by Boot's.)
- 'Not to be used for the other use.' (On a Japanese food processor.)
- 'Product will be hot after heating.' (On a bread pudding sold by Marks and Spencer.)
- 'Do not turn upside down.' (On the bottom of the box containing a dessert sold by Tesco's.)
- 'Fits one head.' (On a pack containing a shower cap in a hotel.)
- 'This product may contain aspirin.' (Warning notice on a bottle of aspirin sold by a pharmacist.)

- 'Contains Milk.' (Label on a milk carton.)
- 'Removing the wheel can influence the performance of the bike'. (Warning in a bicycle manual.)
- 'Platform ends here.' (Notice at the end of a railway station platform.)

★ ★ ★

Laws are hardly ever repealed. New laws are piled on top of old laws and new, new laws are quickly added to the pile of new laws.

Most troubling of all, of course, is the fact that so many new laws are pouring out of Brussels.

Traditionally, ignorance is no excuse for breaking the law.

As the days, weeks, months and years go by it will become increasingly clear that we are all ignorant of the law and quite unaware of the way in which it can affect our lives.

Chapter 18

Why We Should Welcome The Death Of The National Health Service

The NHS now kills more people than it saves. On balance we will be better off without it. A well-intentioned social experiment has been smothered by bureaucracy and the NHS monster now exists not to care for patients but to provide secure, unchallenging employment for its staff. If the money spent on the NHS were distributed to citizens to use on private health care, the quality of care received would soar.

The NHS is a foul, cancerous and pustulent mess. It has been dying for years and today it is sustained by and for those who work for it and whose political future depends upon it. If it was an animal even the most loving human would have had it put down years ago. The NHS is run by people who have long since lost any genuine interest in the welfare of sick people, and any compassion or sensitivity they once had has long ago been replaced by limitless self-interest.

When Labour came to power they promised to get rid of mixed-sex wards. They didn't even manage that. Today, Britain is one of the few countries in the world where men and women must share a ward and a bathroom. Even Third World countries have got rid of mixed-sex wards.

NHS hospitals are filthy dirty. The food is inedible. Patients are treated with neither respect nor dignity. Doctors are hardly ever seen. Nurses are lazy. A Tory peer who was treated in an NHS hospital described his nurses as 'grubby, drunken, promiscuous and lazy'. Charles Dickens' wonderful creation Mrs Gamp would have fitted into the modern NHS very well. NHS hospitals are as dangerous today as they were in the middle ages. Patients who enter them do so at their own risk. The chances of a patient leaving an NHS hospital in better health than they were when they entered it are not high. The inescapable conclusion is that hospitals are run for the benefit not of patients but of the staff.

Everything in the NHS moves frighteningly slowly, and with scant regard for the welfare of patients. When it was announced in January 2009 that the World Health Organisation had devised a simple checklist which had been proved to cut surgical deaths by more than 40% and surgical complications by over a third, hospitals in England and Wales were ordered to use the checklist by February 2010. In other words, the Government allowed hospitals thirteen months to adopt a simple checklist system. Is this what we have become? Is this the world we have created for ourselves? A bureaucracy so powerful that it takes thirteen months to photocopy a list?

The money poured into the NHS in recent years could have been spent on providing the population with an endless supply of cocktail umbrellas for all the good it has done. A recent survey of more than 3,000 doctors showed that the majority believe that Labour has utterly failed to improve hospitals despite doubling the amount of taxpayers' money spent on them.

The problem, of course, is the bureaucracy. The figures aren't a secret. There are more bureaucrats working for the NHS than there are nurses. There are more bureaucrats than beds in our hospitals.

And the result is a patchy, unfair, destructive, lethal system which kills more people than it saves.

★ ★ ★

Back in 1971, I was a regular presenter on a BBC television programme called Pebble Mill At One. One week I stood beside an old-fashioned blackboard easel on which had been placed a map of the United Kingdom. I used the map and a pointer (this was, of course, long before computer graphics) to show how patients in one part of the country were receiving a completely different service to patients just a few miles away. 'It isn't a 'national' health service,' I pointed out.

Virtually the same programme (updated with fancy graphics) was broadcast while I was writing this book over a third of a century later.

Nothing has changed.

★ ★ ★

Walk into an NHS hospital and you will find demented patients in awful pain. You will find patients with terrible bedsores (the bedsore is a classic sign of bad nursing). You will find patients who are starving to death or dying of dehydration because the staff can't be bothered to feed them or give them fluids. You will see patients so dehydrated that their lips are bleeding and sore. You will see patients dumped in a chair, sitting in urine-soaked incontinence pads which have clearly not been changed for hours. You will see obvious signs of malnutrition. These aren't patients in Third World countries. They aren't patients in badly-run care homes. They are patients in major NHS hospitals. I know it is true because I have seen it time and time again with my own eyes.

★ ★ ★

Patients awaiting surgery are sent home because the hospital has run out of money and can't afford the sutures and other surgical equipment needed to operate on them. An 83-year-old woman with dementia was sent home from hospital in the middle of the night without her family being informed. The next day she was found dead, alone, in her bedroom.

A pregnant woman rang an NHS hospital to say that her baby was on the way and that she was coming in as planned. 'There is no room,' said the hospital. 'We are full.'

'What do I do?' asked the woman.

'Look in the Yellow Pages and find another hospital,' she was told.

Britain. The NHS. The 21st Century.

In Britain twice as many people are killed in hospitals by infections as are killed on the roads. The total number of deaths from hospital superbugs such as MRSA and clostridium difficile (c.difficile) reached 5,436 in one recent year. The reason? Filthy wards, unhygienic practices, scandalously poor cleaning, grubby operating theatres and staff who never wash their hands. There are more such infections in British hospitals than anywhere else in the world. Why? Simple. British hospitals are dirtier than hospitals anywhere else in the world. Why? The staff in British hospitals are the most incompetent hospital staff in the world.

★ ★ ★

There are two main reasons why hospital infections are a serious problem. First, doctors have for years now been over-prescribing antibiotics. And farmers have been routinely feeding antibiotics to animals destined for the dinner table. (Giving antibiotics to animals increases the meat available.) The result is that bugs have acquired immunity. Second, hospitals are filthy dirty. And the incompetent idiots who staff them probably can't even spell hygiene. Having talked to many doctors and nurses I am convinced that most don't know the basic principles of how diseases are spread – and how they can be controlled. An unhealthy majority, for example, seemed unaware that there is an important difference between an 'infectious' disease (spread through the environment – including by air) and a 'contagious' disease (spread by contact). I quizzed a dozen doctors and nurses in one large NHS hospital, including several who had specific responsibilities for controlling the spread of infections such as MRSA and c.difficile and none of them understood the basic principles of disease spread. Quite senior NHS personnel have, for example, tried to convince me that gastrointestinal infections can be transmitted through the air and that this, not poor hygiene practices, explains why such bugs tend to sweep through hospital wards. When I produced evidence showing that they were wrong the NHS staff then tried to argue, apparently quite seriously, that bugs behave differently in hospitals to the way they behave elsewhere. If you don't know how a disease is contracted you aren't likely to have much success in preventing its spread. Many don't even seem to realise that common causes of vomiting such as the norovirus are spread largely through inadequate cleaning of contaminated wards.

★ ★ ★

I have, since the 1970s, been warning about the return of serious infections. The rise and rise of problems such as c.difficile and MRSA was quite predictable. And other bugs will come back in a big way too. In my book *Paper Doctors* (1977) I pointed out that two things would result in a rise in infectious diseases: a lack of hygiene in hospitals and the abuse of antibiotics. I predicted the rise in antibiotic-resistant infections. In practice, avoiding infections such as MRSA and c.difficile is not difficult. The best way to avoid them is to clean the wards and to persuade doctors, nurses and other members of staff to wash their hands in between seeing patients.

Today, the NHS is institutionally dirty. Public lavatories in France are cleaner than British hospitals. The area between beds is swept but the area under the beds is left. Equipment is often filthy. Communal baths, showers and toilets are disgusting. Staff don't understand anything about hygiene. And no one cares.

Nothing is done about these problems because the complaints system is designed to protect the system rather than the patient. Hospitals are not interested in learning from their errors. They are only interested in denying the truth and avoiding responsibility. Medical records are kept not only to provide information but also with one eye on future litigation.

When the Healthcare Commission performed unannounced tests at 51 health trusts recently they found that nine out of ten health trusts had failed to meet hygiene standards put in place to reduce hospital infections. Two out of three hospitals did not manage to complete a 'deep clean' of their wards before a deadline set by the Government.

★ ★ ★

New hospitals are built with carpets or carpet tiles on their floors. Anyone planning, equipping or running a hospital who puts carpets on the floor should be fired instantly and sent to work on a trawler, an oilrig or somewhere else with a high mortality rate. Carpets are incredibly difficult to clean and quickly become a storehouse for bugs. Vast expenses of linoleum may not look pretty but linoleum is easy to clean.

★ ★ ★

In one hospital I watched in horror as a ward auxiliary went into a private room where a patient with MRSA was supposedly being barrier nursed. The auxiliary was pushing a food trolley (she had just finished cleaning the floor but had not bothered to wash her hands) and she wheeled the entire trolley into the private room. She took no precautions whatsoever to prevent carrying the bug out of the infected room. When she came out of the private room she simply carried on dishing out food. Several nurses sat and watched her. They were busy eating chocolates.

★ ★ ★

One of the problems is that hospital staff (like other public service employees) are almost impossible to sack. When one former NHS chief executive was forced to resign her £150,000 a year job over Britain's deadliest superbug outbreak she demanded a £150,000 pay off. The woman left her job after at least 90 patients died from c.difficile. And after leaving her NHS job she set up a healthcare consultancy company (to tell the NHS how to improve hospitals). She set up the company with her partner who had quit a senior NHS job after the trust where he worked accumulated debts of £30 million. It is clear that those who do leave the NHS are well compensated for their failure. And the concept of 'shame' seems as alien to the modern bureaucrat as the concept of 'duty' or 'responsibility'.

★ ★ ★

In the future two things are likely to happen.

First, the number of serious, deadly infections in our hospitals will rise. There will be periods when the infections will appear to be under control. But they will not be. Our hospital staff are institutionally lazy. Incompetence and ignorance are defended, protected and rewarded with promotion. Second, the superbugs will escape from hospitals and will start to kill people in their homes and places of work. It is already happening. Medical officers in Holland have found that 50% of Dutch farmers are carrying a new strain of MRSA that is passed from hormone-fed pigs to humans. Already, a new, more virulent strain of MRSA has been found in the community. And the number of elderly people killed in care homes by the superbug c.difficile has officially tripled in the last two years. (Since killer bugs are often not mentioned on death certificates the true figure is undoubtedly far higher than this.) This sad development is hardly surprising when one considers that nurses and local authority personnel who have responsibility for standards in care homes were trained in our hospitals.

★ ★ ★

In late 2008, a tiny report appeared in some newspapers headed 'Mutant superbug is found on farm'.

Upon investigation it appeared that a superbug, a new variety of E.coli resistant to antibiotics had been found among cattle on a dairy farm in the north of England. It was, apparently the first time the particular strain of the bug had been found in Britain and it was only the third time the bug had ever been found anywhere in the world. A government spokeswoman said that 'no additional precautions are warranted'.

Really.

★ ★ ★

How can you defend yourself against these problems?

There are probably three reliable ways.

The first is to try to keep your immune system as healthy as possible. There is extensive advice about how to do this in my book *Superbody*.

The second is to go abroad if you need hospital treatment. You are much less likely to acquire a serious infection in hospital if you are treated outside the UK.

The third is to spend money and have private treatment. Deadly infections are virtually unknown in private hospitals in the UK.

★ ★ ★

One of the problems is that people don't understand that the amount of money available for health care is finite. Lobby groups push for money for their small area and inevitably the lobby groups which are best organised get most of the money. And so non-diseases such as autism and ADHD receive massive funding. Breast cancer, which is fashionable and media friendly, receives enormous amounts of money. But less attractive areas (preventive medicine and bowel cancer for example) receive very little attention or funding.

Every time someone has infertility treatment or cosmetic surgery, someone somewhere dies of undiagnosed, untreated bowel cancer.

★ ★ ★

Dirty sheets are reused in hospitals, just as they are in the dirtiest, cheapest, nastiest doss houses. But hospitals aren't supposed to be doss houses. They are places where the people in the beds are, by definition, all ill. Many of them with infectious diseases.

I can understand bureaucrats accepting this. They are often nasty, uncaring people. But doctors and nurses?

★ ★ ★

Rats and cockroaches are frequently found in British hospitals. There are more food-related infections in British hospitals than in Chinese restaurants. 'This is nothing to do with MRSA,' said a Government spokesman. Bollocks. It has everything to do with MRSA. A dirty hospital is a dirty hospital.

★ ★ ★

When my mother was terminally ill in hospital I was summoned to a meeting to discuss her being sent home. I was told that the hospital didn't have enough beds. The meeting was held in a completely empty ward which was being used for meetings. At a second meeting to discuss her eviction there were no less than nine bureaucrats present. As Albert Einstein once said: 'Bureaucracy is the death of any achievement.'

★ ★ ★

Your child breaks an arm. You have to rush him to hospital. This is not a routine appointment for varicose veins. This is an emergency. Which is why you take him direct to the nearest Accident and Emergency Department. (Your local hospital may not have one of these and if you turn up at a hospital without an accident department you will be turned away and told to take him elsewhere.)

You expect, of course, that your child will be seen within minutes and that he will be treated straight away.

Wrong.

The officially acceptable wait for treatment in an Accident and Emergency department is four hours. The average wait is seven hours. Can you imagine the Blairs or Browns standing waiting for seven hours?

NHS staff complain that they get shouted at, abused and occasionally attacked. I'm not surprised. In fact the only thing that surprises me is that every NHS staff member isn't walking on crutches. Only the English, self-effacing to the point of being self-destructive, would put up with waiting seven hours for emergency medical treatment.

★ ★ ★

Doctors are now the third most important cause of illness in the UK. Adverse drug reactions kill 18,000 people a year and cause 600,000 hospital admissions in the UK every year. That's a fact.

★ ★ ★

The incidence of mental health problems is increasing. Officially, one in two people in Britain is incurably mentally ill. But the number of beds available for mental health patients is constantly shrinking. This is, of course, because the mentally ill make an ineffective lobby.

★ ★ ★

A third of Britain's general practitioners (GPs) would prefer private treatment for themselves and their families. Hospital consultants are the same. Here's what one NHS consultant had to say recently 'In the past we knew we would get good care on the NHS. I don't trust it any more. Even I can't bully my way through the system.'

★ ★ ★

Politicians think the NHS is wonderful. They wouldn't dream of going private. But then they don't have to wait and they are put into private rooms where they are waited on hand and foot. It doesn't cost them a penny.

★ ★ ★

Civil servants working at the Department of Health are entitled to be members of the Benendeen Healthcare Society which serves one million British Telecom, Post Office and civil service workers. If they fall ill they get to go to a luxury private hospital.

★ ★ ★

One NHS manager who fell ill and needed hospital treatment admitted that he 'got into difficulties finding out who was his doctor, what medicine to take and when he was getting out'. This was the man in charge of the complaints system in a London hospital.

★ ★ ★

Trades unions defend the NHS and oppose any reforms but many of them have done deals with private sector organisations to provide private health care insurance so that their members don't have to use the NHS. More than half of the TUC's members have some sort of private medical insurance. This is a higher proportion than any other socio-economic group in the UK.

★ ★ ★

NHS patients who write complimentary letters about the NHS to their local paper are doing more harm than good. They are encouraging the survival of a stagnant, rancid system which kills patients and destroys the souls, spirits and integrity of doctors and nurses. It's like someone who'd been in Auschwitz whooping about the excellent conditions because they were befriended by a guard and given an extra biscuit occasionally.

We have allowed a vast bureaucracy to grow and kill the NHS. We are still dedicated to an ideal which has long since been proved unworkable.

★ ★ ★

The Government is closing hospitals and casualty departments and concentrating services in bigger and bigger hospitals. This is being done to please the EU. Patients who need a GP are being told to telephone for advice rather than to visit the surgery. (The excuse for this is that it will save the planet by reducing the use of petrol). Patients who are injured in accidents are told to telephone ahead and get permission in advance if they think they need to be seen in a casualty department.

This may all sound bizarre. But it's true.

★ ★ ★

The NHS will continue to decline. And private care will also deteriorate. The quality of private medical and dental care in Britain has now fallen to the quality of NHS medical and dental care thirty years ago. Many dentists who were previously working exclusively in the NHS have carried their bad manners into private practice and many patients don't know to expect better. And visit a private hospital and the chances are that you will sit waiting in a crowded waiting room. After a lengthy wait you will be hurried in to see your consultant who will rush through your consultation so that she (or he) can get onto the next one. 'Payment in advance please, please see the receptionist. Cash, cheques and all major credit cards taken.' Private patients now routinely have to wait days (or weeks) to receive the results of simple blood tests, X-ray tests or tissue sample tests. And they have to wait weeks (or months) for essential, life-saving surgery. Paying privately in Britain now buys you better food, slightly more polite nurses and a television set that you don't have to feed with tokens. But it doesn't necessarily buy you better or quicker medical care. (Which is, I suspect, what most people hope they're going to get when they spend vast amounts of money on private health insurance.)

Not surprisingly, a growing number of Britons now go abroad for health care; travelling to India or Thailand for medical and surgical treatment. Hospitals in these countries are already far cleaner, far more modern and far better equipped than British hospitals. And the prices (which often include first-class hotel accommodation for accompanying relatives) are, even when the costs of travel are included, often considerably lower than the price of treatment in the UK.

★ ★ ★

The quality of medical care in Britain will continue to deteriorate because the official answer to all the bad things that happen is not to train people better (or, heaven forbid, to punish the worst offenders) but to add another layer of impenetrable bureaucracy to ensure that no one can ever be held responsible for anything they do. No one must be punished or even reprimanded because once you start down that slippery slope you end up with some higher level official having to accept responsibility and that cannot be contemplated. And so nothing ever improves. Problems merely create more cover-ups. The only concern is to avoid anyone having to say 'sorry' or admit that they have made a mistake. Patients and their relatives may remain unsatisfied, aggrieved or concerned that someone else will suffer in exactly the same way that they did. But no matter. No jobs have been lost or even threatened.

★ ★ ★

Despite having more bureaucrats than beds or nurses the NHS is a financial mess.

In December 2008, it was announced that £327,000,000 of debt would be wiped from ten hospital trusts that were in severe financial trouble. There was not, of course, any suggestion that any of the bureaucrats responsible would lose their jobs. There isn't much hope that things will get better when totally incompetent half-wits who can't manage a budget are let off the hook and allowed to keep their jobs.

In the bad old days (when wards had sisters and hospitals had matrons) each ward would have a clerk. The clerk would keep the records up-to-date and neatly filed in a little cabinet. These days, wards have a row of administrators. Four or five of them sit there constantly scribbling. There are no nurses. Just clerks sitting scribbling. What are they all writing? I have no idea. But I can tell you that whatever it is it is bound to be unnecessary, self-serving guff. Look at the overall plan of a modern hospital and it looks more like an administrative building with a hut for a few patients tacked on. Patients are an unnecessary afterthought; a nuisance without whom hospitals would run far more efficiently.

★ ★ ★

In 2007, the NHS lost £489 million as foreign governments failed to reimburse it for treating foreigners who fell ill while holidaying in Britain. In the same year, Britain paid £527 million to cover the costs of British tourists treated in Europe. Is it beyond the wit of NHS bureaucrats to work out a way to hold back some of the money we pay out and put it against the money we are owed?

★ ★ ★

Political correctness is one of the reasons for the mess the NHS finds itself in. In 1971, when I was a junior hospital doctor I worked all the hours available. It was not uncommon for a junior house officer to work 168 hours a week, snatching hours of sleep whenever there was a lull in activity. We didn't complain about this because it was an accepted part of our training. Every patient was looked after by a designated consultant team. The consultant, registrar and house officer were responsible for patients from their admittance to their discharge.

And then in 1974, the politically correct intervened. More and more female medical students were admitted to medical schools (today, 57% of our graduating doctors are female). And this changed the whole philosophy of medical care. In particular, it changed the concept of continuity of care.

Women doctors didn't want to work 168 hours. Even as young graduates they got married, had babies and wanted a life outside the hospital ward. Just like female MPs, they demanded a regulated 'work-life balance' and expected the job commitments to be adjusted to suit them. They weren't (and aren't) prepared to give the commitment that male doctors have always given. And they destroyed the basic principles of medical care. When they moved into general practice they wanted to continue with their part-time responsibilities. As a young GP I was happy to do two or three nights on call every week. But for female GPs, accustomed to an easy life in hospital, the idea of doing several nights a week on call, as well as ordinary working hours, is quite unacceptable. (Much the same thing has happened in Parliament, of course. The influx of female MPs has resulted in drastically reduced working hours in the Commons. And female Ministers have refused to work at evenings or weekends.)

In the 1990s, the European Union made things even worse. European health ministers insisted that the European working-time directive be applied to doctors as well as coach drivers and factory workers. They did this because there were thousands of unemployed doctors in southern Europe and the directive enabled governments to pay lower salaries and cut medical services. The doctors could always earn a little extra by moonlighting for private medical facilities.

Britain accepted the EU rules for doctors. Our health minister could have refused but he didn't. As our politicians always do, our ministers bowed down to the EU's demands.

And so today the entire NHS is in a mess, doctors no longer provide patients with anything like half way decent medical care, and patients are dying like flies because the quality of care has deteriorated. Iatrogenesis (doctor-induced disease) is one of the big three medical killers in Britain. Doctors kill more people than infections. And they kill far, far more people than terrorists. (You think I'm exaggerating but I'm not. Every week doctors kill more Britons than terrorists have killed in the last 50 years.)

Moreover, things are getting worse.

When doctors qualified in the 1970s, specialists only became consultants or GPs after around 30,000 hours of experience and training. Today, thanks to political correctness and reduced working weeks, young doctors can become consultants or fully qualified GPs after 6,000 hours of training. So, today's specialists have one fifth the experience of their predecessors just 30 years ago. How can that possibly be acceptable? If airline pilots were suddenly allowed to fly passenger planes after a training period that had been cut by four fifths there would be a public outcry.

And now, to make sure that doctors stick to the EU's regulations, hospitals actually employ highly-paid bureaucrats whose sole job is to make sure that young doctors clock off on time and don't spend a moment more than they should looking after patients. Hospitals employ Working Time Directive Project Managers (salaries around £40,000 a year) whose job description involves ensuring the compliance of young professionals with the 48 hour working limit.

The General Medical Council, which is supposed to spend its huge income preserving medical standards, might be expected to have done something about all this. However, the GMC, which was once a rather lumbering but reasonably reliable organisation run by the medical profession to maintain a register of doctors and to dish out punishments to the bad ones, is, it seems to me, of no practical value to patients or doctors but of enormous practical value to politicians and bureaucrats. The GMC's main role seems to be to create ever more complex rules and regulations to keep its bureaucrats busy and to justify its vast overheads.

So, with one thing and another, it is hardly surprising that it is often difficult to find a doctor on a hospital ward these days. And it is hardly surprising that the standard of care in our hospitals is falling rapidly. An NHS hospital scheme to reduce follow-up appointments and to discharge patients earlier has led to a 12% increase in emergency admissions. And it is hardly surprising that more and more patients are getting fed up with the poor quality of care they receive from doctors. In 2007, the number of complaints heard by the General Medical Council was twenty times as great as it had been in 1997. A high proportion of the complaints relate to services provided by foreign born doctors. Naturally, no one is allowed to mention this although it has been the case for some years.

★ ★ ★

Politicians and administrators have taken control of medical care. Their brains are uncluttered with scientific stuff and they know best.

When the London Assembly (in reality the best known EU Regional Assembly in England) invited members of the public to send in thoughts on vaccination for their 'rapporteurship' I sent them a copy of my book *Coleman's Laws*, which contains a lengthy medical explanation of why vaccination is irresponsible and dangerous and a significant cause of illness. An administration officer for the London Assembly wrote to thank me for my views which would, I was assured, be included in their analysis of evidence for the report.

However, there was no mention of any of my evidence in their report and the details of the evidence I had submitted did not appear in the list of references included at the back of the report. I was not surprised by this. Nor was I surprised to see that the report followed the official line. Their first conclusion was that the Department of Health should make childhood immunisation a key performance indicator for Primary Care Trusts. (In other words, GPs should be given extra money if they met vaccination performance targets.) They also recommended that all London Primary Care Trusts 'should appoint an immunisation champion to work with GP practices in order to boost immunisation rates'.

I could find no mention anywhere in the report of the existence of evidence suggesting that sticking needles and potentially dangerous substances into small children might not be a good thing. There was no discussion of the evidence that vaccines are dangerous and might cause serious damage to young children and infants.

Ironically, the title of the report was 'Still Missing the Point?'

I think they are.

* * *

The idea of patients having a personal general practitioner whom they know, and who knows them, is history. The average GP now works a four day week. He has nights and weekends off. He is available on the telephone one day a week. He does home visits one day a week. She or he is paid according to 'performance related activities'. Practices are driven to satisfy targets (so many patients vaccinated, so many treated for heart disease and so on). As a result the average GP no longer provides any sort of personal service. She is paid around £120,000 a year. Family doctors are now doing less work for more money. Over 150 GPs earn £250,000 a year or more. Today's primary care service is run by and for bureaucrats. Doctors can no longer choose where they work. And patients can no longer choose the doctor they want to see.

NHS bureaucrats who negotiated the deal allowing GPs to avoid 24 hour responsibility showed just how poorly they understood the basic principle of GP care.

* * *

One in five GP practices could soon close under Government proposals for super surgeries or polyclinics which will each house up to 25 GPs and provide on-site pharmacies and a variety of other therapists. These are, of course, an EU proposal and so despite the fact that neither doctors nor patients want them, they will come. Polyclinics are much loved by socialists and have long flourished in communist eastern Europe.

★ ★ ★

Now that GPs don't work out of hours (presumably because bureaucrats believe that illness should only strike in normal office hours), primary care trusts have to take responsibility for providing some sort of cover so that patients who are inconsiderate enough to fall ill or have accidents at weekends, evenings and nights can be dealt with. They have to introduce their own walk-in centres and they pay private companies to provide this service.

It is now so difficult to get weekend medical treatment that a year or two ago I went back onto the medical register so that I could sign prescriptions for antibiotics and other essential supplies. I don't have any patients but I want to be able to have access to life-saving drugs in case I or my family need emergency medical help. What does that tell you about the NHS? (It is bound to be against the rules for me to do this, of course, and I am quite certain that someone reading these words will report me to whomsoever it is who takes note of such things. I will happily explain in court precisely why I felt the need to do this.)

★ ★ ★

GPs, now earning over £100,000 a year, plus all sorts of bonuses and expenses on top of that, are forcing patients to dial premium rate numbers (0845 and 0870) in order to make an appointment, order a prescription, or request a visit – even in an emergency. And, of course, calls are lengthened and made more expensive by the usual cornucopia of choices: 'press 1 for details of how to make an appointment or to speak to a receptionist', 'press 2 to be given the address of the nearest hospital', 'press 3 for advice on how to stop uncontrollable bleeding', 'press 4 for the telephone number of a reliable undertaker who makes home visits'. Patients in around one in ten practices are charged 40 pence a minute to call their doctor. Doctors take the profit from every call. Every one of the doctors who runs such a scheme should be hung, drawn, quartered, infected with flesh-eating bugs and forced to spend their last remaining minutes on earth watching re-runs of the Danish version of Celebrity Big Brother.

* * *

If you live in Britain and have to go to hospital for any operation or procedure, you now have a 50% chance of getting a worse disease from being in the hospital. That's official. And if you do survive the experience and get to go home there is a good chance that you will leave malnourished. Staggeringly, one in five NHS patients leaves hospital officially malnourished. Some patients don't eat because the food is inedible. Others stay hungry because no one helps them eat. Orderlies dump food on a patient's table and then collect it, untouched, half an hour later. The patient, starving hungry, hasn't eaten because he or she couldn't reach the food. One patient who was blind couldn't see the food put before her. No one bothered to feed her. 'It's not my job to feed the patients,' I've heard the orderlies say. Other patients complain that the food they are given is shrink-wrapped in impenetrable plastic. It's a sort of modern NHS torture. The patient can see the food but they can't get at it. Nurses are too self-important. It is the greatest indictment of our hospitals that patients actually die in them because they have not been given food or fluid. It was recently announced that in future nurses will be able to decide that a dying patient should not be resuscitated. Why not? Nurses in Britain already decide that patients should die by not being fed.

* * *

Some readers may be shocked to know that the National Health Service already operates a selection system for treatment. But it has done so for many years. (English patients are particularly likely to be affected. Scottish hospitals have plenty of money; though it comes, of course, from English taxpayers.) When treatment is expensive it is provided for those patients who are regarded as the most deserving. And how does our system decide which patients are most deserving? Simple. A young married man with lots of children will be at the top of the list. An elderly man who lives alone will be right at the bottom of the list.

And so the NHS will provide life-saving treatment for an unemployed scrounger of 36 who has a wife, a mistress and eight children. But a great painter or composer will be allowed to die.

* * *

And yet when criticisms are aired there is invariably a flood of protest from 'satisfied' patients and relatives who are either too stupid to know what they should expect a hospital to be like or who have been coerced into writing by relatives who work in the NHS. No one who knows what a hospital should do could possibly be satisfied with the NHS. Every attempt to put things right is thwarted by undemanding dunces whose expectations are set somewhere in the darkest part of the middle ages. The result is that nothing ever changes.

The main problem is that staff have learned that if they follow the letter of the law, and obey all the administrative regulations, it doesn't matter a damn how they treat the patients. Staff are only ever fired if they are convicted of the mass murder of patients.

A million people work for the NHS and they have a vested interest in it remaining inefficient. They work too little and are paid too much. There are too many administrators and the whole health service is suffocating under red tape. The NHS is not going to improve because it is not in the interests of the staff to change anything. And so medical care in the UK will continue to deteriorate. With standards so low in the NHS, private care will also continue to deteriorate.

The NHS isn't going to get any better because its primary aim now is to look after its staff rather than to look after the people who use it. The whole institution (like all state-run institutions) has been manipulated and adapted so that the requirements and rights and interests of the staff are put first. Commercial organisations (such as private hospitals) cannot survive if they operate in this way, but state-run organisations can do so very well because the link between the person paying the bills and the people being paid for providing the service has been broken.

The bottom line is that if the NHS was closed, and the money which we now spend on it used to buy private healthcare insurance for the whole population (so that every man, woman and child in the country was entitled to private medical care), there would be billions of pounds left over with which to buy sickness insurance for every man, woman and child so that everyone would be insured against financial loss when needing to take time off work through illness. That's how bad the NHS is today.

Don't believe me? Look at the figures.

We spend around £100 billion a year on the NHS.

There are around 60,000,000 people in the UK.

Divide 60,000,000 into £100 billion.

And you have £1,666 per head.

I could buy damned good private health cover for £1,666 year. And so could you.

★ ★ ★

Meanwhile, I strongly suggest that you will survive for longer if you avoid the NHS as much as you possibly can. Private health care in Britain isn't a lot better than NHS care (it is much, much worse than health care elsewhere in the world and is now, I suspect, at about the level the NHS was at in the 1970s) but you will be safer in a private hospital because you will probably be given food and you will be considerably less likely to develop an MRSA infection.

Chapter 19

The EU: The Euro, High Food Prices, Gypsies And A Whole Lot More

Just about every truly bad piece of legislation that has been introduced during the last decade has come directly from Brussels.

The EU is destroying Britain and it will continue to do so for as long as it exists.

With little thought we have handed over our heritage, our culture, our independence and our freedom to a bunch of bureaucrats in another land. We might have thought more about disposing of an old pair of shoes than we have about abandoning our past and giving away our future. The real irony? Like the half-wits we must seem to be, we have paid, and paid heavily, for the doubtful privilege of selling ourselves.

The EU's sticky, interfering fingers can be found everywhere. The EU has cleverly left in place each nation's institutions (for example, the UK still has Parliament, the monarchy and the civil service). But these are now just cardboard fronts; the power is all in Brussels and in the hands of the unelected bureaucrats who make our laws and tell us, in minute detail, how to live our lives and how many hours a week we can work. Employment problems caused by EU legislation are massive. Employers struggle to cope with a constant torrent of EU legislation (much of it incomprehensible and much of it nonsensical). And, by 2009, even employees were beginning to understand some of the problems created by the EU. For example, one EU law (it's called a directive but that's just their word for a law) allows foreign contractors to undercut local industry agreements. Not surprisingly, British workers feel angry and resentful. The end result will be xenophobia and nationalism. But British politicians can do nothing, and nor can British voters, because the laws are made by unelected officials in Brussels.

There are now 490 million people living under the oppressive EU regime. It's the world's first truly fascist state though one could, I suppose, equally well describe it as statist, socialist, Stalinist or communist. All that really matters is that it is a form of political collectivism which opposes individualism and freedom.

There is a myth that the EU is most vigorously opposed by those of the right. It is not. The EU is the right. It is the clearest manifestation of pure fascism the world has ever seen. Those who oppose it are active freedom fighters. Democracy exists only in the hearts and minds of those who dream of the end of the EU.

It was the EU which gave us all-day drinking and made many of our town and city streets no-go areas for all of the evening, most of the night and much of the daytime. And it is because of the EU's competition laws that it is not possible for the Government to stop the sale of cheap alcohol. The EU gave us binge drinking and turned millions of frail, elderly or nervous citizens into prisoners in their own homes. For this we give the EU vast amounts of our money.

It is thanks to the EU that home owners have to pay £700 for a worthless and entirely pointless new Home Information Pack if they want to sell their home.

It is thanks to the EU that our towns are now scarred with ugly bits of knobbly pavement and absurd bits and pieces of street furniture.

The EU sponsored promotion of ethanol will increase taxes and damage the environment and add to the cost of fuel and food. The politically powerful ethanol industry (basically, a bunch of very rich farmers) is receiving research grants, development grants, construction grants and loan guarantees. Farmers who produce ethanol receive very generous subsidies. The problem with ethanol is that it contains one third less energy than petrol so you have to buy a third more fuel to go the same distance. And if you add up all the oil needed to make and transport ethanol (the fertiliser, herbicides, fuel for farm machinery and delivery lorries, gas for distillation plants) it takes more energy to produce ethanol than it provides. And the environment gets worse. Oh, and plus the water table is dropping and scarce water resources are becoming scarcer because it takes so much water to grow the corn to produce the ethanol. Finally, heavy corn production results in groundwater pollution (because of the chemicals used in the farming), increases the level of greenhouse gas emissions and exacerbates soil erosion.

It is thanks to the EU that councils won't collect our rubbish.

It is entirely thanks to the EU that most of our villages now have no shop, no post office, no bus service and no church. For the first time since the Norman Conquest, over half the villages of England no longer have a pub. Many of the ones that survive have been bought up by faceless chains and filled with plastic. Even general practitioners' surgeries are under pressure. According to GP magazine one in seven practices are threatened with closure or relocation to a polyclinic. It will, of course, be villages which will be the first to lose their surgery.

The Government isn't satisfied with bringing in EU laws which result in the closure of village post offices, village shops and village pubs. Hundreds of small schools in England are now also threatened with closure because of Government targets. Small schools cannot, for example, provide out-of-hours tuition as required by EU targets. And so the Government plans to close a total of 300 local schools – devastating village communities and forcing parents to drive miles to take their children to school. (It's difficult to see how this helps solve the global warming problem which politicians – and EU bureaucrats – are forever warning us about.)

It is difficult to avoid the observation that in schools where the in-hours tuition is satisfactory the out-of-hours tuition will not be necessary.

★ ★ ★

The men and women who gave us the Common Agricultural Policy and the straight cucumber have also banned smoking in public places.

In theory this was undoubtedly a 'good idea'. And as a doctor and a non-smoker I would support it. In theory.

But this ban has had a number of serious effects. It has dramatically affected bingo halls and working men's clubs. And it has had a deadly effect on village pubs (which are, at the beginning of 2009, closing at a rate of 36 a week).

Closing pubs in villages which have already lost their local shop and local post office doesn't do much to protect the social life of villagers. And it doesn't do much to reduce smoking or drinking either. The consumption of alcohol and tobacco hasn't been affected by the ban on smoking in public places. Instead of going to their local pub people are buying their booze and fags in their local supermarket. And because booze and fags are cheaper when bought in the supermarket people are smoking and drinking more.

Brilliant.

Another example of the EU's ability to get things dangerously wrong by failing to understand how people live, by failing to listen, by imposing draconian pan-European legislation on countries with different social needs and by failing to think things through.

★ ★ ★

Residents within the EU should be aware that most decisions on financial matters are made by the European Union. For example, during the bank crisis of autumn 2008 some European countries (including the UK) wanted to increase the bank guarantee offered to savers to £100,000. This would have done a great deal to reassure savers that their money was safe and it would have probably helped protect the banks. However, the EU eventually ruled that the guarantee should be limited to £50,000 per bank, per saver. Why was the limit kept so much lower than had at first been suggested? One (or possibly more) of the newer Eastern Europe entrants to the EU decided that £50,000 was high enough. From the point of investors in Britain, France, Germany, Spain, Ireland, Italy and numerous other countries the lower limit was distinctly unsatisfactory and undoubtedly led to millions of investors moving their money out of their banks and transferring it to other institutions, thereby adding to the uncertainty which damaged the banks so much.

★ ★ ★

We sometimes laugh at the EU bureaucrats for their daft rules and regulations about the acceptable size and shape of duck eggs and the straightness of cucumbers and bananas but the EU is no laughing matter. It is worth remembering that Oswald Mosley, a man with more than one black shirt in his wardrobe, founder of British Union of Fascists, and father of motor sport's favourite whipping boy Max Mosley, was a staunch and enthusiastic supporter of a United Europe. Ossie would have loved the modern European Union. All those rules and regulations would have had him drooling and breathing heavily.

The brainless bureaucrats of Brussels have produced the equivalent of 120 miles of legislation since the EU was set up. The paperwork weighs more than a ton. By the end of 2006, the EU had produced 666,879 pages of laws. European companies, charities and individuals have to comply with them all. The EU tells us what we can eat (and what it is called) and what we can drive. It is thanks to the EU that gypsies are now allowed to build bungalows in your back garden. The EU has given us Regional Parliaments and taken away our democracy. It is EU legislation which we can thank for the fact that unemployment will go high and stay high for longer than necessary. In America the normal gap between losing one job and getting another is four weeks. In Britain the gap (even in 'good' times) is six months. Why? Blame the EU. Because of EU legislation, getting rid of an employee takes forever. There is a process to follow: verbal warnings, written warnings, meetings and monitoring. Every word has to be thought about carefully, lest lawyers become involved. And because getting rid of employees takes forever companies think long and hard about taking on new employees. Big companies often prefer to hire employees on short-term contracts. Small companies often prefer to stay small. A bloke with a small garage is not going to take on an assistant if it means that he has to heat everywhere to an EU acceptable temperature and provide a dedicated employee a toilet good enough to satisfy EU standards.

I can understand the EU bureaucrats introducing this nonsense to protect themselves and their own miserable jobs. But why did they have to impose their nonsense on the rest of us?

You can, incidentally, see the effects of the EU's regionalisation programme everywhere. It is, for example, because of the EU that local control rooms for the fire and the police are being closed. And it is because of the EU's regionalisation policies that traditional army regiments and police force boundaries are being changed.

Scotland has its own European Union Regional Parliament. The Scots think this is the first step towards independence and they pompously and erroneously refer to it as the Scottish parliament. It isn't anything of the sort, of course. Wales and London also have EU Regional Parliaments. (The EU Parliament in London is known as the London Assembly.) And there are more Regional Parliaments in existence around the rest of Britain, though the members of these Parliaments are appointed rather than elected.

The EU encourages us to have our children jabbed full of vaccines which contain mercury but bans mercury from barometers and thermometers on the grounds that it is one of the most dangerous substances known to man, woman or child. Doctors are paid extra to pump vaccines into small children and health visitors go door-to-door thugging young mothers into having their children vaccinated. The children who die or are brain damaged are merely a statistical inconvenience. The EU is contemplating making vaccination compulsory.

Most things which are inexplicably stupid can be traced back to the EU. If you have noticed that your town has recently been spending rather too much of your money turning roads and pavements into obstacle courses, narrowing already over narrow roads and building absurd pavement extensions then you may assume that your local councils have gone barmy. But exactly the same absurd things are happening all over Europe. It's officially being done to cut road accidents and satisfy targets on road deaths. It does not, of course, do either.

Thanks to the EU, British prisoners are being given the right to vote. (So the MP for Dartmoor will be Sid 'The Knife' who will doubtless be let out to attend the House of Commons.)

It is impossible to argue against the belief that everything the EU does costs money, puts up prices and makes life more complicated and less enjoyable. Switzerland and Norway remained outside the EU and are now richer per head of population than any country within the EU.

The EU has told Britain that for the first time the country can levy income tax on prostitutes. British Governments had previously been sensitive to accusations that if they taxed prostitutes they could be accused of living on immoral earnings. But thanks to the EU, prostitutes can now be taxed. The EU approves so it's OK.

★ ★ ★

Europhiles claim that there is no plan for an EU superstate. If that is true why does the EU have its own flag, anthem, passport, citizenship and currency? Why is it establishing its own police force and its own armed forces?

The EU produces a vast body of laws which govern and oppress every aspect of our lives. Polls done by the EU itself show that less than half the citizens of Europe support the EU. A poll published by the *Financial Times* showed that by a margin of nearly two to one, people in five of the EU's six largest countries think that life has got worse since their country joined the EU. The exception is Spain which, since it joined in 1986, has been given nearly £100 billion by taxpayers from the other five EU countries. The British hate the EU more than most. Twice as many people would like to see us leave as want us to stay in, though no major political party in Britain offers this as an option. As the EU celebrated its 50th birthday in March 2007 a survey in Europe showed that 75% of Europeans wanted a referendum on any treaty giving more power to Brussels. In the UK, 83% wanted a vote and more than 3 to 1 would vote against (67% to 21%). Politicians everywhere except Ireland responded by making sure their citizens had no referendum and no vote. The Irish voted against the Treaty of Lisbon but will vote again and the EU will help ensure that they will get it right the second time. It was always obvious that the people of Ireland (who had the temerity to vote against the Lisbon Treaty) would be told by the EU to vote again. This is the way the EU usually does things if a democratic vote goes against it.

In order to ensure that the Irish Government could 'sell' the wretched treaty to an untrusting electorate the EU abandoned many of the basic principles of the treaty. The Irish were told that the treaty would not affect Irish military neutrality, or its national tax system or its abortion laws. And the new Irish-friendly treaty was given new material upholding the protection of workers' rights.

I assume (though we haven't been told this) that the re-written treaty will affect all the other signatories. (Although, I suppose it is perfectly possible that the Irish might end up signing a different treaty to the other member countries.)

In a normal world you might expect that since the Treaty has now been changed significantly the other countries would have to look at it again, and decide whether or not they still wanted to sign it.

Not a bit of it.

Gordon Brown, who had signed the Lisbon Treaty and broken a promise that he would hold a referendum before signing it said that the concessions to Ireland did not materially affect the Lisbon Treaty and so there was no need to re-open the ratification process. (A ratification process which had consisted of Brown slinking into a room in Lisbon and signing a treaty he had promised he wouldn't sign unless the British people gave him permission.)

★ ★ ★

The EU philosophy is to decide what to allow us to do, not what to stop us doing (which is the traditional English way, as defined in a thousand years of law). The EU's way obviously gives the bureaucrats and the policemen far more power.

EU staff are among the best paid and most mollycoddled in the world. When Peter Mandelson voluntarily left his job as an EU Commissioner he could look forward to an EU salary of £78,000 a year for the next three years (although he wasn't actually working for the EU this was intended to bring his £100,000 a year cabinet salary up to his £182,500 Trade Commissioner salary). And this money is taxed at the preferential tax rates devised by EU officials for EU officials. Protests were met with the response that this is 'normal' practice within the EU. Anyone stupid enough to leave a well-paid, secure, lowly taxed EU job still gets paid by the EU if they accept a job paying less than their highly paid EU job.

When John Prescott was offered the job of European Commissioner his wife was reported to have said: 'My God, can I go and buy that Brueghel print at WH Smiths?' Prescott allegedly replied: 'You can buy the original on the money that comes out of Europe.'

I have in front of me a huge advertisement from the European Commission inviting applications for six new senior management officials. Applicants have to come from Bulgaria, Cyprus, Czech

Republic, Estonia, Hungary, Latvia, Lithuania, Malta, Poland, Romania, Slovakia and Slovenia. Applications from English citizens will not be accepted.

What do you think might happen if I advertise for a new member of staff and insist that I will only accept candidates who are English?

Precisely.

The EU leaks money in every direction. The whole thing is an exercise in waste and excess. It costs £170 million to transport the European Parliament between Brussels and Strasbourg every month. £160,000 is spent hiring lorries to carry all the files. My book *The OFPIS File* is packed with information about the European Union – including details of why British politicians support the EU and how the British Government 'gold plates' legislation which is ignored by other nations in the EU.

★ ★ ★

In *The OFPIS File* I pointed out that many of the bad things happening in Britain are a direct result of orders from Brussels. Some critics (most of whom hadn't actually bothered to read the book) grunted that my book was filled with nonsense. The commonest complaint was that my remarks about the EU being the reason for the closure of our post offices was untrue.

But everything I said was absolutely true. The first rules affecting British postal services appeared in December 1997 when the EU announced that its competition rules apply to the postal sector. EU Directive 97/67/EC, issued on 15th December 1997 is entitled 'Privatisation of Postal Services' and was responsible for reducing the Royal Mail's monopoly. The EU then instructed the Post Office to reduce the size of its network by around 2,500 branches. This, strangely enough, is precisely the number of post offices which were closed by the Labour Government in its initial blitz on rural post offices. (As always the British Government was much quicker to accept the ruling from Brussels than other governments were.)

It is, of course, the EU's intention to run a trans-European postal service.

So, why don't Labour politicians admit that these unpopular closures are a result of edicts from the European Union's unelected officials?

Simple.

In 1971 the Foreign Office published a document entitled FCO 30/1048. In paragraph 24 the Foreign Office states: 'there would be a major responsibility on HMG and on all political parties not to exacerbate public concern by attributing unpopular measures or unfavourable economic developments to the remote and unmanageable workings of the Community.'

The Community is, of course, now known as the European Union.

The EU's rules encourage waste. The daft regulations are allegedly designed to make things safer but in reality they are designed to encourage new product sales. Manufacturers, shops and individuals have to dump perfectly good equipment, even though it may be safe and work perfectly well, if it doesn't obey the latest edit from Brussels.

Thanks to the EU we are awash with rules and regulations. There is a glut of legislation. We cannot open an account, close an account or sell a house without providing gas bills, passport copies and sworn statements. Companies and businesses spend much of their time dealing with absurd administrative nonsenses dreamt up by officials in Brussels who have never done a decent days work in their lives. But none of these rules, none of this legislation, none of these miles of financial red tape help protect us.

* * *

Nothing illustrates the EU's devotion to waste more succinctly than the Common Agricultural Policy (CAP).

The way EU bureaucrats have managed agriculture within the EU's boundaries is a good example (for those who have forgotten the Soviet Union) of the way that state intervention tends to produce inefficient, bureaucratic and costly industries.

For decades the EU has provided farmers in Europe with subsidies. Excess food grown in the EU has been dumped overseas and has held back agricultural development in Africa and elsewhere. The EU's Common Agricultural Policy has been a direct cause of millions of deaths from starvation and disease around the world. Anyone who supports the European Union is, therefore, guilty of sentencing thousands, if not millions, of innocents to death from starvation. That isn't rhetoric; it's a simple truth.

Everything the CAP does is unfair. It is difficult to think of a more immoral, corrupt, bureaucratic, expensive, wasteful way of supporting European farmers and destroying farmers in developing countries. British taxpayers (the main contributors to the fund) are forced to subsidise the production of food for which there is no market. And British consumers are forced to help keep the prices high. Taxpayers and consumers lose out twice. The excess food is then dumped on Third World countries at very cheap prices (making local farming unviable) or simply destroyed. To make things worse the EU's policies encourage the overuse of pesticides and the destruction of hedgerows and, inexplicably, pays money to farmers who do absolutely nothing with their fields. Smokers and tobacco companies have benefited enormously by the EU subsidising tobacco growing. Farmers in the Netherlands receive subsidies which are twice as big as farmers in Poland. And the richest landowners, with the most fertile land, get the most help. The Queen of England and Prince Albert of Monaco both receive six figure handouts from the EU.

For over a generation the British have been struggling to bring an end to the CAP. But the French created the CAP, the French love it and the French want it to continue. So it will. Indeed, under France's direction, the European Union is going to extend farm subsidies, damage Britain (the EU's main contributor) still further and do even more harm to farmers in Africa.

Finally, the waste of food, and the cost of food, are both exacerbated enormously by the absurd 'best before' dates which now have to appear on all foodstuffs (and which are, indeed, so universal that I even found myself looking for them on bars of soap the other day). The 'best before' dates are often absurd and the result is that, thanks to the EU, vast quantities of perfectly edible (and perfectly safe) food is thrown away.

★ ★ ★

Nothing illustrates the EU's determination to destroy the middle classes and impose its fascist rule upon us all more than the rules requiring local authorities to provide campsites for gypsies.

Councils throughout Britain are currently using satellite spy cameras to find private land where they can build gypsy sites. Once they have spotted potentially suitable land, councils who have been told to find 7,500 sites, use proactive planning powers, including compulsory purchase orders, forcibly to take land they have chosen. Even land which has been denied planning permission is being taken to create gypsy campsites. The Government (or, rather, the EU) has imposed targets which mean that local authorities must provide a specified number of sites. In theory, the gypsies using the sites will be expected to pay council tax. Around £100 million of taxpayers' money has been allocated for the project.

And don't think that your home is safe because the land near to it is difficult to access. One proposed site can only be accessed by a three yard wide gap between two houses.

The first householders hear about plans for a new gypsy site is a letter from the council. Protests are, inevitably, regarded as politically incorrect (though one suspects that remarkably few of these 7,500 gypsy sites will be situated next door to homes owned by Britain's thousands of EU representatives or employees). Those who object will be dismissed as unpleasant racists and probably visited by the police.

Many householders have submitted written objections to gypsy sites being set up next to their homes. Here are some of the commonest reasons for opposing such sites:

1. The council should be more concerned with taxpayers' rights than those of travellers.
2. A traveller site might have an adverse effect on property prices in the area.
3. A traveller site might lead to more litter.
4. A traveller site might lead to an increase in petty crime in the area.
5. Having travelling families nearby could mean an increase in noise levels.

Every one of those fears has been officially dismissed as racist. (One could argue, however, that forcing such sites onto local areas, against the wishes of the locals, particularly if the action results in a massive change in the nature of the native population, is itself a racist action and certainly likely to encourage racist attitudes.)

Why is the Government doing this?

Well, actually it isn't the Government.

It's, the, er, European Union.

The whole programme is being drawn up by regional assemblies which are, as readers of my book *The OFPIS File* will know, unelected quangos created by and serving the European Union and having the responsibility for 'strategic planning'.

(None of this was, of course, mentioned by the bits of the media which bothered to tell their readers, listeners and viewers about the gypsy site plans. The EU is never given the credit for its amazingly unwanted, unpopular and downright undemocratic schemes. And nor does the Government ever make it clear that this is an EU project. Both media and Government are determined to protect the EU from criticism – however justified that criticism might be.)

Meanwhile, anyone who has a home with land might consider moving. And anyone considering purchasing a home with a little land attached or nearby might reconsider. The people living near to existing or planned gypsy sites report that their homes are now unsaleable and, therefore, effectively worthless.

Alternatively, it might be wise to buy a home located near to a senior politician or EU employee. Curiously enough, gypsy sites rarely seem to be put in such areas.

★ ★ ★

And then there is the euro.

The EU currency, the euro, is hated everywhere and a vast majority of citizens who use it as their currency want their old currencies back. Of all the European countries who use the euro only the people of Romania, Denmark and Malta would vote to keep it. The rest want to get rid of it. There was a demonstration in Paris in February 2009 demanding the return of the French franc. (French shops never abandoned the franc. Even in 2009 there were shops still quoting prices in both euros and francs. With the franc price given first.)

The euro is a fake currency for a fake state.

Just before Christmas 2008, Jose Manuel Barrosa, president of the European Commission announced that 'the people who matter in Britain' believed that the UK should join the euro. (He didn't define 'the people who matter in Britain' but it's a pretty safe bet he wasn't talking about you and me.)

I have little doubt that the Government will use the economic crisis as an excuse to push for Britain to join the euro. The Labour Party promised that there would be a referendum about joining the euro. But there is no doubt that if a referendum was called the public would vote against our joining the EU's common currency. And so, the promise will probably yet again be ignored. Brown, if he is still Prime Minister, will find some way to wheedle out of his moral obligations and there won't be a referendum. Brown will simply sign the relevant documents and the pound sterling will be history.

But there is one snag.

The other euro countries might well turn us down. They might well point out that Britain is now the weakest country in the EU. And they might feel that the pound needs to be stronger (and higher against the euro) before Britain joins the single currency. And there are undoubtedly those in the EU who will point out that Britain's debts are so great that the nation's debt/Gross Domestic Product (GDP) ratio far exceeds 60% and may indeed be considerably more than 100% of GDP. (The Maastricht rules require member states of the EU to reduce their public debt to no more than 60% of GDP.) And for Britain to join the euro with the nation so burdened by debt would be a breach of the EU's own rules.

In the long run, none of this matters much.

In the long run, the euro will not exist.

I have for years believed that the euro has no future. If there was any doubt then that doubt disappeared during the economic crisis of 2008. Instead of working together to create and preserve a strong currency, the countries in the eurozone all did whatever they needed to do to protect themselves. Long centuries of nationalism cannot easily be rubbed away by a few power-hungry bureaucrats. And the financial markets recognised the fundamental weaknesses of the euro too. Gaps widened dramatically between the yields offered by German bonds and those offered by Spain, Ireland, Portugal, Italy and Greece. In theory, these countries share a currency and a common economic future. In practice, things aren't quite that simple. Some economies are considered more equal than others. As I write the yield on Greek bonds is 2.3% higher than that on German bonds; that spread is now ten times higher than it was a year ago. The perceived default risk for euro countries has risen dramatically and at least one ratings agency has warned Greece, Ireland, Spain and Portugal that their national debt might be downgraded. Individual countries which are in a special mess can do nothing to help themselves. They can't let their currency appreciate because their currency is the euro. And they can't lower interest rates because interest rates for all the countries in the 'eurozone' are fixed by the EU.

The credit crunch showed the weakness of the EU as politicians in individual countries within the EU forgot about their pledges to EU bureaucrats and started thinking of their own political futures.

The euro will not last many more years. And the collapse will be terrifying for those in the eurozone. France and Germany have retained their links with their old currencies and will be best placed to survive. Ironically, although it was France which has long controlled and promoted the European Union it will probably be the people of France who will be responsible for the euro's demise.

★ ★ ★

The vast majority of people in Britain want to leave the EU. But all three main parties are committed to maintaining our membership of the EU. A study of the way the EU operates makes it simple to understand why. In the end, the EU will be destroyed by a rise in nationalism inspired by poverty which will be blamed on immigration. The euro will go first. And then the EU itself will implode. Neither will be mourned.

Chapter 20

Edukation, Educashun, Educasian

One in five of all British school leavers cannot read or write properly. But the number of students leaving college with diplomas in media studies, brewing, tourism and hairdressing is soaring.

We spend more on education than ever before. But after ten years of a Labour Government devoted to education (the political slogan 'education, education, education' was actually stolen from East Germany) one in five of all 11-year-olds in Britain cannot read or do simple arithmetic.

Despite an endless production of new regulations, all the evidence shows that education standards in Britain are constantly falling. One in seven children struggle to write their name after a year at primary school. And academics claim that an A grade in today's A levels equates to a C grade 20 years ago. An increasing number of observers now suspect that the alleged explosion in the incidence of dyslexia in Britain is a result of illiteracy resulting from the failure of incompetent schoolteachers to teach children properly. According to the United Nations, the well-being of British schoolchildren is the poorest among industrialised nations.

Illiterate citizens are far, far more likely to commit crimes than literate ones. Over 80% of all inmates in British prisons have a reading ability no better than an 11-year-old.

More than a third of employers are today worried about the ability of their staff to read, write and add up correctly. Many firms have been forced to invest in remedial training in basic literacy and numeracy at a cost to the economy of £10 billion a year. I have a letter on my desk from a woman applying for a job at Publishing House. She assures me that she has a keen eye for detail and claims that at her former position she was responsible for 'stationary stock levels'. Listen to senior police officers being interviewed on television and you quickly get an idea of the quality of education in Britain.

It is hardly surprising, perhaps, that a 16-year-old Polish boy, a son of immigrants, said that he was appalled by the standards of education in Britain. He went back to his parents' home town to continue his schooling in Poland. An international survey of literacy levels put Britain 19th out of 45 countries.

One huge problem is that teaching in state schools no longer concentrates on the essentials or the basics. Traditional subjects are constantly being corrupted by political agendas. Britain now has 150 quangos, 5,000 Government officials and countless local authority employees telling teachers how to teach (and, between them, getting through a third of the entire education budget). In 2008 the Department of Education spent £72 million on 'consultants'. That would have paid for another 2,000 teachers which would have helped reduce class size (the proven way to improve learning.) Disciplined learning has been banned. New and untried methods of teaching have replaced traditional and effective teaching methods. Children as young as five will soon be given compulsory sex education and the Government says that four-year-olds must learn about same sex families. Children are allowed 'freedom of expression'. Teachers have no sanctions over children and, therefore, cannot control what happens in their classrooms. Teachers have been told to stop teaching pupils about British history and British values. Children are taught nothing about Henry VIII, Elizabeth I, Cromwell or the British Empire. Schools have abandoned direct teaching and pupils sit in groups learning (or attempting to learn) by 'discovery'. Errors go uncorrected because it is believed that this might discourage children. Sports days are banned because 'competition causes distress'. (And if there are no sports days the playing fields can be given planning permission and sold for housing.) Even examiners are incompetent. In early 2009, Britain's exams regulator said that Britain's examinations system was so error-ridden that it was 'inevitable' that some pupils would get inaccurate grades. How many is 'some'? Up to a third. What, pray, is the point of having an examination system with a possible 33% error rate? Why hasn't everyone involved been sacked?

British schools are legally obliged to involve themselves in multicultural activities. In practice this means that Christian crucifixes are banned from the classroom but Muslim headscarves are allowed. It can hardly come as a surprise that a quarter of all adults in Britain today cannot name the birthplace of Jesus Christ.

English is now a minority language in 1,300 British schools. There are 800,000 pupils in British schools who do not speak English as their first language. Schools spend £500,000,000 a year teaching English to migrant children. According to Government figures, white British children are in a minority in 20% of local education authority areas. In parts of London white children are outnumbered nine to one. More than 100 languages are spoken in schools in Suffolk. There are now so many Polish students in England that a Polish University is opening a branch in London. Last year, thousands of foreign students gained entry to Britain by being accepted at British universities. But 10,000 of them didn't turn up, though they are assumed to be in Britain somewhere.

The problem, of course, is political correctness and multiculturalism. Eleven-year-olds are taught that sex outside marriage is fine. One school let pupils boycott a Shakespeare test because they claimed, absurdly, that Shakespeare was anti-Semitic.

There is micromanagement and endless interfering from politicians who have their own agendas to sustain. Teachers have been allowed (and encouraged) to worry more about the 'educational experience' than the quality of their teaching. And the bad teachers, the really bad ones, don't get sacked. When, in the year 2000, Ofsted said that there were 15,000 incompetent teachers in our schools the then Education Secretary (the utterly useless David Blunkett) introduced a fast track procedure for firing poor staff within a month. And in 2001, the General Teaching Council was set up to protect children from under-performing staff. Councils are legally required to pass details of incompetent teachers to the watchdog but two thirds of all councils have not made one referral yet. So, guess how many teachers have been fired since 2000? Go on, guess. I'll give you a clue. It's less than 15,000 (the number who were judged incompetent nine years ago). In fact it's 10. That's how easy it is to stay in work if you're an incompetent public sector employee with a fat salary, a cushy life and a huge, index-linked taxpayer-funded pension when you retire.

It's attractive and easy for schools to concentrate on 'soft' subjects (such as 'media studies') instead of tougher subjects such as mathematics. The schools which head the official list of 'good schools' are invariably the ones which specialise in such weak, undemanding subjects. Teachers encourage pupils to follow certain subjects because it is in their personal interest (the more students there are taking a particular subject the bigger the department will be and the more money the teachers can earn). And of course some subjects (notably media studies) are much easier to teach than others. (They are easier to study too. Media studies students, for example, put in less than 20 hours work a week. It is hardly surprising that graduates find life in the real world too hot to handle.)

The same thing is happening at universities. Science, maths and languages are dying out in British universities. One in ten maths and science courses and 15% of French courses have closed under the Labour Government's control. University students, like school pupils, opt for media studies or tourism and other lighter and trendy subjects.

The Government encourages children to go to university and pretends this is so that everyone can have the same, advanced education. It is, of course, a cynical nonsense. Educational standards have fallen appallingly. University students now take courses in bar management or beauty care and graduates find that, despite their huge personal expenditure they are no more employable than they would have been if they had left school at 16. The everyone-must-go-to-university philosophy is one of the most cynical ploys in British history. The primary aim is to cut unemployment figures. And since students now have to take out loans to pay their fees the whole trick doesn't cost the Government a penny. Instead, truckloads of unemployable graduates with utterly useless degrees are chucked out of their university after three years with no prospects and huge debts. Ten years later these unfortunate souls have been so busy paying back their loans that they have no savings, no pensions and no homes.

★ ★ ★

And although they aren't doing much teaching, schoolteachers have now become an integral part of the 'let's drug our children to keep them quiet' movement. It is partly because so many teachers are prepared to diagnose the imaginary disease Attention Deficit Hyperactivity Disorder (ADHD), and to enthusiastically promote the virtues of drugs such as Ritalin, that half a million children in Britain are now diagnosed with ADHD and taking a drug I wouldn't use for landfill.

ADHD is a disease created to provide a purpose for a drug. Since 2002, the number of prescriptions being written for anti-hyperactivity drugs has risen to 535,000 a year. That figure is double what it was in 2002. And yet researchers have shown that a 20 minute stroll in the park could be just as effective for treating hyperactive children as a drug such as Ritalin. Parental enthusiasm for the diagnosis and the drug may well be influenced by the fact that once a child is on Ritalin its family is in line for up to £10,000 in benefits.

For more information about why ADHD doesn't exist and why Ritalin should be banned see my book *How To Stop Your Doctor Killing You*.

★ ★ ★

Today, our education system doesn't teach children to think. Specifically, it doesn't teach them to think about probabilities or uncertainties. And to be acceptable, books must be 'politically correct, relevant and accessible' (whatever that means).

The long-term consequences of all this are impossible to overestimate. We are creating a generation of greedy, egotistical, self-centred, politically correct semi-literates with useless diplomas in media studies, tourism and hairdressing. Their skills and qualifications will ill prepare them for the real world. If Britain's future depends upon its youth then the nation is in for a hard time.

Back in the dark days of the 1950s, nearly half of the children born to the poorest parents grew up to be higher earners. Today only around a third manage to escape from poverty. Thanks largely to the mess they've made of the educational system, the Labour Party's policies have taken away opportunities.

Chapter 21

Disappointment And Resentment Among The Young Will Grow

There will be a massive increase in the incidence of depression among the young as they slowly discover that they cannot all be reality TV stars.

Today's generation is known as the 'smug generation'. Full of self-confidence and high expectations they 'know' that they are brighter and better looking than their parents. They know they deserve fame, adulation and riches. We have created a generation which craves instant success and wealth. One in seven teenagers believe they will get all the fame they desire not through hard work but through appearing on a reality TV programme. Their aim is to go on TV, do something memorable (this need not be something that requires skill, talent or manners and, indeed, it probably won't be) and 'write' a book about their experience. They will be given a radio talk show as a result of the book. And then a TV series. And they will be paid huge sums to travel around the world visiting nightclubs. Sorted. They are full of ambition and self-regard. But the majority have little genuine drive and not much affection for hard work. The inevitable result will be under-achievement, disappointment and long-term sadness.

* * *

British teenagers were asked to list their role models. They chose:

1. Tony Blair (a vacuous war criminal)
2. Kate Moss (a thin model)
3. Pete Doherty (a man who wears a hat)
4. Paris Hilton (a relative of a hotel chain)
5. Jordan (a woman who became famous for having huge, artificial breasts)

★ ★ ★

Young people don't want unexciting jobs making things or doing things or serving people. They don't want to have to work for money and fame. They want it to be handed to them on a plate. Television reality shows have taught them that there is a short-cut and so just as millions now rely upon the lottery to provide them with a pension when they are old so millions rely upon the television reality show to provide them with a route to stardom, publicity (at any price) and wealth.

A comparison of school children found that members of the class of 2006 were far more confident than members of the class of 1975. Their fawning parents and teachers had bathed their egos determinedly, pumped them up with undeserved praise and inflated exam results, and created a smug generation. Teachers report that growing numbers of pupils are so spoilt at home that they are unable to behave and accept even basic rules at school. Never having been set boundaries they find it difficult to cope in any sort of structured society; they blame others for their own failures and refuse to do anything difficult or boring. I read an interview with a student recently who said that since he didn't think he would be able to find employment as an investment banker at the moment he would become a management consultant.

They are, of course, mostly doomed to disappointment. They will eventually be known as the disappointed generation.

It's not their fault, but just as their hopes have been raised by an educational system which has failed to prepare them for the real world (schools have been designed to eradicate any real sense of competition among pupils because competition, leading as it does to the chance of failure, is regarded by potty educationalists as damaging to the developing mind) so the real world has suddenly become extremely and exceptionally challenging.

As millions of young people slowly realise that they are not all going to become television presenters/pop stars/models/millionaire footballers so there will be widespread resentment and anger.

And eventually there will be depression.

The smug generation hasn't been prepared for the prospect of failure and disappointment and they will not know how to deal with it.

I wrote the first draft of this chapter in early 2008.

And then in early 2009, the Prince's Trust published the results of a survey of 16 to 25 year-olds which showed that 1 in 10 young people believed life was not worth living or was meaningless. The survey, of over 2,000, showed that more than a quarter felt depressed.

It's already happening.

Chapter 22

House Prices Are Going To Fall For Years (And They're Going To Fall A Lot)

The Labour Government's policies encouraged borrowing and were responsible for an unprecedented and unsustainable housing boom. House prices rose to absurd levels during the Labour Government's first decade. Sadly, things that go up have a regrettable tendency to come back down again. And since house prices went up far too high they will probably collapse to astonishing lows before they start to rise again.

It has been painfully obvious for years that house prices in Britain rose far too much during the first decade after 1997. By the start of 2009, houses in Britain were still more absurdly overpriced than anywhere else in the world. Houses and apartments in London have for several years been considerably more expensive than similar properties in New York, Paris, Tokyo or Monaco. At the end of 2007, I saw an advertisement in a magazine for a small building site in Cornwall. The price? An eyewatering £3,500,000. For a building plot for one house. In Cornwall.

People have been buying houses and apartments not because they saw them as good homes to live in but because they saw them as good investments. There is, of course, a massive difference in attitude and expectation. And there's a difference in the amount you are prepared to spend and how you are prepared to finance the purchase. Greed inspires risk. Badly-run banks and building societies encouraged the greed. (Because the people who ran them were, of course, also inspired by their own greed.)

Before it was nationalised, Northern Rock was offering mortgages of six times salary. Several other banks would lend buyers 125% of the value of their proposed new home. So, if you wanted to buy a modest home costing £200,000 (and how absurd it will soon be that a modest home should cost £200,000) you could borrow £250,000. And what could you do with the extra £50,000? The banks' suggestions included: home improvements, buying a car or going on holiday.

Mortgages could be obtained for periods in excess of half a century. There was an industry selling fake pay slips so that people could persuade their mortgage lenders to let them have bigger loans than they might otherwise think wise. There was a lot of nudging, winking and closing of eyes going on. If you were unemployed but wanted a fake pay slip to show that you had a £50,000 a year job with a blue-chip company you just typed 'duplicate pay slip' into an Internet search engine and chose your 'discreet and confidential' adviser. Then, you took your evidence to the bank and came away with a loan for a quarter of a million pounds.

Curiously, although bankers, estate agents and mortgage brokers were blamed for encouraging people to borrow too much money, hardly anyone said a word about the people who borrowed too much. Virtually no one pointed out that the greedy individuals who were borrowing money they couldn't hope to pay back, so that they could live in houses they couldn't possibly afford, deserved what they got.

'We hear so much about how the banks 'recklessly lent' to buyers but it is never mentioned that individuals recklessly borrowed. If the Government now helps to bail out these 'reckless borrowers', where is the financial lesson for those of us who actually thought about what we could afford when the banks were so generous?' Wrote a reader to the *Financial Times*.

★ ★ ★

There were two other things that made the situation worse.

After Brown deliberately and cold-bloodedly destroyed pensions for those Britons not employed by the Government, more and more people put their savings into property rather than pension funds. Brown's policies directly encouraged the rise in the buy-to-let market.

And obtaining planning permission to build new houses became increasingly complicated and expensive. A straightforward house application would have taken 8-12 weeks a few years ago. Under the Labour Government the bureaucracy increased so much that a similarly straightforward application could take 18 months. The cost of steering a way through the bureaucracy added to the cost of building a house – and also helped increase house prices.

Partly deliberately and partly through incompetence and stupidity, the Labour Government forced a tremendous increase in house prices. Gordon undoubtedly welcomed the housing bubble. It was, after all, the dramatic and rather absurd increase in house prices which gave the nation the false growth it needed to pay for Gordon's mania for spending.

* * *

House prices will go down much further than seems sensible or logical because people will panic and they will sell at any price. And just as they lost touch with reality when prices were going up so they will lose touch with reality as prices come down. Greed took house prices up. (Though there was also the misplaced fear amongst buyers that if they didn't buy quickly then they would never be able to buy). Fear, and nothing but fear, will take prices down.

In my book *Gordon is a Moron* I wrote: 'Looking at the figures dispassionately it seems that by mid 2007, property in Britain was between 20% and 30% overvalued by every possible sensible criteria. But this doesn't mean that if house prices fall they will fall by 20% to 30%. When markets get out of kilter, as they do from time to time, and as they have under Gordon Brown's direction, the correction which invariably ensues always goes as far in the other direction. So, if house prices are overvalued by (say) 25% then the chances are that house prices will fall not by 25% but by 50%. By then, of course, no one will be buying houses.'

Banks, I predicted, would not be lending because they would be up to their eyeballs in bad debt.

* * *

Naturally, Gordon (aided and abetted by his pals at the Bank of England) followed his instincts and did everything he could to make things worse.

In late 2008, the Bank of England cut interest rates to get the economy moving and to help house owners who were struggling to pay the mortgages they should never have taken out and were now realising they couldn't afford. By the end of 2008, it seemed likely that borrowers could see mortgage rates fall as low as 0%. And banks which had lent money to borrowers at a rate guaranteed to be below the official bank rate would then find themselves having to pay people to borrow money. Hardly fair to savers (receiving no interest on the money in their deposit accounts) and, indeed, hardly likely to help the banks work their way back towards solvency.

Gordon announced all sorts of measures specifically designed to ensure that the housing crisis lasted for longer and ended up causing even more damage. He told banks that they had to carry on lending money at the rate at which they had been lending in 2007. He alone seemed unaware that the housing crash had been made worse, if not created, by banks lending too much money to too many people who couldn't afford to pay it back.

Brown even introduced a scheme enabling greedy house buyers to put off paying their interest for two years. Brilliant. You have a £500,000 house which you couldn't afford to buy but which the bank and the Government encouraged you to purchase with a massive loan. The plan is simple. The Government will help you stay in the house you could not afford and should never have bought. It didn't occur to Brown that after two years the value of the house might have fallen by half. So, you would then be forced to sell. And either pay off a £250,000 debt or go bankrupt. Or sue the bank for letting you stay in your house for too long. It's like the Government telling casinos and bookies that they cannot take money from people who have lost. Honest, careful, prudent taxpayers will be subsidising the greedy and the cheats. This is economic madness; a policy designed to win votes not to save the country.

But if the people who had greedily bought houses they couldn't afford were being protected from their own greed, the people who now wanted to jump onto the stationary bandwagon were having a tough time of it. Banks weren't lending because they were broke.

'We have to do something,' insisted Government ministers. Why? Britain would have been far, far better off if Brown, Mandelson and the rest had gone and sat on a yacht for a few years.

In the UK, the ultimate irony of the credit crunch was that

Gordon 'the moron' Brown brought disgraced former minister Peter Mandelson back into his cabinet to help deal with the crumbling economy. No politicians, journalists or commentators seem to have noticed that on one of the previous occasions when he had to resign Mandelson's crime had been to lie on a mortgage application form in order to persuade his mortgage lender to let him have money they would not otherwise have been prepared to lend him. He had borrowed £373,000 from a fellow minister and then lied to his mortgage lender to obtain by deception another £150,000 to buy a house he couldn't possibly afford. It was, of course, precisely that sort of despicable behaviour that triggered the credit crunch. So, one of the many greedy individuals whose irresponsible behaviour had helped bring the system to the brink of total collapse was brought back, at enormous public expense, to deal with the consequences of the communal greed.

* * *

By the start of 2009 house prices were still way overpriced.

Look at this example.

If you wanted to buy a nice, but fairly ordinary detached house in the provinces you would have to find £500,000. We're not talking mansions here. We're talking three or four bedrooms, one bathroom and a small garden. Something nice and middle class.

Pop into the bank for a loan and, even if they would consider lending you any money, they would want you to find 20% of the cash yourself. They might provide the other 80%. So that means you'd have to find £100,000. Cash. If you didn't have the loot lying around in your bank account you would, of course, have to sell your own house in order to raise the money.

And the other £400,000?

Well, the bank would only lend you money at the old-fashioned rate of three times your salary. So you'd need to prove that you had a reliable income of £400,000 divided by three. That's £133,333 a year.

Now, I don't know about you but I don't know all that many nice, middle class people earning £133,333 a year.

So, at the start of 2009, I was pretty confident that house prices still had a long, long way to fall.

* * *

It is a myth that there is a shortage of homes in Britain. At the start of 2009 there were almost one million empty properties across Britain. And rents were falling fast as more and more landlords struggled to find tenants. Nearly half of all buy-to-let landlords were in negative equity, and desperate.

★ ★ ★

Household debt has risen faster in the UK than anywhere else in the world. Encouraged by Brown's policies, consumers have loaded up on credit and run down their savings to historic lows. The nation went on an unprecedented, and unmatched, spending spree. It is inconceivable that this madness will not now be matched by an equally lengthy period of retrenchment. Consumers will spend less as households struggle to pay off their debts and then build up some savings. To make things worse, nearly half of all homebuyers with interest-only mortgages have no specific savings plan to repay their debts. During the great mortgage binge of the early 21st Century a total of £66 billion was loaned to 1.3 million homebuyers without any formal agreement on how the money was to be repaid. The homebuyers and the loan companies all seemed to be hoping that something would turn up. Oh dear.

★ ★ ★

In 1992, when Britain left the wretched Exchange Rate Mechanism (ERM) the official interest rate rose as high as 15%. Banks were charging their customers much more than that.

How many British mortgage holders will still be able to pay their monthly mortgage bill when interest rates rise to 15% again?

An interest only charge on a £200,000 mortgage will be £30,000 a year. How many people in a modest semi-detached house will be able to find that sort of money out of their after tax income?

Especially when tax rates are raised to pay for the huge debts incurred by Gordon Brown and his Government.

I suspect house prices are going to be falling for quite some time. I stick by my long-held prediction that they will fall 50% from their peak. And I believe that when they have stopped falling they will remain stagnant for a long time. The days when people were earning more from their house than from their work are unlikely to return in the foreseeable future.

Chapter 23

Our American Inspired Oil Wars Will Continue

If we really want to fight a war to defend ourselves, our sovereignty, our history and our freedom we should be fighting a war against the EU bureaucrats in Brussels. But, thanks to the Labour Government and a docile Parliament, we have spent much of the last decade fighting two wars against people who have neither harmed nor threatened us.

There are two types of war: the type in which a country is attacked and defends itself and the type in which a country starts a war by attacking another country for some sort of gain. As with gunfighters, it is good countries which fight only to defend themselves and bad countries which start the shooting. Since Britain has, in the last decade, started two major wars (and murdered countless thousands of innocent citizens in Iraq and Afghanistan) we are now a bad country.

The wars we have been fighting (and are still fighting) were started by us, even though we were not attacked. The wars have resulted in the deaths of hundreds of thousands of innocent people, and hundreds of British servicemen and women have died. The wars have cost us billions of pounds, and will cost us billions more. Moreover, the wars will put every British citizen at risk for many years to come. The sole beneficiaries? The Americans who want the oil those countries can provide.

★ ★ ★

British troops are likely to be withdrawn from Iraq in 2009. The Government and the military are, of course, claiming that this is because we have won a famous victory in Iraq. These are either blatant lies or an example of extraordinary stupidity. The oil-inspired invasion of Iraq was always doomed to be an expensive failure. The main beneficiaries have, of course, been American companies and American politicians. (I forecast much of what eventually happened in Iraq in my book *Rogue Nation*, which was published before the invasion took place.)

As troops are pulled out of Iraq (leaving that part of it which isn't producing oil so destabilised and vulnerable that Iraqi citizens are able to apply successfully to be accepted into the UK as asylum seekers), so they will be sent into Afghanistan where we are, with the Americans, fighting another oil war. Our soldiers can genuinely said to be between Iraq and a hard place.

Invading forces have repeatedly failed to conquer Afghanistan. Our efforts there will merely antagonise Muslims still further and make Britain the world's premier target for terrorists. The UK has been sending 17-year-olds (officially children according to UN) to fight in the Iraq war and 17-year-olds will doubtless be sent to fight in Afghanistan too. As far as I am aware no senior politicians have so far sent their children into either of these unjustifiable wars.

And it will, of course, be the Americans, not the British, who will benefit from any energy gains derived from the war. Britain will be left with a lot of mourning families.

★ ★ ★

You might imagine that now that Iraq is controlled by the Americans, the Iraqis will be happy and feel safer than when the ogre Saddam Hussein was swanning around trying to choose a Palace du Jour. Not a bit of it. The Iraqis are leaving the security and peace offered by American and British invading armies in far greater numbers than ever. Flights out of Iraq are fully booked weeks in advance. Flights into Iraq are virtually empty – containing only a few campaigners flying in to remind the Iraqi women of their feminist rights. Traffic jams at the borders happen only in one direction. According to the UN High Commission for Refugees one in ten Iraqis has fled their country and now lives abroad. If things go on at this rate there will soon come a time when the only people left will be the invading armies. In sheer numbers of people it's a bigger crisis than the one in Darfur. It's the largest migration in the Middle

East since Palestinians fled Israel in 1948. The American-led war has resulted in there now being 2.4 million Iraqi refugees. Many have moved to Europe, claiming political asylum as they flee from the Americans. Countless thousands, forced out of their country, are in refugee centres in places like Sweden. Vast numbers have moved to Jordan and Syria.

★ ★ ★

Dozens of British soldiers have been killed by American troops in Iraq and Afghanistan (the Americans seem, however, to be less likely to kill other Americans). The American murderers (usually pilots) invariably get away with it. For example, in one of the very few instances where someone was accused of something, a Major Harry Schmidt, an American pilot was found guilty of dereliction of duty after dropping a laser-guided 500 lb bomb on Canadian troops. He was fined £2,500 and reprimanded.

If you count as your enemy the people who kill most of your side then the Americans are our enemy. They seem to kill more of our troops than the Iraqis and the Afghanistanis who must, therefore, be considered our allies in these conflicts.

★ ★ ★

Most of the Americans who are found guilty of murdering or abusing Iraqi or Afghan civilians get away very lightly. Most are simply demoted, have their pay docked or get a simple reprimand. According to civil liberties groups Human Rights First and Human Rights Watch, only about half of the hundreds of allegations against American troops and other personnel have been adequately investigated. Around 330 credible cases of torture, killings and abuse have been documented but of the 600 American soldiers and officials implicated only around 40 had been given custodial sentences.

★ ★ ★

How brilliant it was of the Labour Government to allow unlimited numbers of Muslims into Britain while at the same time starting two wars against Muslim countries.

★ ★ ★

The Labour Party's wars mean that Britain's military expenditure is now second only to that of the USA. We spend more than France, Germany, Japan, Saudi Arabia or, indeed, any other country in the world except the USA. Amazingly, the British Government spends £823 per head on arms and armed forces. China, in comparison, spends just £35 a head. Our gross expenditure on military matters is £50 billion. Russia, in comparison, spends just £32.5 billion.

* * *

Former boxer Chris Eubank was arrested for driving through London with an anti-war poster attached to his lorry. He was arrested for a breach of the peace. Protesting against war is a breach of the peace. Enough ironies there to keep us all going for a while. And how can anyone breach the peace when we are at war with half the world? How about arresting Blair and Brown for causing a breach of the peace?

* * *

The death rate in Iraq is double what it was before we invaded – in other words we are killing twice as many Iraqis as Saddam Hussein was. At least 655,000 Iraqi civilians were estimated to have died by the start of 2007. The number killed is now considerably more.

* * *

The war in Iraq will end when the Americans are satisfied that they have control of the oil. The war in Afghanistan will continue indefinitely. Wars in Afghanistan always continue indefinitely.

Chapter 24

Health And Safety: Onward Blindly And Without Purpose Or Good Sense

Inspired and led by EU bureaucrats, Britain's highly paid army of health and safety experts know bugger all about health and safety. They suppress the harmless and the life-enhancing and ignore the real problems because they don't understand the principles of risk any more than they understand how diseases and illnesses are caused.

A ten-year-old boy was banned from cycling two miles to school because of health and safety rules. The boy wanted to ride his bike to be environmentally friendly, but was told by his school that he could do so only if his mother drove behind him.

Volunteers at a hospital were banned from selling home-made cakes to raise funds for the hospital because of health and safety fears. The volunteers baked and sold the cakes to raise money for NHS equipment but were told that they couldn't do it again. Too dangerous.

Health and safety Gestapo officers confiscated salt cellars from fish and chip shops and replaced them with approved salt shakers which had fewer holes. This exercise in health fascism cost the local taxpayers more than £2,000. (The customers, of course, simply shook for longer.)

Before Christmas 2008, it was announced that men and women wanting temporary work as Father Christmases would have to go on health and safety courses to ensure that they didn't hurt themselves by balancing children on their knees.

Most bizarrely, and cruelly, of all, perhaps, was the news that Labour plans to ban children from school if they have not had the MMR jab. It would then presumably arrest the parents for not sending their children to school. (Vaccination is, at best, a controversial issue. I have shown in numerous books (most recently *Coleman's Laws*) just why I believe that vaccination is a major cause of illness and why vaccination should be stopped.)

The madness is everywhere. Residents have been told that they cannot have doormats outside their homes because they are a health and safety risk and must be removed. Some councils have even threatened to take residents to court if they ignore their advice. (One council has said that it will not enforce a total ban but will assess each mat on an individual basis. They will presumably soon be advertising for Mat Assessment Officers. More £30,000 a year non-jobs.)

When gales blew sand into a pensioner's garden he kindly carted the sand back to the beach. But the council warned him that if he did it again they would prosecute him for fly-tipping and he would face a fine of £50,000 or a jail sentence. A spokesidiot for the council said: 'The council has no responsibility to clear sand from private land, the owner must do this. However, dumping anything from your garden on to the beach constitutes fly-tipping.'

Cat-owners have been threatened with prison for letting their cats get fat. A council is spending £15,000 of taxpayers' money on telling grown ups how to cross the road. In Hartlepool, a children's sack race was cancelled because the cost of insuring the competitors was over £400. The race was due to be held on grass. Everywhere in England, wheelbarrow races and three-legged races are a thing of the past. Children are not allowed to play conkers unless they wear goggles.

An author who wrote a book honouring First World War soldiers was told that his book could not be stocked in the local tourist information centre unless he paid £150 for £5 million worth of insurance in case the book fell on someone's foot. Or, horror of horrors, they got a paper cut.

Police refused to chase a thief who'd stolen a motorbike because he wasn't wearing a helmet. (Another example of the rights of the thief being put above the rights of the victim.)

Cheshire county council ordered a local council to remove goalposts from a field in case ramblers bumped into them.

The health and safety police have even entered our graveyards where they have been wandering around pushing on gravestones to see if they topple over. (You might think that if you are a gravestone and you have been standing in a graveyard for 175 years then you are entitled to topple over in your own time if the fancy takes you without some po-faced, dried up health and safety weed giving you a push to see if you are safe.)

A church I know has health and safety warnings stuck to every pew, reminding worshippers of the terrible things that might happen to them just at the moment when they are trying to achieve some spiritual relief from a world full of chaos, uncertainty and danger and where, indeed, they may have gone to pray for safety and protection. Putting health and safety notices in churches is a state intrusion, a barbaric memory of the fascist world in which we live, a reminder of statist atheism, a sacrilege.

The Government is spending £400 million on a campaign to 'heal Britain's obesity problem'. Does it really cost £400 million (that's around £8 a head) to tell people to eat when they're hungry and to stop when they're full? The £400 million will be spent on advisors and self-proclaimed dieticians and nutritionists who, in order to justify their existence and their vast salaries, will over complicate something very simple. And once again people will be encouraged (and taught) not to take responsibility for themselves but to expect someone to take on that responsibility for them.

A baker has been told by officials that she must rename her Robin Tarts because they don't contain robins, that she mustn't sell tarts called Miss Piggy because although they have sugar pigs on the top, they don't contain any pork and that she must stop calling one of her cakes 'Paradise Slice' because, it doesn't come from paradise. The local trading standards buffoon said that 'consumers have a right to know what is in food'.

The Scottish Executive spent £2.5 million of English taxpayers' money on a campaign to teach Scots how to wash their hands. The State produced a guide to the ten stages of hand washing and employed 14 'hand-washing co-ordinators' on salaries of £50,000 a year.

Park benches throughout Britain are to be replaced (or simply discarded) because they are three inches too low. Health and safety laws state that benches must be at least 17.75 inches high so that the elderly and the disabled can get off them easily.

A charity placed a knitting box (containing wool and needles) in a hospital waiting area so that patients could knit a square of a blanket for charity while they waited. The hospitals removed the knitting needles claiming that they presented a safety hazard.

A self-employed painter and decorator was fined £30 for smoking in his van while driving to the shops to buy some teabags. The man was told that because his van counts as his place of work he couldn't smoke in it. The painter pointed out that he decorates houses not vans. The van was insured only for private use and had no markings. Thanks to the EU, smoking is banned in places of work and all public places. The only places where it is legal to smoke in Britain are the bars in the Houses of Parliament. MPs banned smoking in every club and bar in Britain, except their own.

My 86-year-old father had to pay for his car's MOT test twice (and drive his car to and from the MOT test centre twice) when the car failed the test. I have the 'Refusal of an MOT Test Certificate' form in front of me. The car failed because the 'Offside lower windscreen has a sticker or other obstruction encroaching into the swept area by more than 40mm outside zone A'. The obstruction which resulted in the car's failure was the cardboard badge allowing my father to park in disabled parking bays. He had left the badge tucked up against the windscreen and because of this he had to drive all the way back to the test centre on a subsequent day. I find it appalling that anyone can be so callous and so uncaring as to use legislation to trick an elderly man in such a way. But I find it equally appalling that the legislation allows and endorses such behaviour. It would have taken the mechanic who failed the car a fraction of a second to pick up the disabled badge and put it to one side. (I didn't find out about this until some time afterwards. This is probably a good thing for, although no one could describe me as a violent person, there is little doubt that if I had heard about it at the time I would by now be serving the appropriate sentence for driving a wooden stake through the place in the motor mechanic's chest cavity where one might normally expect to find a heart.)

It is now illegal to wrap fish and chips in newspaper in case we are poisoned by the ink. (I have, incidentally, been unable to find any evidence of chip eaters being made ill by newspaper ink.) Instead of newspaper our chips are served in horrible polystyrene boxes. Presumably, witless council experts believe that using polystyrene boxes that take 500 million years to rot, and have to be manufactured specially, is somehow more ecologically sound than using old newspapers.

The lunacies are endless. Councils are banning Punch and Judy shows on the grounds that they glorify domestic violence. (Curiously, they don't seem to worry about television programmes such as the BBC's Eastenders which have apparently made domestic violence a constant theme.) Shopkeepers who put displays of vegetables or flowers on the pavement outside their shops are arrested because they might be obstructing the free passage of wheelchairs (even if they aren't). No ice cream van can play its chimes for more than four seconds every three minutes. Woe betide the ice cream van driver whose tune tinkles for a second too long. I have absolutely no doubt that councils all over Britain now employ Ice Cream Chime Timing Consultants at £40,000 a year. I also have no doubt that the anti-ice-cream-van-chime legislation originated in the Belgian capital.

Even postmen are getting in on the act. There has, in recent years, been a dramatic increase in the number of homes where the Royal Mail won't deliver letters because of health and safety issues. Postmen have, to my knowledge, refused to deliver for the following reasons: stairs were too slippery, the road was too narrow and steep, shrubs were overgrown, a driveway was too bumpy, the letter box was at the bottom of the door (meaning that the postman would have to bend down) and the letter box slammed shut too hard. Oh dear, what a pity. Whoops. There, there, never mind. Maybe postmen are just becoming wimpy.

Where does all this nonsense come from?

Well, not all of it comes from Brussels. It seems that some of it is self inflicted; created by idiots who like to interfere. An organisation called BSI British Standards (which already has 27,000 current standards) even wants to introduce standards for trees. They have proposed that every year each landowner or householder should check the trees on his land. The trees would be formally inspected by a trained person every three years and inspected by a more qualified arboculturalist every five years. The scheme would, of course, create a huge industry of tree experts and colleges to train them. What utter, utter madness. I suggest that the people who think up these crazy things should be sat in darkened rooms, wearing straight jackets, and observed through a metal grille twice a day.

Meanwhile politicians want to add fluoride to our drinking water. In February 2008, the Health Secretary, a former postman, announced that he believed that adding fluoride to the water supply was an effective and relatively easy way to help prevent tooth decay. He presumably thinks it is easier than persuading parents to stop feeding their children on junk. I'm glad he didn't add the word 'safe' to his commendation. Dumping fluoride in the drinking water may cut the costs of providing a free dental service to those feckless citizens who can't be bothered to clean their teeth properly but it may also kill people. (How long will it be, I wonder, before councils start hiring Dental Cleansing Advisory Officers. Maybe they have. I daren't look.)

An airline called easyjet would not carry stem cells needed for a transplant operation because the packaged contained more than 100ml of fluid and so 'posed a security risk'. The cells, which had taken five months to grow, had to travel from Bristol to Barcelona within 16 hours to be of use.

Sometimes the health and safety police become confused. Most are desperately politically correct and this can cause problems. So, for example, playing conkers is banned but marathon running is allowed. Why? After the 2007 London Marathon, a 22-year-old runner died and it was reported that 77 others needed hospital treatment. This was the ninth death since the start of the London Marathon in 1981 and it means that the London Marathon is more dangerous than Grand Prix racing.

The real problem, of course, is that Britain's army of highly paid health and safety experts actually know bugger all about health and safety. They ignore all the real problems because they don't understand the principles of risk any more than they understand how diseases and illnesses are caused.

For example, food infections in Britain are constantly rising and will do so as long as cake shops, bread shops and supermarkets are allowed to display their produce on open shelves where it can be coughed on and fondled by any passer-by. In one store where sweets are sold in open bins (sometimes covered by an easily lifted plastic lid) the manager regularly instructed new members of staff not to take sweets from the bins. This was not because he was worried about pilfering but because he knew that the sweets were so badly contaminated with bugs that anyone who ate them would probably be sick (and unable to work).

'I wouldn't eat anything from there,' one restaurant worker told me, nodding towards a salad bar where the food was on open display. 'When you've seen people coughing, sneezing, dribbling and dripping into the coleslaw it rather puts you off.'

The health and safety people visit regularly but never say anything about the open-plan coleslaw.

Chapter 25

Biased Broadcasters Suppress And Distort The Truth

Declining broadcasting standards are damaging every aspect of British life, encouraging exhibitionism and voyeurism and sustaining politically correct bigotry and multicultural prejudices.

The BBC is the broadcaster we all pay for. It belongs to us all. But it doesn't represent us all. The BBC may not exist to defend the Government and to promote Government policies but in practice that is what it does. Although licence payers provide the money, the system is run by and protected by the Government, and BBC staff know very well that if they annoy the Government too often then they don't have a future (and most of them would fail to get work outside the organisation because they are institutionalised and too inefficient and incompetent to find work in the real world). Of course, the BBC will occasionally broadcast something vaguely critical of the Government. But they do this in the same way (and for the same reasons) that tabloids publish material that makes them look fair-minded and even-handed. It is done to bewilder and confuse the readers and it is done so that they can, if pressed, produce evidence of their impartiality. In practical terms, BBC staff are civil servants and are, therefore, unlikely ever to do anything honourable, creative or critical of the establishment.

In practice, the BBC is a perfect example of what goes wrong when you separate capital from labour. The people who pay for the BBC (licence fee payers) have no rights and no control whatsoever over the people who receive the money (BBC employees). The result is that the BBC is out of touch with the people who pay the bills. Here's a small example. When snow fell in February 2009 I was in Paris. I turned on the radio to listen to the 'news' and heard a man laughing and joking about how he'd skipped off work and taken the day off to have fun in the snow. It was agreed that this was a fine thing to do and that more people should behave like this. The man was a schoolteacher. His salary was paid by private sector taxpayers who had, by and large, struggled through the snow to get to work so that their businesses had a better chance of surviving the global recession. Schoolteachers taking the day off had, of course, made life very difficult for workers with children.

A report commissioned by the BBC concluded that the organisation is out of touch with great chunks of the public and guilty of 'unconscious self-censorship' on issues it finds unpalatable. In other words, the BBC has a politically correct bias which has left it out of touch. The BBC is legally required to be 'independent, impartial and honest'. It is none of these things. The BBC supports the Labour Government, the European Union (and European federalism), the State and Statism, mass immigration, minority rights, multiculturalism and progressiveness in the education and justice systems. The BBC, a Soviet style State broadcaster which exists only to defend the fascist establishment, rarely questions the official establishment line on science and medicine. After the Israelis bombed a United Nations school in the Gaza strip, the BBC declined to show film of the wounded on the grounds that the pictures were too disturbing. The BBC must have known that it was images of children being pulled like broken dolls from the ruins of their homes which did Israel's reputation enormous, and probably irreparable, damage in 2006. Mention of the elected Palestinian Government is usually accompanied by the word 'militant'.

Israeli spin-doctors want to trick the world into believing that the cruel and oppressive war they are fighting is part of the 'war on terror'. The facts hardly support this outrageous fabrication. Many organisations are working to bring war crimes indictments against Israel's leaders. According to a tally of Geneva Conventions and United Nations resolutions which have been defied and ignored, Israel is said to be the most lawless regime on our planet. BBC viewers and listeners may not know this.

Shortly afterwards the BBC appalled the nation by refusing to air an appeal for aid to be sent to Gaza, claiming, inexplicably, that to do so might damage its reputation. Channel 4 (which is, of course, also public funded), ITV and Channel 5 all agreed to broadcast the appeal. All the BBC did, of course, was convince many that suspicions about the BBC's lack of impartiality were well-founded. The impression I was left with was that the BBC was doing what it could to protect Israel's interests and damaged reputation. This is perhaps not too surprising when you realise that the Labour Government, to which the BBC shows clear and sustained allegiance, licensed the sale of £18,847,795 worth of arms to Israel in the first quarter of 2008 alone. So the bullets and bombs raining down on the women and children of the Gaza strip were ours. In its heavy-footed, clumsy, arrogant way the BBC produced the opposite result from the one it claimed it wanted. Viewers were convinced that, once again, the BBC had exhibited partiality and they were also reminded of the cruelty and wickedness of the Israelis. The BBC's argument made no logical or moral sense. If a cameraman sees a child bleeding to death does he keep filming and refuse to help because to do so might affect his credibility or independence? That is, effectively, the argument the BBC seemed to me to have put forward.

★ ★ ★

In January 2009, I learned that the BBC was spending £15 million of licence fee payers' money a year on a new BBC TV channel aimed at Iran. The question 'Why?' demands answers which I know I'll never get.

★ ★ ★

There is no longer any dispute that the BBC is biased. The only argument now is about the extent of the bias. The rest of the media do not, of course, like to discuss this. This is because those who don't work for the BBC want to be invited onto chat shows when they have something to promote or, better still, live in hope of being invited to present something on the radio or television and receive a very large chunk of licence fee payers' money for their trouble. BBC television and radio pay their presenters far more than commercial stations. Collectively, the BBC seems to have a long memory. Those who annoy just one tiny part of it suspect that their disrespect will be long remembered and when their colleagues have their books, films, records, plays or whatever reviewed and promoted with awe, their productions (whatever they may be) will either be ignored or reviewed without credit.

It is not the BBC's place to take a view on contentious issues. But it does. Andrew Marr, a former BBC political editor, described the corporation as 'a publicly funded urban organisation with an abnormally large proportion of younger people, of people in ethnic minorities and almost certainly of gay people, compared with the population at large.' What he didn't say was that the BBC's licence fee is paid largely by white, middle-class English people whose views are most certainly not represented.

The BBC receives £3 billion but spends it on programmes like Eastenders and highly paid 'personalities' such as Jonathan Ross. Licence fee payers (who are forced to pay the BBC's own very special tax) have no genuine control over programming and no control over which presenters are hired or how much they are paid. The taxpayers don't even have any control over who runs the BBC. For those inside the BBC the organisation must be a perfect quango: plenty of authority and absolutely no responsibility to the people who provide the money. The BBC is a wildly prejudiced organisation; it is quite out of control and those who work for it have long since abandoned any sense of fair play or decency. The organisation is corrupt, insensitive and immoral and careless of its responsibilities to the licence fee payers who are forced, by law, to pay its bills. The BBC has a number of agendas but the organisation's main corporate agenda is preserving its own status as the sole recipient of the licence fee. In order to do this it uses its programmes to provide employment, and a platform, for those members of the establishment who support the BBC and the licence fee. I suspect that individuals who are regarded as a threat to the establishment and the BBC are, whenever possible, kept out of its studios.

The BBC is also endlessly, painfully, pathetically politically correct. At the end of 2008, for example, the BBC broadcast what I can only describe as the first feminist version of John Buchan's classic novel *The 39 Steps*. In the BBC's version of the story, written and produced by women of course, a delicate heroine (invented by Hitchcock for his film version of the book) turns into a tough, hard-talking suffragette spy. The hero, Richard Hannay, seemed to me to have become little more than arm candy for the BBC's feminist heroine. Now I have no objection per se to the BBC broadcasting feminist propaganda (though I'm not sure that such a policy fits neatly into its remit as a public service broadcaster), but why bastardise classic stories to do it? Giving Buchan's adventure story a tough feminist heroine made as much sense as turning Jane Eyre into a story about a Polish transsexual or making Miss Marple a transvestite docker.

★ ★ ★

It has been shown, quite conclusively, that the BBC is biased in favour of the European Union. A 2005 report showed that pro-European voices outnumber Eurosceptics by two to one on the BBC. The director-general of the BBC has admitted that the BBC's political coverage has long been systematically biased in favour of the political elite driving forward the European Union. This is utterly outrageous. News reports do not give a balanced view of the EU.

The BBC's blatant bias in favour of the EU makes me wonder if this is why the organisation seems to go out of its way to ignore 'England' and 'English' issues. News reporters seem to prefer to interview foreigners rather than English folk. There is a BBC Radio Scotland and a BBC Radio Wales but there is no BBC Radio England. And yet the BBC is spending £11 million a year on a new Scots Gaelic channel, which has a potential audience of fewer than 60,000 people. In the past I often appeared on programmes produced by BBC Scotland and BBC Wales. I don't think I was ever interviewed by an English presenter in either country. But vast numbers of the presenters fronting programmes for English viewers and listeners were born in Scotland and Wales. It sometimes seems to me that it is quite rare to hear a genuine English voice on the BBC these days. The English have a Government run by Scots. And they hear about its doings by listening to programmes presented by Scots. Why do the English put up with it so meekly?

One of the arguments in favour of the BBC is that it exists to ensure that national sporting events are available, without extra charge, on terrestrial television. If this is the case why are sporting events involving national English teams (rugby and cricket for example) so rarely shown on the BBC? The BBC can hardly say it doesn't have enough money to pay for sports programmes. In 2008, it committed itself to paying a rumoured £45 million a year for five years to show Formula One Grand Prix racing. Licence fee payers did not need the BBC to spend licence fee money on funding Formula One. The races were already being shown on ITV and viewers were perfectly happy with the service they were getting. I couldn't help wondering if it was really a coincidence that the politically correct, multicultural BBC had decided to show Formula One Grand Prix racing in the year that the sport acquired its first black world champion.

★ ★ ★

In the summer of 2008, 472 BBC staff were involved in a conference call to discuss the BBC's coverage of the USA party conventions. According to one insider, the BBC had a bigger presence at the USA conventions than any of the American networks, including CNN and Fox. (I couldn't help wondering about the size of the BBC's carbon footprint.) Not surprisingly, none of the main players could be bothered wasting much time talking to the BBC (they were more interested in speaking to American stations which would reach potential voters). Why couldn't the BBC's existing American correspondents cover the election?

★ ★ ★

The BBC's top 50 executives are all paid more than Britain's Prime Minister. The director general took home £816,000 in 2007. And far too many presenters are paid multimillion pound salaries for doing very humdrum jobs. The BBC spends a fortune on champagne and taxis. At Christmas 2008, as the nation shivered and worried, the BBC put £5,000 of licence fee takings behind the bar at the Radio 1 Christmas party so that BBC employees could enjoy a free bar. The BBC's taxi bill between April 2007 and March 2008 was a staggering £13,800,000. In summer 2008, the BBC was fined £400,000 (paid for by licence fee holders) over unfair television and radio competitions in which competitions were aired which audiences had no chance of winning. After a year of scandal the BBC's directors rewarded each other with enormous pay rises worth £107,000. And 12 BBC trustees claimed £147,368 in expenses. BBC trustees even claimed expenses for their subscriptions to Sky television's satellite channels. (So, BBC licence fee payers were paying for BBC bosses to watch Sky TV.)

★ ★ ★

A better way has been suggested.

Licence fee payers should all be given pin numbers allowing them to vote online every year on the BBC's performance. Licence fee payers should be allowed to comment on programme quality and on whether or not producers, presenters and management are doing a good job. Employees who get a poor report should be sacked. To ensure fairness licence-fee payers should set the questions to be asked.

And every year licence-fee payers should be allowed to vote on whether or not the licence fee should be retained or scrapped. The BBC cannot possibly complain about such a proposal. It is, after all, how a real democracy operates.

Meanwhile, why do so many people continue to pay the damned fee?

Doubtless the aggressive activities of the bullying bureaucrats at TV Licensing are responsible. As numerous people have reported, TV Licensing commonly gets away with threatening innocent and entirely honest citizens. People who have paid the licence fee complain that they have nevertheless received threatening letters and been told that their names are about to be added to the TV Licensing authority's National Enforcement Database. Letters to TV Licensing are ignored. Employees of the licensing authority seem unaware of the fact that 'it is an offence to harass someone with demands for payment so as to subject him or members of his family or household to alarm, distress or humiliation'.

One solution for besieged innocents is to make a formal complaint to the local Trading Standards department. And the Information Commissioner advises, on its website, that citizens should 'write to the organisation explaining what the problem is and where appropriate provide them with evidence to show what the information should say. Keep copies of this correspondence. If, after a reasonable amount of time (we would recommend 28 days) the information has not been corrected, you can make a complaint under the Data Protection Act.'

But if 10,000 people simply refused to pay the television licence fee what would happen?

★ ★ ★

There is much accumulated anger against the BBC. People are angry at the arrogance and institutionalised prejudices of an organisation we are forced to support but which sneers at us by providing us with a toxic mixture of rubbish and propaganda. It would make just as much sense if we were all forced to become members of the British National Party.

I don't mind paying a tax to receive broadcast programmes (I pay taxes for just about everything else I do). But I object strenuously to the whole of the tax being handed over to a bunch of state broadcasters whose political aims are quite opposed to my own. The BBC cannot even claim that its non-news output is of artistic or cultural value. BBC programmes have, in recent years, included Fuck Off, I'm a Hairy Woman, My Man Boobs And Me, Dog Borstal and Tittybangbang. In addition, of course, the BBC produces the unedifying and deeply depressing soap opera Eastenders. When the BBC cut jobs to save money the cuts were largely made among news and documentary staff. Bad television is destroying society and the people who produce it just don't care. ('I'm just doing my job, it's what people want.') Violence and sex. Twenty four hour nastiness. Modern programme makers seem to delight in working out new ways in which people can be nasty to one another.

Today the BBC has divided the country into two halves. On one side are those who work for the organisation (and enjoy its generous patronage): these individuals tend to regard it as a wonderful and impartial broadcaster. On the other side are the citizens who pay the licence fee: these tend to regard it as neither. If there was a referendum on whether or not the licence fee should be abolished the outcome would be dramatic: 99% for abolition.

I strongly suspect that increasing numbers of people will find ways to avoid paying the tax without attracting the attention of the authorities. Will some, for example, choose to watch television programmes on computers? And if so how will the television licence authorities find them? Will television receiver detection vans prove effective at tracking down miscreants? How many people will simply refuse to allow television licensing investigators into their homes – preferring to shut the door on them and send them on their way?

Incidentally, the BBC isn't the only broadcaster to receive a big chunk of public money. Channel 4, which is a taxpayer asset ultimately controlled by the British Government, receives £100 million a year of taxpayers' money. Its most successful programmes include Big Brother, Celebrity Big Brother and Wife Swap. Just why taxpayers should pay for these programmes is quite beyond me. If Channel 4 was wanted by viewers it would attract enough advertising to survive without a subsidy. Broadcasting standards have been deteriorating steadily for decades. But they took a huge lurch downwards with the launch of the television series Big Brother on Channel 4. The Big Brother series encouraged voyeurism and exhibitionism and persuaded a whole generation to accept (and even welcome) the idea of their every movement being filmed by intrusive television cameras. Worse still, the programme makers devised games that encouraged contestants to act in a self-serving way. Viewers, often young and impressionable, saw that disloyalty and dishonesty were rewarded while honour and decency got you nowhere.

Many of the programmes now broadcast on terrestrial television in the UK bear an alarming resemblance to the sort of freak shows which were so popular among the Victorians. It won't be long before some television channel produces a real 21st Century version of the Roman gladiatorial contests. The only difference will be that the lion's victims won't be slaves but volunteers – desperate for a chance at glory and a million pound prize.

Chapter 26

Why And How The Internet Will Continue To Do More Harm Than Good

The Internet is a boon for mail order companies and pornographers. It encourages poor research, the suppression of information and copyright theft. It makes it easy for governments to spy on us.

When the Internet first appeared it was said by enthusiasts to be the most important invention ever made; more important than the wheel, the internal combustion engine, the aeroplane, electricity, the telephone or even the computer. There are still many who believe this. There are probably some who believe the Internet is more important than oxygen.

And it is true that the Internet has become a vital part of our lives. Many forms which need to be filled in can now only be accessed online. If you don't have access to the Internet then you're stuffed. It won't be long before HM Revenue and Customs make it compulsory for taxpayers to fill in their forms online.

If you don't have Internet access you cannot now travel to the USA (though why anyone would want to go there I cannot imagine). Potential visitors have to fill in an online form 72 hours before arrival in the USA. Those who have failed to do this risk being detained and then sent home. So much for international relations.

But, despite the respect with which governments now treat it (it is, after all, the easiest way they have of keeping an eye on what we are all doing, where we are going, who we are communicating with and what we are saying) the Internet has done enormous damage to many aspects of our life. It has contributed little, if anything, that could be described as adding to the quality of human life but it has destroyed much of our social fabric and, it has produced much unemployment. It hasn't done small businesses much good either. A study of small and medium sized enterprises showed that almost half of all small business owners feel that the Internet has made it harder to run a company. And considerably less than half feel that the Internet has increased their operational efficiency.

Many school teachers now tell their pupils to use the Internet as a research tool. A Minister recently announced that books aren't necessary because research can be done on the Internet. There are a growing number of schools which no longer have libraries. 'Books are old-fashioned and pointless,' said one teacher, explaining why his school no longer bothered to keep a library. 'The Internet is much faster and more fun for students.'

Well, it may be more fun. And it may be faster, too.

But anyone who thinks that the Internet is a reliable and useful research tool for students obviously knows nothing about research and frighteningly little about the Internet. (I don't have a vested interest because I don't write the sort of books which are, by and large, likely to end up in school libraries.) The truth is that it is enormously difficult for anyone (however experienced) to obtain accurate, reliable information from the Internet.

There are two problems. First, many of the sites which offer information (and which may appear to be independent and impartial) are created by or for commercial organisations which want to promote a particular product or point of view. And a large number of sites accept money from commercial organisations to promote specific products or points of view. Since users won't pay to access websites the only way to make money is through overt or covert advertising. And covert advertising is much more effective. Second, the search engines which guide users to websites accept money to put websites at the top of the list when you type in a specific search request. The best and only honest information on a particular subject may be on the 23rd page of search engine results. How many students are going to plough through 23 pages of results to find that site? And how will they possibly know that the best site is there, or that the information it offers is objective and accurate? You really have to know what you are looking for before you can find trustworthy and genuinely valuable websites.

As a research tool the Internet is about as useful as a television commercial. And it frightens me that teachers think that their pupils can do research by using commercial search engines.

The Internet has damaged our towns (by making it possible for shoppers to buy exactly what they want, at the lowest price, without leaving their homes). Small shops have been battered by greedy councils and ever-growing supermarkets but the Internet has to take a good chunk of the responsibility for wrecking our town centres.

★ ★ ★

Many Internet sites which have acquired a reputation among fact-seekers are quite unchecked. For example, one of the well-known ways to find information on the Internet is by using a site called Wikipedia. This is, supposedly, a sort of online encyclopaedia. I am told that I have for years had an entry in this online encyclopaedia. I've never looked at it. No one has ever asked me to check it. I have no idea whether or not any of it is true. If it is taken from newspaper cuttings it is probably mostly untrue. I did see an article about me that appeared on the *Daily Telegraph* website. It contained a number of inaccuracies but when I wrote to the editor drawing attention to these errors I didn't even receive the courtesy of a reply. I have no idea whether or not the article is still available. The piece was illustrated with a photograph stolen from my website and used without permission.

Stealing is now normal on the Internet. There are whole books of mine now available on the Internet – handed out free on other people's websites and used to attract advertising so that the site owner can make money out of my work. This now seems to be normal, accepted practice on the Internet. Google, the search engine, has just agreed to hand over money in settlement of a lawsuit brought against it after it scanned in copyright books and displayed excerpts on the Internet without permission. Google denies the claims but has nevertheless agreed to pay out a total of $79 million. I somehow doubt if I will see much of that. And, if approved by the court, the settlement will authorise Google to scan in copyright books in the United States of America and maintain an electronic database of books. Google, it seems, will be able to sell access to individual books and place advertisements on pages dedicated to books. The pittance Google will pay will not provide much compensation for the many authors whose work is being appropriated.

The Internet makes it easy for students to steal material. Plagiarism is now so common among sixth-formers that teachers often receive identical essays from pupils who have merely stolen their 'work' from the Internet. It is not uncommon for homework to include advertisements accidentally copied from the Internet sites from where the students stole the material they are putting forward as their own. And most of what they read on the Internet is wrong – not by accident but by design.

Everywhere you look the Internet is changing our world for the worse.

The Internet has encouraged people to expect information to be given to them without any charge. Newspapers and magazines which have been destroyed by the Internet are looking at the possibility of running on-line editions of their publications. It won't work for the simple reason that there won't be enough people prepared to pay subscriptions. A few publications will survive on the advertising income they receive but the most successful will doubtless be the ones which are sponsored by organisations, governments or large companies. And anyone who thinks that such 'publications' will offer unbiased information obviously doesn't know how the world works these days.

Bookshops and publishers have helped destroy books in ways that could never have been imagined just a few years ago. Publishers use the Internet to destroy themselves by putting books online free and by making books available in a software version. Once a book is available for downloading on the Web the author will be extremely unlikely to receive much in the way of royalties in the future. A book that has been put online will quickly reappear on other websites.

The Internet has produced a new generation who believe that all published work is, or should be, community property and that authors or musicians who want to earn a royalty from their work are somehow cheating the people who pay.

The Internet has proved most effective as a distribution medium for pornography and those selling pornography have proved clever and effective at using search engines to sell their products. In Argentine, 114 stars have sought restraining orders against search engines such as Google and Yahoo over the fact that when their names are put into search engines the list of top ten searches includes sex sites. Such litigation could not even get off the ground in Europe since European law has kindly provided exemptions from liability for companies such as Yahoo and Google.

Naturally those who speak for the search engine companies claim that attempts to control the search engines in any way is unacceptable censorship and 'an attempt to limit freedom of expression'. What they don't mention is the fact that search engines happily allow some governments to decide what content is available. For example, Google allows the Chinese Government to control what material the Chinese Internet user can access. That, of course, isn't considered to be censorship. It's commercial expediency.

The Internet was never going to change everyone's life. It was really only ever a new way of selling (stuff and services) by mail order. And an excellent way for the authorities to keep a check on what we write (and to whom we write), where we are and what we buy.

★ ★ ★

The Internet will be the primary provider of news by 2012, according to one leading European publisher. Traditional publishers are losing circulation (and staff) and it seems clear that the Internet has done to newspapers what motor cars did to horse drawn vehicles (and what the television tried, and failed, to do to the cinema). Sadly, however, although newspaper websites attract many readers they don't bring in much income. Most Internet users expect everything on the Web to be free and only a small number of publications seem able to attract enough subscribers to stay alive (and, even then, they do it by keeping down costs to a minimum and pasting advertisements all over the place).

National newspapers are going to start appearing only on the Internet. Maybe *The Independent* will be the first to give up printing a paper. The current economic climate will probably mean the end for a newspaper with such a small circulation.

CHAPTER 27

The Persecution Of The Prudent

Despite his claims and protestations, Gordon Brown has been the most imprudent Chancellor in British history. His spend, spend, spend philosophy (more suitable to a pools or lottery winner) has left the nation weakened and in debt and has encouraged millions of citizens to make the same terrible mistake.

In Labour's world, prudence is not valued or appreciated. Spend all your money and the State will look after you. Save, and the Government will do everything it can to grab all the money you have put aside.

This is bizarre and irrational and unfair and it leads to resentment and injustice. It has also led large sections of the population to regard imprudence and improvidence as the only rational course of action.

For most of the 20th Century, people saved around 8% of their money. By the beginning of the 21st Century, after a few years of a Labour Government, the savings ratio had fallen to 0%. Millions of people had no savings whatsoever.

The UK saving rate has been negative for the last four years.

For four whole years the average person in the UK has spent more than they have earned. They have borrowed money on their credit cards. They have dug into savings. And they have borrowed against their house.

Savings rates in Britain are the worst since records began.

When (not if) things get really tough the British will be more vulnerable than ever before. The coming recession is going to be far worse than anything we've ever seen before.

* * *

The majority of students who've left university since 1997 have no savings, no pensions and no housing equity. There are five reasons for this. First, students have been too busy paying back the loans they had been forced to take out in order to continue their studies. Second, thanks to Gordon Brown's policies, a whole new generation have no faith in pensions. Third, thanks to Gordon Brown's policies, housing has become far too expensive for young people to be able to get on the property ladder. Fourth, Gordon Brown's means-testing policies meant that there is little or no incentive for anyone to save. And fifth, the complete failure of the regulators to control mis-selling and dishonesty by investment companies means that very few people have much remaining faith in the investment industry as a whole.

* * *

On October 8th 2008, at the height of the banking crisis in the UK, as millions of worried savers moved their money out of banks, National Savings and Investments cut the interest rates on its products.

National Savings and Investments reduced the interest rate on some of its variable rate savings products by up to 20 basis points (0.2%). NS&I also cut the Premium Bond price fund rate. The nation's only safe haven for investors, the one guaranteed by the Government, announced that it was cutting its rates to maintain a consistent level of market share and to provide a positive savings experience for its customers.'

So, there it was.

The Government had cut the rate it was paying on the only truly safe savings product in the country in order 'to provide a positive savings experience for its customers'.

Critics accused National Savings and Investments (NSI) of profiteering from the crisis. Billions of pounds had flowed into NSI accounts because savers wanted security for their money. And so the Government had taken advantage of their fear to trim the rates it was paying.

* * *

During the crisis of autumn 2008, it was revealed that one of the people most closely involved in giving advice to the Prime Minister and the Chancellor of the Exchequer was former banker and civil servant Baroness Vadera. Never elected to office, Vadera was put in the Lords and made a Minister by Gordon Brown. In October 2008 she was made Minister for Economic Competitiveness (an Orwellian title if ever there was one).

Shriti 'granny' Vadera, a former adviser to Gordon Brown when he was Chancellor, was made a peer and minister when Brown became Prime Minister. 'Granny' Vadera had a major role in the Government's theft of Railtrack from investors. When investors went to court over their losses it was the loathsome Vadera who was revealed to have dismissed shareholders as 'grannies'.

She and her chums seem to have been left alone to look after the shop a good deal during the crisis. At one point, while stock markets around the world were in free fall, Gordon the Moron was visiting a literary festival in the west country. Sir Francis Drake and the Duke of Wellington both had reasons for showing sang froid at moments of crisis (Drake famously played bowls on Plymouth Hoe while the Spanish fleet approached, and Wellington attended a ball the night before the Battle of Waterloo – both wanted to reassure their men and so dispel panic and boost confidence) but a wiser Prime Minister might have stayed in his office trying to think of something useful to do to save the country he was being paid to lead.

It is, of course, not surprising that Brown should be keen on appointing unelected people to positions of great authority. He himself may be a Scottish MP but he was not elected Prime Minister. Indeed, we should never forget that there is one big very important difference between Gordon Brown and Adolf Hitler: Hitler was elected leader of his country.

★ ★ ★

The hardworking, the prudent, the cautious, the thrifty, the fiscally responsible are the people who have suffered most from Brown's tenure. Savers who put their money into equity investments have seen their savings diminish during Brown's tenure, first at No 11 and then at No 10. Savers who put their money into the bank, on deposit, have endured sleepless nights worrying whether their money would still be there in the morning. And they've seen the interest they receive on their savings cut and cut again.

The only clear message from Gordon Brown has been this: prudence does not pay. Spend your money. Don't save it. Borrow as much as the banks will allow you to borrow. And then spend that too.

The people who have benefited from Brown's time in power have been the feckless scroungers, the 17-year-old girls who regard pregnancy as a career, the fakes who claim their bad back has prevented them from working for thirty years, the parasites who argue that they are too stressed to work, the families who regard the State as a constant source of everything they need, the immigrants who move to Britain in search of an easy life and a regular pay cheque, the public sector workers who retire at 35 on a full pension because they have been exposed to stress while doing the jobs they were well paid to do.

It's not surprising that the country is in trouble. And nor is it surprising that it is going to be a long, long time before it is out of trouble.

Britain will only solve its financial problems when people start saving and investing.

But the Government encourages the opposite.

So, things are going to get worse.

Much, much worse.

However, for those who have savings there is a bright thought.

Brown's policies are going to lead to unprecedented levels of inflation. And interest rates are likely to soar.

When that happens savers will be rewarded for their prudence.

Chapter 28

Rising Political Correctness, Declining Morality And Disappearing Personal Responsibility

Although we now live in a country controlled by the politically correct, our moral values are weaker than they have ever been.

Political correctness is one of the three big evils of our time (the other two are means-testing and multiculturalism).

It began well enough.

Well-meaning people wanted to eradicate the bad things from our society. They wanted to get rid of unfairness.

But they got carried away.

And they forgot that it simply isn't possible to get rid of all the unfairness without creating an unpleasant, Stalinist, statist world where individualism counts for nothing and freedom is ignored.

Look at some of the daft things that have happened as a result of our attempts to impose politically correct views on all aspects of our world.

1. It is now the law that children in primary schools, as young as four-years-old, must be taught about homosexuality. This is apparently being done to prevent homophobic thoughts. How many four-year-olds do you know with homophobic thoughts?
2. A reader wrote to tell me that her local library was closing because to get into it you had to go up some steps. The library was, therefore, difficult for people with 'limited mobility' to

access. So, instead of either creating alternative arrangements the local council simply closed the library. Perfect. Books are bad for the State anyway. They have a tendency to make people think.

3. Celebrating Christmas isn't allowed in many areas. The reason? It might upset Muslims. The Muslims have made it clear that they don't mind. (Which is nice of them since it's our country and it's a Christian country.) Sadly, this sort of bending over backwards creates resentment and racism.
4. Free guided walks of the Lake District were scrapped when it became clear that the only people on the walks were white and middle class. Tourism chiefs said the walks had failed to attract enough ethnic minorities, young people or disabled people. The lottery funding was apparently dependent on the walks attracting people from these groups. No one-legged teenage transsexuals on the walks meant no lottery funding and no lottery funding meant no walkies for the white, middle class folk.
5. The employer of a man who told a fellow worker that she was wearing a nice dress was fined when the woman complained that she had been sexually harassed.
6. Famous red Routemaster buses were taken off the streets of London (against the wishes of more than four out of five Londoners) because they were not properly accessible to the disabled. People with wheelchairs found them impossible to use. (It would have been considerably cheaper, and better all round, to provide a fleet of special free taxis for disabled travellers. But the politically correct police don't feel that they are doing their jobs properly if they don't cause some suffering.) The cost of replacing the buses was phenomenal. And the new bendy buses which replaced them seem to me to be both unsightly and potentially dangerous.
7. The Samaritans charity had a £300,000 grant application refused by the National Lottery because they couldn't prove that they had helped enough disadvantaged people and because they were not targeting asylum seekers, ethnic minority communities, the young and the elderly. (The Samaritans help anyone, and

don't discriminate but were themselves discriminated against.) Instead the Lottery fund gave £360,000 to a group that helps prostitutes and, presumably, was able to prove that it helps crippled prostitutes who come from distant countries and don't speak English, rather than people who are simply suicidal.

8. The Severn Area Rescue Association's request for £5,000 to replace a 14-year-old Land Rover used to launch its lifeboats was turned down because the Association couldn't provide details of the social backgrounds of the people they had rescued. (Early in 2009, it was announced that in future coastguards had to fill in a risk assessment form before responding to emergencies detailing 'reason for journey'.)
9. The Bowland and Pennine Mountain Rescue Team's application was turned down on the same grounds.
10. The Labour Government has made it compulsory for adoption agencies to hand babies to gay couples.
11. Crimes are now labelled as 'racist' if the victim and the perpetrator have different skin colours. This is absurd. Even if the skin colour was relevant (which it might not have been) a crime is no better or worse for the thoughts of the people who committed it. Does it matter to the person who is killed why the killer did the deed? Does it really matter to the bereaved? The crime is the sin. Labelling crime in this way is in itself racist – and encourages racist thinking.
12. A man who called a Welsh woman 'English' was arrested and given a suspended prison sentence and a supervision order. It is now actually illegal to call someone 'English' if they are not. What sort of madness is that?

★ ★ ★

There is a growing rage at the way bureaucrats attempt to force their lunatic ideas on us, ignoring the fact that some people are better suited to some types of work than others.

As one reader put it in a letter: 'I hope the bureaucrats are the people in the burning building when the disabled, wheelchair bound firewoman is outside wondering how to move her chair up the ladder and rescue them.'

The dislike of political correctness in our society was well illustrated when a character in a television series called *Life on Mars* became popular largely because he was politically incorrect.

In our politically correct society we have to pretend that everyone is equal. And everyone has to have equal access.

This is, of course, a doomed policy. People cannot all be equal.

I want to open the batting for England in the next Test Match against Australia. I want to drive a Ferrari in Formula One motor races. I have to accept that I cannot do these things because the world isn't entirely equal.

It's not fair.

The brave, the courageous and the determined do not need stupid laws to defend them from prejudice and inequality.

* * *

In 2007, politically correct 'non jobs' costing taxpayers almost £600 million were advertised. Local councils and quangos advertised 15,700 posts in *The Guardian* newspaper. Each job paid an average of £38,000 a year, with an enormous range of expenses added on and, of course, the obligatory gold-plated, index-linked public sector pension to be paid by taxpayers.

Examples of jobs advertised included a 'community empowerment network programme manager' and an 'assistant chief executive (value for money)'. Many of the job titles (and their job descriptions) were incomprehensible.

* * *

The real irony is that although we now live in a country controlled by the politically correct, our moral values are weaker than they have ever been. We are on the slippery slope of moral relativity. And we are travelling ever faster downhill. It seems that either our leaders don't know the difference between good and evil or they don't care about it.

The idea of taking personal responsibility for yourself, your family and for what you do (both in your personal and your professional life) has all but disappeared – especially among those whose prime driving force is political correctness.

For example, a woman whose daughter was charged with bullying claimed that her daughter was innocent. 'She didn't hit anyone,' said the mother. 'She just watched.'

It's a common excuse these days. And a surprising number of people seem to believe that just being a bystander excuses them from responsibility for bad things that happen.

It doesn't, of course.

After World War II Albert Speer, third ranking member of the Nazi hierarchy pleaded guilty at Nuremberg and was sentenced to life imprisonment. Speer later said that he, like others, was often asked 'Didn't you know what was going on?' and he always replied 'We wanted not to know.'

That it seems, rather sadly, is the response of many Britons today.

★ ★ ★

Another problem is that adopting the principle of political correctness has enabled many to separate authority from responsibility.

Around 40 years ago I wrote an article for the old *Daily Telegraph* magazine expressing concern at the way that authority and responsibility had become separated. The division has continued to widen and will do so, with dire results.

Politicians and public servants don't apologise, take responsibility or resign these days. Whatever happens they always have an excuse – and someone else to blame. As long as they can say that they behaved in a 'politically correct' way they will deny any wrong-doing.

This appalling habit has seeped out into all other areas of public life. And it's going to get worse.

Bankers, for example, avoid apologising, avoid taking responsibility and avoid resigning. Shame and embarrassment they know not.

Those who work within the system have become primarily concerned with protecting themselves and their jobs. And that means simply following the official rules – rather than following any personal sense of right and wrong or any personal sense of responsibility. Obeying the rules, rather than providing an honest service, has become their most important aim. Consequently, instead of learning from their mistakes they spend their time covering up errors and finding ways to avoid blame. This is now true for hospital staff, the police, schools and all other public sector services.

And it's all going to get worse.

Chapter 29

The Elderly Will Be Treated With An Increasing Lack Of Respect

The elderly are already abused and disenfranchised and regarded by politicians, doctors and public sector workers as a growing financial embarrassment.

As the economy slides further into the coming long-term depression so there will be increasing enthusiasm for 'putting the elderly out of their misery'. Committees of obscure moral philosophers and quango professionals will decide that it is a 'good thing' to help the frail, the weak and the mildly demented to 'move to a better place'.

According to Help the Aged, half a million older people in Britain are, at any one time, being neglected or abused. Health care professionals are the most likely cause of neglect and abuse. If children were treated the way old people are treated there would be a national outcry. But, sadly, nobody cares much about the elderly.

In an average British winter, 30,000 British pensioners die as a direct result of being too cold. Politicians don't care two hoots about pensioners. And dead pensioners concern them even less. And yet, imagine the fuss if 30,000 children died every year because they were too cold?

Other countries find our attitude difficult to understand. In February 2009 it was announced that a shipload of warm clothes and blankets for British pensioners would arrive in Grimsby. The clothes and blankets were sent by concerned Icelandic citizens who had heard of the terrible conditions facing the UK's elderly and had organised a charitable appeal. Iceland's entire economy (including their banks and their Government) had collapsed shortly beforehand.

A third of doctors say that the elderly should be refused operations if they are unlikely to live long enough afterwards to enjoy the benefits. One third of doctors said that the NHS should think twice before carrying out hip and knee replacements and other routine operations on older patients – however fit and healthy the older patients might be. Many doctors, it seems, now regard the provision of infertility treatment, plastic surgery and sex change operations as more important than providing health care for the elderly who may be in pain or dying. Half of the doctors who took part in one major survey said that the NHS couldn't afford to treat everyone and that even though tests and drugs would benefit the elderly they would withhold them because 'the elderly aren't worth caring for'. This, let me remind you, is the view not of yobs, muggers or politicians but of people masquerading, and being paid as, doctors. In a decent, honourable world doctors who spoke this way would be struck off the medical register and never allowed back on again. Where do we train these people? The University of Josef Mengele? The Auschwitz School Of Medicine? The Dr Harold Shipman College Of Medical Caring?

In some parts of the country this sort of blatant age discrimination is actually official and doctors are not allowed to refer patients over 75 to hospital. In nursing homes old people are now legally sedated (against their will) with drugs hidden in their food. When old people die the police and coroners' courts seem largely indifferent. The attitude is: 'Well, they were old!' When I say that doctors get away with murder I am not using hyperbole to make a point.

Elderly and frail patients don't receive basic care for conditions such as osteoarthritis. Much better provision is provided for patients who can earn their family doctor an incentive payment and although there are incentive payments for treating heart disease, diabetes and high blood pressure there are no incentive payments for treating the sort of problems that afflict the elderly. General practitioners receive incentive payments to poison small, healthy children with vaccines which may make them ill (and certainly won't do them any good) but they don't get incentive payments for helping elderly patients whose lives are being ruined by relatively easily treated problems such as incontinence.

The elderly who need to go into council care homes are allowed to keep just £21.90 a week of their own money to pay for everything including clothes, toothpaste and other toilet items, newspapers, books, telephone calls and so on. Everything they have above the £21.90 a week is taken off them and used to pay for their care. This is little more than State enforced mugging.

It has even been suggested that frail and vulnerable pensioners could be fitted with electronic tags (just as prisoners are tagged to enforce curfews) to save cash on night time cover in care homes.

It's going to get much worse. Euthanasia will become accepted, then popular and finally it will probably be compulsory. If you think I am exaggerating, just remember that it is now perfectly legal for nursing home staff to give sedatives and tranquillisers to the elderly without their permission.

When death comes after life's passions have been spent it is acceptable. But when life is taken before life's passions have been spent, where there are still aims, and hopes, and ambitions and joys then the taking of life (or murder) is not acceptable. It is wrong whatever the age of the person whose life has been taken. It doesn't matter if it is a child or an elderly person.

Our society doesn't seem to want to recognise that.

The pressure to approve euthanasia with or without the consent of the patient will increase.

★ ★ ★

An old woman who had been mugged was left to die alone on the pavement. No one bothered to stop and help her.

★ ★ ★

A man who left a 96-year-old war veteran blind in one eye after attacking him on a packed train was given a three year supervision order. The man, who launched an unprovoked attack on the 96-year-old in Croydon, South London, was found guilty of grievous bodily harm after the attack was caught on closed circuit television.

Now, try replacing the words '96-year-old war veteran' in the first sentence with these alternatives:

1. A 35-year-old American banker with connections to the White House.

2. Gordon Brown's wife.
3. Prince Harry.
4. A six-year-old girl.
5. A policeman.

★ ★ ★

A 78-year-old man suffering from Alzheimer's disease rebuked a yob for urinating in public (outside a supermarket). The 22-year-old picked up the old man and hurled him to the ground. The yob and a friend then strolled into the supermarket to steal alcohol. On his way out the yob stepped over the pensioner. The old man died 13 days after the attack. The yob was arrested, taken to court and given two years in jail.

★ ★ ★

During the next few years it will be increasingly common for the elderly to be denied medical and surgical treatment that might save their lives (or alleviate their symptoms).

Only those with the resources to pay for private care will be able to survive.

Chapter 30

Taxes Will Have To Rise, Rise And Rise Again

The new Labour Party policy on tax seems to be: 'Squeeze them all until the pips squeak.' Huge debts, massive public spending commitments and ever-increasing public sector pension obligations mean that taxes are going to have to rise and continue rising.

Thanks to Gordon brown's tax and spend policies, most of us are worse off than we were in 1997. By 2012, the average hardworking couple with two incomes and no children will be £2,208 worse off than they were in 1997. If the Government increases taxes they will be worse off than that. (There is no chance of the Government reducing taxes).

The average couple's chance of buying their own home and starting their own family are slimmer than ever. Only public sector employees (whose salaries have risen enormously), unemployed single parents, and non-earning couples with children are better off than they were in 1997. Labour's tax changes have meant that scroungers are £2,901 better off than they were in 1997, while unemployed single women with children are £2,491 better off. These are the days for the lazy and the feckless.

* * *

Taxes have risen dramatically since 1997 when Labour took over ruining the country. Brown's taxes have damaged the standard of living for everyone who works or saves – including the lowly paid and the elderly. (Since 1997, when Labour came to power, the number of pensioners paying tax has increased by 1.5 million.

And, of course, Gordon Brown's raid on pensions has dramatically damaged pension funds and pension payments for those not fortunate enough to be entitled to the sort of generous pensions enjoyed by former Government employees, but paid for by taxpayers.)

The massive increase in house stamp duty brought in by Brown in 1997 is, effectively, a wealth tax on home purchasers. If Brown had put as much effort into strengthening the economy as he has put into thinking of new ways to tax people (and new ways to complicate the tax system) Britain would be in a much stronger position.

New Labour has already announced that income tax will go up after the next election. Their flagship rise will be a new rate of 45p in the £ for all incomes over £150,000. But the pittance that tax will raise won't help much. Indeed, independent think tank the Institute for Fiscal Studies says that the 45% tax rate will reduce – not increase – the Government's total tax take since wealthy earners will find ways to avoid paying the new top rate tax. Some will put more money into pension funds. Some will do less work (and so earn less). Many people in England are now taking advantage of new laws and choosing to work half-time or part-time. They say they want to spend more time with their families but what they really mean is that doing this enables them dramatically to reduce the amount of tax they pay and to avoid the Government's cruel means-testing policies.

And many more earners will emigrate.

How long do you think it will be before the 45p becomes 50p and then 60p? And how long before the £150,000 is reduced to £100,000 and then £50,000? How long before the normal top rate of tax is raised to 60% and the lower tax rate raised accordingly?

The Government has already said that it will increase National Insurance contributions and a whole armoury of wealth taxes have been introduced and will, doubtless, be added to in the future. (Only politicians regard National Insurance contributions as anything different to income tax.)

And they are going to have to raise taxes more and still more. As the economy slides ever further downwards the money the Government receives from corporation taxes, income taxes, VAT receipts, National Insurance contributions, business rates and so on will shrink.

Moreover, the Government (and Her Majesty's Revenue and Customs) seem determined to attack all forms of tax avoidance, rather than targeting tax evasion (which always used to be the one regarded as fraudulent and illegal). What they perhaps have not realised is that many of the most popular tax avoidance schemes are those – such as Individual Savings Accounts (ISAs) – which are organised and promoted by the Government itself. What fun it will be when the authorities start prosecuting taxpayers who have put their money into Government sponsored savings schemes.

Meanwhile, the number of people receiving unemployment benefit or incapacity benefits will rise. So will the number of public sector workers retiring and wanting their index-linked pensions. And the number of public sector workers to be paid. And the number of people requiring State pensions.

How long will it be before the number of people who are dependent on the State exceeds the number of people who are doing proper jobs and paying taxes?

Not long, I fear.

★ ★ ★

The latest edition of *Tolley's*, the UK tax guide, has more than doubled in size since Gordon Brown took over as Chancellor. The 2008 *Tolley's Yellow Tax Handbook* is 10,134 pages long and fills four volumes. When Brown took over at the Treasury, *Tolley's* filled two volumes and was 4,998 pages.

And as tax law becomes increasingly complex (and incomprehensible for the average taxpayer) so the tax authorities acquire more and more power. From the 1st April 2009, Her Majesty's Revenue and Customs have been given the power to enter business premises and private homes used for business. Tax officers can inspect and remove information and documents. If you do any work in your home the taxman can wander around at will. He can rummage through your bedside cabinet and underneath your bed in his search for anything relating to your past, present or future tax liabilities in the UK or other EU states. (I think it is safe to assume that taxmen from other EU states will also be able to wander around your business premises and your home.)

★ ★ ★

It isn't only individuals who are emigrating because of Britain's tax regime.

More and more companies are leaving the country. A poll of 50 big businesses in the UK in 2009 showed that the proportion considering moving their tax residency jumped from 6% in 2007 to 14% in 2008. Moving a company's tax residency is a complicated and expensive business and yet a growing number of companies think it worthwhile. They leave (even if they still have offices and factories in the UK they have officially 'left' if their head office is abroad somewhere) not just because they are fed up with paying high taxes. They leave because the tax system in Britain is now so complicated that it is incomprehensible. Even the experts get confused. Companies waste vast amounts of time trying to understand what they can and cannot do. They leave because Gordon Brown has been changing the tax rules retrospectively and overnight. Nothing is predictable. And if you are running a huge company then you need to have some idea of what the tax laws are likely to be tomorrow, next week, next month and next year. (You also need to know what the tax laws were last year. Under the Labour Government even this has become impossible.) Finally, even the companies which aren't actually leaving are finding ways to avoid paying taxes. Here's one simple trick. A company which makes a drug and which appears to be based in the UK because the tablets it sells are manufactured and put into bottles in the UK can still make most of its money in another country (and thereby limit the amount of UK tax it pays). How? Simple. The raw materials from which the pills are made are purchased by a subsidiary or associate company in another country (where taxes are lower and simpler and more reliable) and are then imported into the UK. But the subsidiary or associate company charges a huge price for the raw materials. And so most of the profit from the pills stays in the low tax country. The company in the UK can, of course, take advantage of whatever benefits and incentives are being made available by the British Government.

A national audit office analysis of the 700 companies whose affairs are handled by HMRCs large business service revealed that 50 of the businesses paid 67% of the total tax collected, while 220 paid no tax and 210 paid less than £10 million.

★ ★ ★

We pay more and more tax and get fewer and fewer services. Many things which used to be 'free' now cost us money. The Government has a vast number of premium rate phone numbers. Ring up an advice line and you will probably find yourself paying far more than for an ordinary phone call. Today I received a tax bill and a VAT form to complete. I noticed that when I posted back the cheques I had to put stamps on the envelopes. That's a new one.

★ ★ ★

The Government does two things: it collects money and spends it. Why are they brilliant at the first and so bad at the second?

★ ★ ★

Louis XIV's economic policies led to a state of constant crisis. His wars and extravagances cost money and so taxes were forever rising. Jean-Baptiste Colbert, his chief adviser, was a statist who believed in higher taxes and more government regulations. When Colbert asked businessmen what he could do to help make them more profitable he was told: 'Leave us alone.'

★ ★ ★

'If public spending had only grown in line with inflation since 1997, we could have abolished income tax, corporation tax, capital-gains tax and inheritance tax, leaving the taxpayer £200 billion better off.'

THE ADAM SMITH INSTITUTE, DRAWING ATTENTION TO THE CONSEQUENCES OF GORDON BROWN'S DECADE LONG RECKLESS SPENDING SPREE.

★ ★ ★

Two things annoy most taxpayers about HM Revenue and Customs. The first is that they are, by and large, rude and overbearing. The second is that they are desperately unfair and unreasonable. Almost anyone who has dealt with them can give examples of the rudeness. And as for the second, well, overpay your tax and HM Revenue and Customs will pay you 0% interest (even though the mistake will be theirs) but underpay your tax and you will pay 3.5%, whether it is your fault or theirs. (Those were the figures early in 2009). Fair? Of course not.

★ ★ ★

While taxes have been soaring, the nation has been deteriorating in just about every way imaginable. Crime rates have soared, the quality of service provided by the NHS has fallen so low that Turkish immigrants now go back to Turkey if they need medical treatment, and British schools have fallen down international league tables. Our roads and our railways are the laughing stock of Europe. Private pensions have been destroyed. The Government's tax-credit scheme has lost £14 billion in fraud and overpayments since it was introduced by Gordon Brown in 2003. And yet, like everything else introduced by Brown, it is so complicated that the people who should be benefiting aren't. One in three people entitled to receive pension credit do not claim it because they don't understand it. The benefit seems to have been created for the joy of bureaucrats (whose empires are built on it) and scroungers (who put all their effort into understanding every piece of legislation which might result in them getting more money out of taxpayers). Oh, and the nation has huge debts which future generations will be forced to pay off for years to come.

Today, the nation as a whole is, as I predicted it would be, the worst placed in the world to deal with the problems ahead. Britain is entering a deep depression (which will, I believe, segue straight into the problems created by peak oil) with a rapidly deteriorating structural deficit (public sector borrowing as a proportion of national income). Britain already has the second highest structural deficit of any G7 country bar America. And America does, at least, have the world's only reserve currency.

When Brown took over as Chancellor, in 1997, Britain was, in economic terms, a relatively healthy country. Now even the EU forecasts our national deficit is going to hit extraordinary heights – and require a massive increase in taxes to sort out. Today, it doesn't matter who wins the next election: services will deteriorate and taxes will rise. I'll go further: services will deteriorate dramatically and taxes will rise dramatically.

'I prefer not to prophesy before the event. It is much better to prophesy after the event has already taken place.'
WINSTON CHURCHILL

Biography Of The Author

Vernon Coleman was an angry young man for as long as it was decently possible. He then turned into an angry middle-aged man. And now, with no effort whatsoever, he has matured into being an angry old man. He is, he confesses, just as angry as he ever was. Indeed, he may be even angrier because, he says, the more he learns about life the more things he finds to be angry about.

Cruelty, prejudice and injustice are the three things most likely to arouse his well-developed sense of ire but he admits that, at a pinch, inefficiency, incompetence and greed will do almost as well.

The author has an innate dislike of taking orders, a pathological contempt for pomposity, hypocrisy and the sort of unthinking political correctness which attracts support from *Guardian*-reading pseudo-intellectuals. He also has a passionate loathing for those in authority who do not understand that unless their authority is tempered with compassion and a sense of responsibility the end result must always be an extremely unpleasant brand of totalitarianism.

He upsets more people than he means to but apologises only to those who are upset by accident rather than design.

Vernon Coleman is the iconoclastic author of well over a hundred books which have sold over two million copies in the UK, been translated into 23 languages and now sell in over 50 countries. His best-selling non-fiction book *Bodypower* was voted one of the 100 most popular books of the 1980s/90s and was turned into two television series in the UK. The film of his novel *Mrs Caldicot's Cabbage War* was released early in 2003.

Vernon Coleman has written columns for numerous newspapers and magazines and has contributed over 5,000 articles, columns and reviews to hundreds of leading publications around the world.

Many millions have consulted his advice lines and his website. Vernon Coleman has a medical degree, and an honorary science doctorate. He has worked for the Open University in the UK and is an honorary Professor of Holistic Medical Sciences at the Open International University based in Sri Lanka. Vernon Coleman has received lots of rather jolly awards from people he likes and respects. He worked as a GP for ten years and is still a registered medical practitioner. He has organised numerous campaigns both for people and for animals.

He likes books, cafés and writing and once won a certificate for swimming a width of the public baths in Walsall (which was, at the time, in Staffordshire but has now, apparently, been moved elsewhere). He likes cats, pens, cricket and notebooks. His favourite place is Les Invalides, his favourite author is P.G.Wodehouse and his favourite piece of music is whatever he is listening to at the time (because that's why he put it on). He can ride a bicycle and swim, though not at the same time. He likes desolate country places, small country towns and busy cities. His favourite cities in the world are London, Paris and Vienna and it is no coincidence that it was in these cities that coffee houses first appeared and it is in the last two that cafés are now still at their best.

(Some critics have sneered at his affection for the Europe on the other side of the Channel, arguing that it is absurd for someone opposed to the EU to enjoy going anywhere that isn't in Britain. What these idiots don't understand is that opposing European bureaucracy does not preclude loving European history, culture and architecture. Indeed, one of the reasons why he loathes the EU is that it wants to turn the whole of Europe into a homogenous greyness.)

Vernon Coleman enjoys chess, malt whisky and old films and is married and devoted to Donna Antoinette who is the kindest, sweetest, most sensitive woman a man could hope to meet and who, as an undeserved but welcome bonus, makes the very best roast potatoes on the planet. They live in Bilbury, Devon, surrounded by animals and books.

Vernon Coleman is balding rapidly and is widely disliked by members of the Establishment. He doesn't give a toss about either of these facts. Many attempts have been made to ban his books (many national publications ban all mention of them) but he insists he will keep writing them even if he has to write them out in longhand and sell them on street corners (though he hopes it doesn't come to this because he still has a doctor's handwriting).

For a catalogue of Vernon Coleman's books please write to:

Publishing House
Trinity Place
Barnstaple
Devon EX32 9HG
England

Telephone 01271 328892
Fax 01271 328768

Outside the UK:
Telephone +44 1271 328892
Fax +44 1271 328768

Or visit our website:
www.vernoncoleman.com

Other books by Vernon Coleman

Gordon Is A Moron

In *Gordon is a Moron* I've explained how Brown's stupidity and incompetence have weakened Britain for generations to come.

If you share my horror at the lowering of quality and standards in public life you will, I suspect, also share my belief that no one exemplifies the lowering more dramatically than Gordon the Moron. I have tried to deal with Brown in an objective and academic way but I make no apologies if any of my contempt has seeped into my prose. What have we done to deserve public servants such as Brown? It must have been something pretty terrible.

taken from the Preface of *Gordon is a Moron*

"Thank you, thank you. An amazing book. Skillfully written, entertaining, frightening and long overdue." (A.J BY E-MAIL)

"Brilliantly perceptive biography." (J.W. NORTHANTS)

"If you want to know the damage that the Moron has done to the economy of Britain, this is the book you should read. A Page turner filled with factually backed accusations. The effect of Gordon Brown's actions on the finances of his country, its institutions and its Constitution are all examined and picked apart – £25 per copy as opposed to the publisher's price of £9.99." (P.H. AMAZON REVIEW)

"Thank you for writing *Gordon is a Moron*. I have just packed one for David Cameron and one for William Hague. I have asked both of them to read it, and I have also advised them that this book should be sent to every college and school and to all authorities." (S. P. J., WALES)

"Why, you will ask, has no one in the media charted the cataclysmic damage caused by this dour control freak in a way that makes clear what has happened? You won't get it on the state sympathetic BBC, and you won't hear it talked about in the Westminster Village. None of the matters discussed can be genuinely rebutted because they are all true. Read it and weep." (R.B. AMAZON REVIEW)

Other books by Vernon Coleman

The O.F.P.I.S. File

"The Most Powerful And Revealing Book About The EU Ever Published"

- Were we taken into the EU illegally?
- The EU and our money
- Fraud in the EU
- The EU's regionalisation of Britain
- The EU, the law and your disappearing freedom
- The EU is destroying business
- The damage done by the British Government 'gold-plating' EU legislation
- It's the EU that insists we carry ID cards
- The EU's policy on immigration: a ticking time bomb
- The EU and the stupidity of the biofuels directive
- The failure of the media to inform us about the EU
- The Lisbon Treaty, the EU Constitution, the Queen, a good many lies and the end of Britain
- Why the EU is just like the old USSR
- Why English (and British) history is being suppressed
- The case for leaving the EU: why England should declare independence

"Had to thank you and praise you for your incredible work getting out your informative book on the EU." (M.W., Wales)

"I have just finished reading my latest Vernon Coleman book, *The OFPIS File*, and think it probably the best yet, not only because it lights up the EU scam in a way that few can, but has such a great deal of relevant detail." (J.M., Lancs)

"Thank you for sending me your *OFPIS* book which I managed to read in about two days flat. Your books are very readable and are hard to put down once started (the secret must lie in your writing style)." (A.K., Middlesex)

"Vernon Coleman is well regarded in our circles as the author of several fine books exposing the machinations of the Europhile elite, and for others in which he emerges as a sincere and thoughtful English patriot. He most definitely is neither a crank nor an alarmist." Identity Magazine

"Whenever I read one of his books he never ceases to amaze me." (C.N., Dorset)

Other books by Vernon Coleman

Living in a Fascist Country

We are losming our freedom and our privacy. The world is changing so fast that it is difficult to keep up. Britain and America are now fascist states. Why? What is going on? Whatever happened to democracy? Who is behind it all? How did we come to find ourselves in what the politicians boast will be an everlasting war?

'Everybody ought to have a copy of this book.' FOURTH WORLD REVIEW

"I suggest you buy this book, to give you perspective on what's underway and what to do about it personally."
HARRY SCHULTZ "HSL NEWSLETTER"

'... like a bedtime book of nightmares ... scary stuff indeed.' Nexus

'With its accounts of how the government is fooling the people ... how ID cards and under-the-skin chips will destroy personal liberty, how public infrastructure has been offloaded to the highest bidder, and how the banks and other institutions are in on the take, this book is a manifesto aimed at alerting people to the fact that they're being manipulated big-time and calling on them to rise up to assert their rights before it's too late.' NEXUS MAGAZINE

How To Protect And Preserve Your Freedom, Identity And Privacy

Thousands of people fall victim to identity theft every year. The consequences can be absolutely devastating and can take years to sort out.

Banks and Government departments take poor care of the vital, private information they demand. It's hardly surprising that identity theft is the fastest growing crime in the world.

Amazingly, there are scores of ways that your identity can be stolen. The majority of people aren't aware of just how vulnerable they are until it's too late.

How To Protect And Preserve Your Freedom, Identity And Privacy gives advice on:

- What to do if you're a victim of identity theft.
- The type of phone that can protect you against fraud.
- The tricks fraudsters use at cash machines.
- The signs which show that your identity may have been stolen.
- What you should watch out for when using your credit card in shops and restaurants.
- How you can protect your security before you go on holiday.
- Why you should be wary of the 'postman' knocking at your door – and the e-mails you should be frightened of.
- How answering your phone could leave you vulnerable to fraud.
- Why you should be wary about the clothes you wear.
- Why just leaving your Internet lead plugged in could leave you open to fraud... and much, much more.

Vernon Coleman's best-seller contains crucial security tips for personal survival in the 21st century. It's a book you can't afford not to read.

Moneypower

Moneypower doesn't offer you the names of shares you can buy to make a fortune. Nor does the book contain long lists of useful web sites or tips on using charts. It doesn't even contain boastful examples of successful investments I've made.

This is a guide book to investing designed to put power over money into your hands.

You remember the old Chinese adage about fishing?

Give a man a fish and you feed him for a day but teach him how to fish and you feed him for a lifetime.

This is a 'teach you how to invest' book.

It is, I hope, the honest, impartial book that you can give your children and grandchildren to read – so that they grow up understanding something about money.

This is a book to teach you the things you need to know in order to invest profitably.

taken from the preface of *Moneypower*

Oil Apocalypse

How to Survive, Protect Your Family And Profit Through The Coming Years of Crisis

Why the oil apocalypse is inevitable. How and why our dependence on oil will end in tears. And how you can prepare yourself and your family.

Also includes

- Our Unhealthy Addiction To A Gift Of Nature
- Peak Oil: The Beginning Of The End Of Civilisation
- Oil Wars: Past, Present And Future
- What Will Happen When The Oil Runs Out
- A New Energy Blueprint
- Your Personal Survival Plan
- Investing To Survive The Oil Apocalypse

The world you know is going to change dramatically and permanently. Anyone under fifty, with a normal life expectation, will live to see a world almost unrecognisable from the one they grew up in. Five billion people will die within a very short time. There will be no cars, no lorries, no buses, no aeroplanes and no supermarkets. The rich will travel by horse and cart. The middle classes will use bicycles. The poor will walk. The oil is running out and, as a result, our civilisation is reaching its end.

You will never read a more important or more alarming book than this one. The disaster inexorably heading our way will make any natural disaster, any tsunami, seem inconsequential. Forget global warming. Forget terrorism. They are trivial problems.

If you want to know the truth, and you think you can deal with it, sit down, turn to the first page and read this book now. It will change your life. Forever.

Vernon Coleman